THE PLANETARIZATION OF CONSCIOUSNESS
From the Individual to the Whole

1969

Dane Rudhyar

The
PLANETARIZATION
of
CONSCIOUSNESS

by DANE RUDHYAR

Preface by OLIVER REISER

HARPER COLOPHON BOOKS
Harper & Row, Publishers
New York, Evanston, San Francisco, London

This book was originally published in 1970 by SERVIRE
Publications, Wassenaar, Holland in two hardbound ed-
itions:
A de luxe autographed and numbered edition of 100
copies
An ordinary limited edition of 1200
Copies may be obtained by writing to Dane Rudhyar,
P.O. Box 636, San Jacinto, California 92383

First HARPER COLOPHON edition published 1972

LIBRARY OF CONGRESS CATALOG CARD NUMBER: 71-184855

STANDARD BOOK NUMBER: 06-090241-8

PREFACE

by Oliver L. Reiser

This new book by Dane Rudhyar which comes as the culmination of his life-long meditations, will held in no small measure to satisfy a growing need. What is required today, and even more so in the years ahead are scholars, writers and thinkers -- men and women of vision and wisdom -- who can do the necessary pioneering work in unifying the sciences, the arts, and the religions of mankind. Mr. Rudhyar is a modern prophet who proclaims his vision of the "new being," to employ Paul Tillich's language. Essentially a creative artist cast in the Renaissance mold, Mr. Rudhyar succeeds in fusing into one purview the vision of the poet, the mystic, the musician and theologian. To encompass this synthesis in our time and for our world requires considerable knowledge of Eastern and Western civilizations, and in this respect, Mr. Rudhyar is not found wanting.

The creative thinker is always in a dilemma. Like Professor Whitehead, he faces the alternatives of using an old terminology to convey new ideas, thus risking misinterpretation, or he must invent new terms for his mutant ideas, and these will defy facile comprehension. To steer a middle course is the path of wisdom, and this Mr. Rudhyar achieves in a graceful and flowing style. Readers of his previous writings will recall that Mr. Rudhyar's world-view at some points resembles C. J. Jung's approach to symbolism and depth psychology, but his cosmic and metaphysical outlook now covers a much wider field than the Swiss psychologist allowed himself to envision. Indeed, Mr. Rudhyar's

conceptions should not be steamed and pressed into anteced-
ent patterns, for this would diminish the components of originality. For example, the notions of the "symbol," "truth"
and "values" -- the ways in which they emerge and their
places in the cyclic processes of nature -- all demand a new
frame of reference.

Fundamental to Rudhyar's entire metaphysics is the notion of time as the cyclic rhythm of the world symphony.
Thus this philosopher, a va nt ga rde composer in his own
right, restates the Pythagorean insights of antiquity. This
is "time-binding" at its best. The rhythmic cyclicity in turn
prefigures and proclaims the coming of the "man of plenitude," the "global man," who embodies the "surge of potentialities" which moves toward the coming planetarization of
humanity.

Such a comprehensive sweep is seldom compressed in a
single volume. Well might our professional academicians,
technicians in those "factories of knowledge" which the large
modern universities have become, study this volume as a
model of what a philosophy can be and do when it is devoted
to the sum-total of human achievements in the "sciences" and
the "humanities." Here we have clear anticipations of how
the "two cultures" can be orchestrated into the forms of unity.
It is hoped that Mr. Rudhyar's projected synthesis may serve
as an impetus to a coming planetary civilization.

OLIVER L. REISER
Emeritus Professor of Philosophy
University of Pittsburgh
Author of:
"The Integration of Human Knowledge"
"Cosmic Humanism"
"This Holyest Erthe"

CONTENTS

CONTENTS

For ROBERT L. MOORE

In grateful friendship

This book comes as a latter-day product of a life filled with a great variety of creative endeavors which have been oriented since my seventeenth year toward the formulation of new ideas, new musical sounds, new pictorial images, and new feelings emerging from more open and inclusive interpersonal relationships. The desire to write such a book, and indeed a series of books, came forcefully to me some thirty years ago in my mid-forties during a crisis of reconstruction of my previous philosophical and "spiritual" beliefs and my attitudes toward other human beings. Several volumes were actually completed -- one, MODERN MAN'S CONFLICTS: The Creative Challenge of a Global Society, published in 1948 by The Philosophical Library in New York and for many years now out of print; and THE AGE OF PLENITUDE (a very ambitious project relating various fields of human activity) which was never published.

Seven years ago this book, THE PLANETARIZATION OF CONSCIOUSNESS, was started in Europe; but rather strange events at first and, during these latter years, heavy pressure of work interfered with its completion. In its present form and under its new title this book may in a way be a kind of philosophical testament. I, perhaps more than anyone else, am aware of its incompleteness and shortcomings. But it is offered to the growing public interested in my work in other related fields as an attempt to at least pose crucial problems in a somewhat new way and thus perhaps to make a few people who are deeply and vitally aware of the present need for a new way of thinking and feeling, think and feel more thoroughly and creatively about the radical changes in human consciousness and in social, cultural and religious concepts which are inevitable and impending.

The questions this book raises and attempts to answer range over several fields of enquiry, from the metaphysical and epistomological to the psychological, ethical and artistic. Each chapter should, in a sense, be expanded into an entire volume; and a great many as yet unorganized notes and fragments dealing with these several topics may sooner or later be incorporated into one or more volumes. As it is now, repetitions were inevitable, as certain basic principles have to be restated in terms of the field covered by a particular chapter; but I trust they have been reduced to a minimum.

Unlike the usual books on philosophy, psychology or scientific research, this volume contains practically no precise references to other books and authors. For the last sixty years I have read a vast number of books and obviously have been influenced by many in formulating my thoughts. Some of these influences will be apparent and actually stated. But I have been too much occupied in several fields of activity, and my life has been so "nomadic," that it has been impossible for me to keep well-ordered files of references which I could use at this late stage.

Besides, this is not meant to be a "scientific" book in which I show how much I have learned from colleagues and how related this or that concept of mine is to what this or that author thought and wrote. It is a book in which is expressed what I trust is a deep and vivid intuition of what existence could mean for this and coming generations of men willing to consecrate themselves to the task of building a new humanity. The holistic world-view which I present here is meant to be an incentive to think greater thoughts, to feel deeper, more inclusive feelings, and to act as "agents" for the Power that structures human evolution -- however we wish to imagine this Power. It is meant to integrate some of the most basic concepts, existential attitudes and spiritual realizations of the Asiatic and Western worlds.

All my life I have held, strongly focused in mind, the principle of synthesis. In my twenties I attempted to start one of many abortive projects which had as its motto the words: Synthesis - Solidarity - Service. These words mean very much the same thing at the three basic levels of human activity -- mental, emotional and actional. I still stand, several decades later, by this motto. We are at the threshold of an Age of Synthesis; but unless men are ready to go beyond the egocentric individualism which our society so glorifies and learn to feel and live in terms of the deepest kind of solidarity and service, the kind of synthesis mankind may witness could be oppressive and stultifying in its totalitarianism.

I can only hope that this book may arouse in a number of sensitive and open minds the desire and will to repolarize their consciousness, their thinking, and indeed their loves and allegiances, so that they may join the company of creative individuals who, whether they are fully aware of it or not, are working freely, doggedly, intensely, lovingly -- and indeed humorously also -- for the birth of a new way of life and a new humanity.

Part One

IN THE PSYCHOLOGICAL MODE

Chapter I: THE RELEASE OF SEED IDEAS

Definition and purpose of philosophy in reference to man in his environment (17); The individualistic, depersonalized, quantitative character of our society (18); Probable revulsion against such a human ideal
- Two types of Existentialism (19); Two approaches to the "New Age"
(20); Mankind in a "critical state" and the revolution in consciousness
(21); From local to global consciousness (22); Youth confused over
the nature of inevitable change - A new philosophy as a solution (23);
What the creative philosophy must be (24); The fecundant spread of
Asiatic philosophies (25); The Seed Man concept (26); New Images of
man, spiritual and scientific (27); A critique of our technology (28);
New types of energies possible (29); The real meaning of "synthesis"
(30); Negative results of technology unless in the hands of a new type
of human being (31); Preparing the ground for a new type of consciousness (32); The renewal of the mind (33); Descartes fallacy (34); What
is needed - The limited value of Asiatic traditions (35); The new seed-
ideas (36).

Chapter II: MAN'S PRIMARY EXPERIENCE OF EXISTENCE
             AND TIME

The holistic world-view (38); Existence and Non-existence (39); Order and change (40); The phenomenological approach, and the infant's
primary awareness of existence (41); Repetition as the basis of the
sense of order and foresight (42); Security based on predictability
(43); Insecurity and order (44); Existence as relationship (45); The
interrelationship of order and change (46); Existential time and the
continuous flow of changes (47); The infant's awareness of time as the
"passing" (48); The development of the time-sense (49); Living in the
Now (50); Holistic time and the cyclo-cosmic concept of existence (51);
The cycle as a "time-whole" - The field as a "space-whole" (52);
Structural factors in existence - Space as relatedness; time as the basic rhythm of self (53); Greater and lesser wholes (54); Bergson's
concept of duration - Measurement and motion (55); Dimensional and
scientific time (56); The cycle as Eon, and the Christian misinterpretation of eternity (57); "Timeless" experiences (58); Transcend-
ence and Reality (59); Non-existence -- in Bergson's philosophy and
in Asiatic thought (60); Samsara and Nirvana are one (61); The holistic ideal of "fulfilling time" and eonic consciousness (62); Expansion
in formed consciousness (63).

Chapter III: THE EXPERIENCE OF "I": SELF AND EGO

The search for identity (65); What does the feeling of "I am" really imply? (66); The objective and subjective approaches (67); The baby's gradual distinction between inner and outer events (68); Reflective and focused consciousness (69); The development of the ego-sense (70); The ego as a structure of consciousness and the self as center of power (72); The subjective inward quest for the self (73); Self-denudation and its results, and various definitions of self (74-75); What is reached may not be what is being sought - The bare fact of organismic existence (76); Container must be dissolved as well as contents (77); An inward experience (78); An analogy: The U.S. Government vs. "America" as a people and a land (79); Descartes' famous experience re-interpreted (80); The "I" as a managing Executive (81); The Principle of Wholeness, ONE or SELF (all capitals) (82); Selfhood at the generic and at the individual levels (83); The purpose of ego-development in terms of the full actualization of man's potentialities (84); The interplay of power and consciousness in the fulfilled individual person.

Chapter IV: SELFHOOD AND RELATEDNESS

Relationship and selfhood as basic facts of existence (87); Matricial and associative relationships (88); The family as a psychic womb for the baby -- the archetypal role of father and mother (89-90); Unconscious matricial relationships and conscious associative relationships (91); The negative effect on children of our technological society and of an extreme stress on personal relationships and permissiveness - The child as a potential, not actual, individual (92); Traditional patterns in education and the rebellion against family-cultural matrices - Aggressiveness, a screen for the insecure ego (93-94); Personal growth through associative relationships (95); Man-in-relationship vs. Man-the-individual (96); The development of individual consciousness from the tribal communal state to the Mosaic revelation of the "I am that I am" (97-98); The tribe as thesis, the individual as antithesis - Synthesis in the New Age (98-99); Several levels of integration and the process of individualization (100); The purpose of true occult techniques (101); The spiritual mind-organism after the death of the body (102); The transfer of the power of generic selfhood to the occult Heart Center (103); The guru-chela relationship (104); The Pleroma of Man - The Communion of the Saints - Teilhard's Omega state - The White Lodge (104-105); The individual as a field of existence (105-106); The transformation of mind and the beginning of the New Age (107); The development of planetary mankind as a basic functional Whole within the organic field of the Earth - An inevitable process - The Auroville experiment (107-108-109); Need for a holistic philosophy as basis for the new WE-experience (110); The Path and the state of isolation (111); The way to true individualization - Man's identification with the Eon (112).

I. THE RELEASE OF SEED-IDEAS

Philosophy, in the most authentic sense of this word, is an enquiry into the basic character and the implications of human experience and of existence in its most general sense. The purpose of such an enquiry seems obvious. It is to enable human beings to develop, collectively and individually, their innate potentialities with the best possible chance of success, of total happiness and/or self-transformation toward higher levels of fulfillment.

However, what can be an optimum development of innate potentialities at a certain historical time and in certain geographical-social circumstances may not fit human beings equally well in other times and places. No true philosopher should ever consider man -- individual or collective man -- entirely apart from his environment and from the period in which he lives. If he does so he commits the grave philosophical sin of extreme individualism; he deals with abstractions and not with existential realities.

There are fundamental facts concerning human existence which remain relatively unchanged as long as we deal with man as a participant in the complex activities of the Earth's biosphere; but we should accentuate the term "relatively," for conditions in the biosphere, the whole planet or the whole solar system can change considerably. It is entirely conceivable that such an alteration in the conditions of life on earth is ahead of us, perhaps in the not too far distant future.

Basic facts of human nature pertaining to "man's common humanity" do exist, but the way they have to be dealt with is what changes. Every human culture approaches them in a different way, giving them different meanings and implications.

Philosophy in our modern American universities has become what it generally is today because the official layer of our present society -- the Establishment -- has accepted as its ideal, "technological man" -- or as some would say, "computerized man." The man who seeks above all to measure phenomena and events with reference to the achievement of quantitative and statistically expressed goals, and through the use of machines, standardized tests and psycho-chemical interferences with natural processes -- such a type of human being is today considered by most people in America, and more and more in other countries as well, as the most characteristic and most important product of our civilization.

What is implied in such an over-all attitude toward human existence and toward the world in which man lives is a peculiar and historically novel emphasis on the individual person. This individual person is glorified in his ego-reactions and his ability to be a ruthless master over his environment, and at the same time reduced to a mere number by a quantitative and statistical approach to his collective social existence. We live in a period of intensified individualism, but as well of depersonalization. Everyone for instance is eager to act according to "his own" opinion, his own way of arranging his life -- to "do his thing"; yet these opinions and ways of life are moulded by ever-increasing social-economic pressures, and conform to group-standards and perhaps sooner or later to standards universally imposed in the name of "scientific fact," of "efficiency" and of maximum happiness for the greatest possible number of people. "People," rather than individual persons are considered. Quantitative achievements and the amount of commodities produced regardless of the welfare and happiness of the producers count much more in actual fact than qualitative values and whatever is needed to insure the full development of the individual being as a whole-person, microcosm of the universal Whole in which this person lives, acts and has his being.

In a society where quantity, exact measurements, statistically generated values and mechanization for maximum productivity prevail, philosophy inevitably tends to satisfy the need for strict and precise formulations which can be fed into computers and the variegated mechanisms of social living. Man is seen ideally as a thinking animal seeking to super-rationalize and to dis-animalize his character. The term, reason, divested of the higher meaning it originally had in classical Greek philosophy, becomes intellectualized and technocratized. Will such a society follow the lines of logical development which are being plotted out by the students of the future, the "prospectivists" and "structuralists" of recent fame? A revulsion against such a prospect is already being felt, especially by our youth. It is certainly possible that, sooner or later, we may witness a repetition of the process which nearly two thousand years ago led from the ratiocinations of the Greek Sophists to an emotional mass-dissatisfaction, making possible the triumph of Christianity. The Roman sense of "law and order" wedded to the older Greek rationalism collapsed under the pressure of under-privileged classes, of constant military adventures, and of a sense of emptiness and futility among many individuals of the ruling class. Irrational faith and the inner excitement of self-surrender in martyrdom replaced the older ideals of the Greco-Roman tradition -- C r e d o q u i a a b s u r d u m: I believe because it is absurd.

Our present-day society is already witnessing in many places such a mass-revulsion; some aspects of it are quite obnoxious, even if understandable as psychic escape from a sense of futility and bondage to set life-patterns controlled by the drive for ever greater profit and material productivity. But there are also valuable and promising attempts at developing a new over-all philosophy of existence. Some of them, popularized under the name of "existentialism" were at first heavily colored by despair and the experiences of the two World Wars; other attempts at reorientation and at transforming our modern Western mentality have sought a way of renewal and spiritual-mental rebirth in the ancient metaphysical concepts and the life-ideals of India, China, Japan.

In these Asia-oriented attempts, two trends are noticeable: one of them leads to a mystical or quasi-mystical attitude toward the world and man, based largely on feeling-values and devotion; the other toward a more mental endeavor to discover the "structural" factors operating at the core of existence, whether at the individually human or the cosmic level.

AT THE THRESHOLD OF A NEW ERA

The feeling of a coming "New Age" has become, of late, world-wide. The official academic Establishment in our Western world is not against such a sense of an impending New Age which may mark the coming to maturity of the human mind; but it sees this New Age as the progressive development of what started in the European Humanism of the fifteenth century--thus 500 years ago. There are, of course, the pessimists who speak of global nuclear destruction, wiping out mankind. The optimists think along the lines of the new "science" of prospective (of which the Frenchman, Gaston Berger, was one of the main pioneers) attempting to extrapolate what is now at work into the future. They are committed to the scientific mentality of our day. They study where the present trends will or at least may lead, expecting no radical change of consciousness or in the basic attitudes of man. They are not really seeking to develop a new kind of philosophical insight, but only to plot out ahead of time gradual modifications of what exists today.

This is, in a sense, also the basic attitude of the "Liberal" in politics and in all fields of organization of the collective life. He does not want a solution of continuity in our social sense and in our traditional institutions, or even a too sudden and too radical transformation of basic human values. He still believes in what the 19th century worshipped, i.e. Progress. But this concept of gradual progress from barbarism to some ideal world-civilization has lost much of its convincing power since our World Wars and the electronic revolution. This is the tragedy of Liberalism, and of many idealists who believe in it with a rationalistic and democratic fervor.

In contrast to the scientific-liberal approach to the concept of a New Age, we have a great variety of groups and movements which, quite emotionally in most cases, expect some striking and radical change to bring about a supernatural and relatively sudden metamorphosis of humanity. These groups range all the way from those who fervently expect that "space people" will protect us from nuclear harm and transform us individually and collectively in as easy and painless a way as possible, to individuals who are working intently -- through meditation, invocation, fund-raising, group-building -- to become the disciples and servants of the returning Christ, or of a new Avatar, or of some transforming cosmic Entity who will "make all things new."

It should be evident to every sane and unsclerotic mind that we are indeed living in a period of intense and apparently relentless transition -- a "critical state" between two conditions of human existence, or at least of social organization. And this transition may be as marked as that of the solid to the liquid state of matter. It is not merely a quantitative change in the size and scope of social institutions; for the extension of our human environment and field of communication from the localized provincial-national to the global, planet-wide level implies also a change in the quality of interpersonal and inter-group relationships.

The peasant of medieval Europe, who under the pressures of the new type of national organization was transferred to the state of dweller in the metropolis of a large modern nation, had to experience a change in the character of his relationship to other men and to all kinds of factors in his new environment. We are still witnessing today, in vast numbers of people, the psychological, mental and spiritual dislocation attendant upon this bio-psychic-social change. The change from the national-cultural consciousness to an all-inclusive global or "planetary" participation in a "world-society" can certainly be expected to be as drastic. How drastic it will be can even now be observed; but human eyes very often, alas, refuse to see, because the change is frightening to minds more or less comfortably at ease with the status quo -- even to those who are smugly attached to their own ego-frustrations and spiritual emptiness. One can be clinging desperately to one's familiar sufferings and tragedy just because they are well-defined and familiar!

The essential point, we must insist, is that there cannot be such quantitative changes in the scope and inclusiveness of interpersonal relationships and in the character of the participation of individual persons in the society to which they de facto belong without a corresponding qualitative transformation of their fundamental field of consciousness and of their entire character and their responses to personal experiences. We all recognize the truth in such a statement; but in most cases only vaguely. We are not totally convinced; even less so than the young teen-age girl is really convinced that a successful married life demands of her a basic change in consciousness and feeling-responses to her new type of existence. We want to change, to increase the scope of our human relationships and our experiences; but we are confident we can remain the same. We demand to retain unaltered what has been called our "ipseity," our own character; and this actually means our own ego, our own private "Establishment," our institutionalized "differences" from other persons.

This is the crucial issue facing our present generations. The older ones do not want to, indeed temperamentally cannot, change unless confronted with the utter disintegration of their past; and even then, how many of the old exiled French or Russian aristocrats actually became transformed persons able to realize that tragedy had liberated them from an obsolete even if, in part, beautiful society? As for the present younger generation, they "would very much like" to change, to experience life in a new way; but they really do not know how, for they have no model easily available, no exemplars to imitate, and not enough knowledge or even feeling-awareness of what is really at stake. Thus, notwithstanding a few remarkable exceptions which one hopes to see greatly multiplied, the young people tend to flounder in uncertainty; and, dispirited as well as uprooted, they at times make violent but empty gestures just to prove to themselves that they are alive and vibrant in the midst of the social sclerosis of a dying civilization -- or at least of a chaotic mass of obsolescent patterns of collective and individual living.

SEEDS FOR TOMORROW

What then is the solution? A new philosophy from which will derive a new sense of interpersonal, world-wide relationships, leading to a new kind of ethics and a new type of society in which the principle of management for total and harmonic use will have superseded at all levels that of power-politics -- including the family level where the individual as an infant becomes acquainted with the power-politics of its parents' egocentric attitudes, and often its helpless victim.

This "new philosophy" can hardly belong to the sphere of what most of our present-day universities understand by philosophy. It requires, quite obviously, a new type of philosopher. This new philosopher will have to be able to integrate the seed-harvest of the whole of humanity's past -- and not only what has resulted from the last five centuries of individualism and science in our Western world. He will also have to challenge ruthlessly the obsolete values of our culture and of any culture of the human world. He will have moreover -- and this will be his most essential activity -- to be able to evoke new Images of order, of integral relatedness, of personal fulfillment, and, in the most general sense, of a human plenitude which will include all levels accessible to the consciousness of the global man of tomorrow.

Very few men, indeed, can be expected to perform effectively and vividly these three functions; but the great philosopher should incorporate them to some extent in his synthesizing, challenging and evocative work. He need not be a "man of action" in the external sense of this term; yet he will inevitably consider himself an "agent" for the vast movement of the evolution of humanity, creating the new at least in seed while challenging the old to radically renew its symbols and its behavior and feeling-patterns or to let go of its stranglehold on the human mind. Some philosophers are destroyers as well as if not more than creators. Typical among them was Frederick Nietzsche; yet he was a seer, distorted and incomplete as was his vision.

There have been great personalities during the last century and even more recently who have sought to garner the fruits of old traditions and myth-expressed wisdom as spiritual food, and as a vitalizing ground for new ideological departures and new visions -- often trying to return to the original sources of deviated and materialized traditions so as to touch the essential substance of reality which centuries of cultural living and compromises had so altered as to make it unrecognizable. There is an essential substance of reality for Man on this Earth; it expresses what I called long ago "man's common humanity*" -- that is, the root-factors in global Man; and many attempts have been made since 1870 to discover world-wide meanings in myths and popular tales from all continents and to stress the similarities in the Sacred Books of all major religions.

The work of several great Hindu thinkers since the latter part of the nineteenth century has been characteristic of the attempt to go far back in their culture -- beyond the world-wide evolutionary phase of medievalism and intense devotionalism, beyond the rationalistic period of the sixth century B. C. and the centuries following -- to what modern historians insist on interpreting as a primitive mentality, but which may well also have been a period of great spirituality formulating itself outwardly as myths and Mystery-rituals. The magnificent and revelatory writings of the great Hindu philosopher, poet, yogi and seer, Sri Aurobindo, throwing a totally new light upon the old Vedas, is perhaps the best example of such attempts. European thinkers and students of Asiatic traditions have also done remarkable work in unearthing the real meaning of old texts and of a few still existent groups or Brotherhoods. Sir Woodruff for the Tantra, Richard Wilhelm for the Yi Ching and other Chinese "esoteric" treatises, Evans-Wentz for Tibetan records, G. R. S. Mead for Gnosticism and Carl Jung (and several recent writers) for Alchemy, are but the best known of such workers, reopening old and often desecrated wells of wisdom.

All this work on the past is, however, but background work. As F. D. Roosevelt significantly said: "The past is only prelude." What is, after all, the essential task at the threshold of the New Age that is ahead of us is to fecundate the collective unconscious of mankind

---

*cf. THE FAITH THAT GIVES MEANING TO VICTORY, 1942, published by the Foundation for Human Integration, now non-existent.

with new Images relevant to the expectable
global character of the future society. It may
not be an immediately expectable society and some at
least of the utopian expectations of frustrated and restless
groups of seekers or devotees may at best be dreams that
may take centuries if not millennia to be realized in a global
manner; but every great philosopher should be, to a degree
at least, an evocator of visions of the future -- thus in the
true sense of the term, a prophet, a man who has seen a
vision.

Among some of the Pueblo Indians of New Mexico, particularly in Taos, every boy after having passed through ini-
tiatory rites around the time of puberty is sent to the mountains alone for days of fasting and meditation until he has received a vision. This vision is believed to be the key to his
deeper life. As a Medicine Man from Taos told Carl Jung:
"What can a man do if he has not had his vision?" In many
cultures, the initiate receives a new name, perhaps a mantram; this too is the sacred key to his true life. It sets the
tone to a significant, because symbolic, approach to individual existence. "Christ" is the sacred Name of our Western
civilization, as "Buddha" was that of a vast Asiatic cultural
Age. Alas, what has been done to the basic keynotes of these
historical periods, especially in our theoretically Christian
West!

Oswald Spengler spoke convincingly of the Prime Symbols
which constitute the very soul of a culture: but his vision was
strangely limited and past-oriented. He could not see how,
within the very process of culture-disintegration which he
identified with civilization in the negative sense of the term,
"seeds" are formed which become in due time the foundation of a new culture. On the other hand I have emphasized
for fifty years the concept and ideal of the "seed man" -- and
Arnold Toynbee in another way and about the same time,
came to a similar realization; yet he has been very timid or
bound to the past in his endeavors to envision the coming

civilization which his structural analysis of history portrays as imminent.

New "Images of man" have been presented during the last decades by philosophers or creative artists who have thought to outline what a new type of human being might be. Sri Aurobindo's "Gnostic man" may be one of the earliest, and as well the most inspiring of these new Images. His great work THE LIFE DIVINE ends with a magnificent vision of what such a type of spiritualized being in attunement with the creative and transcendent energies of the universe might be like, and of the society he could build. Teilhard de Chardin also had his vision of the future man, homo progressivus. Charles Morris wrote in his PATHS OF LIFE of the "Maitreyan man," at a time when I was outlining the figure of "the Man of Plenitude" (THE AGE OF PLENITUDE and MODERN MAN'S CONFLICTS: The Creative Challenge of a Global Society, 1945). Oliver Reiser, Lancelot L. Whyte and a few others have sought to present new ideals of manhood which are far more than the mere extrapolations of present trends.

How lifeless and sterile such projection into the future of our present humanity can be is amply demonstrated by the science fiction writers who usually cannot escape from the concept of the Technocrat, which developed between the two World Wars. This concept, popularized for a while by Howard Scott's organization, Technocracy, is based in the last analysis on the premise that the future belongs to modern science and its particular brand of technology and its intellectual methods. But is this a true, a necessary premise? Do we have to postulate that the path that the scientific and strictly rationalistic mind of Western man definitely took some three or four centuries ago in Europe is a path that will be proven in the long (or short) run basically valid for the optimum development of the potentialities inherent in Man? What if, for easily understandable historical reasons,

i. e. as a reaction to Medieval scholasticism, our European brand of humanism, our Cartesianism, our Baconian empiricism and our particular way of approaching technological problems were not essentially sound and wholesome, in spite of what they have achieved? Where will these achievements lead? Could it not be to a society in which powers of self-destruction would be inherent -- as they seem to be already inherent in our present technological society?

We cannot discuss here such a possibility; nor can we give any precise suggestion as to how our Western science might have taken another turn some four centuries ago, and how man could have approached his quest for knowledge and understanding of the processes of existence along very different lines; but a rather simplistic observation may give a clue.

Our technology is based on the destruction of material entities as a means of releasing energy. We burn wood, coal, oil; we split the atom. What is released is "fire" of some sort and heat; and the apparently inevitable result of such techniques for the release of energy is a considerable quantity of more or less poisonous waste products. Our atmosphere, our water -- and the water cycle on our planet is the condition for life -- our soil and indeed our physical bodies are being poisoned by our technology to a degree which is likely to increase by geometrical progression in the immediate future. We all know this as a fact, though we would like to think it simply is not there. Unless a radical change occurs in the social and personal drives of today's humanity there may well be no way to solve this crucial problem, for it has its roots both in the emotions of greed and craving for power and in the intellectual approach to the problem of releasing energy for use.

But do we have to "release" energy, in the sense that matter must be destroyed in order to effect such a release? Einstein's famous formula (and perhaps his entire Theory) may be hypothetically true, yet the only way we can think of putting it to use may be essentially destructive of truly human values and spiritual attainment. Do we need to destroy anything in order to have energy or power at our command?

When men crossed the seas in sailboats, they used a power that was there to be used by the ingenious mind of man -- the mind that knows how to adapt to natural conditions and to increase their yield so as to satisfy human needs for existence. Agriculture and cattle-raising make use of the power of life in the biosphere, that is, of the principle of multiplication of seeds; the more favorable the environmental conditions, the more effective this principle of multiplication of animal or vegetable seeds. Nature is made to work directly for man in a true partnership -- a creative partnership. Nature's energies surround us. All that we need is to discover means of utilizing them to the fullest possible or the optimum extent.

How do we know that we are not surrounded by planetary, solar and cosmic energies which could be used more or less as the sailor uses the power of the wind? Indeed we know very well that such as yet unused energies are all around us and are pervading us through and through. Gravitation, earth-magnetism may be weak, but they could perhaps be concentrated, as diffuse light is concentrated by a lens. We already use solar light to heat water and to provide electricity to orbiting instruments. We may build accumulators for solar winds and cosmic rays. We may learn to use what today we call neutrinos; and there may be many other types of as yet undiscovered energies. Perhaps we will realize sooner or later that our great scientific experiments have been programmed in such a way that we have only a distorted idea of what these unused energies really are -- an idea which makes their effective and wholesome use by man very difficult or even altogether impractical. But such a realization would have to offset the tremendous inertia generated by the very achievements of our technology.

What this implies is that our Western mentality may have developed along lines which could almost inevitably lead to some catastrophy in the not too distant future unless a fundamental "change of mind" somehow occurs. I am optimistic enough to believe that such a change may occur; but how it could take place without quite a radical crisis of some kind -- it could be telluric as well as social or religious -- seems almost impossible. However, should such a fundamental human and planetary crisis occur, what will follow would depend in a large measure on what has been produced as "seed-ideas" before the crisis. If no seeds fall into the ground during late summer and early autumn, there can be no new vegetation when a new spring comes after the long wintry death. To produce such "seed-ideas" is the function of the true philosopher and also of the true creative artist; in a deep sense the two are one, even though in terms of outer achievements they can be and usually are differentiated.

WHAT IS REALLY AT STAKE?

If our Western mentality, its science and technology, have gotten onto a "wrong track" how are we to find the right one?

These terms "right" and "wrong" have been used only to force a basic point upon the reader's attention. They are not adequate terms. The development of the Western mind during the last centuries -- and perhaps already in Greece after Heraclitus and Pythagoras--is not to be considered as wrong any more than the antithesis which follows the thesis in the dialectical process is wrong. It can however lead to destructive ends if the power of the synthesis is not made to operate.

However, what is dialectically called synthesis is not correctly understood by many thinkers. The synthesis presupposes, we believe, a "descent" or focusing of a more encompassing or "higher" principle of action upon the process being considered. If we can speak of levels, then something of the higher level must intervene in the conflict between antithesis and the obsolete forms resulting from the original thesis. If this does not occur the revolutionary energy of the antithesis degenerates in an unholy alliance with these obsolete forms which are thus given a seemingly new life.

We have a tragic instance of such a process in Naziism; for the basis of Hitler's doctrine was a purely tribal worship of blood, folk-culture and land. The tribal state of society may be considered as the thesis of the development of man as a being able to emerge from the compulsive patterns of the biosphere; and originally it held in latency the eventual liberation of the human spirit. But if the still existent biological imperatives of the tribal state become for some reason associated with the antithetic development of the individualistic intellectual and analytical mind, i. e. with the type of methods and research used by modern science -- such as, for instance, vivisection and interference with genetic processes -- then the result can indeed be monstrous.

What the modern science-hypnotized world needs is an "intervention" from some "higher" realm if the process of synthesis is to occur constructively and bring about what we might call a transfiguration of human values. But there need be no "mysticism" attached to the terms, "higher" and "intervention," even though unfortunately they may be loaded with religious emotionalism and a basic feeling of personal frustration. What we consider "higher" is simply, in fact, more encompassing. Tribal man lives enclosed in a small valley watered by a small stream or springs. From the mountain-top of the intellectual mind the vision extends to a large area, and the problems which arise from this vision are those connected with the conquest of this vast Earth-space, with communication between the products of various climates and the men of different regions, languages and customs. Western society has tried to meet these problems through long journeys, intercontinental commerce and -- almost inevitably considering this phase of human evolution -- colonialism and slavery on a vast, interracial scale.

Now the mountain-top consciousness is acquiring globe-circling wings; this could mean synthesis at a higher all-encompassing level in relation to the planetary being of humanity. But circum-global space-travel, and even reaching the Moon whose orbit may well mark the outermost boundaries of the Earth's total being -- its "aura," some may want to call it -- still presents us with a crucial choice. It could lead to negative results, if the old tribal consciousness of man remains effective in a maximized and monstrous manner to animate future man's endeavor into organizing the whole planet along "technocratic" lines; this would indeed result in nearly total destruction. The positive results to be hoped for require more than what the modern technologist and his computers can produce; they need a new spiritual force -- a radical transformation of the character of individual man. And such a transformation inevitably demands a new quality of interpersonal relationships and a new sense of value and purpose.

We may call this a "descent" of spiritual or cosmic power; we may speak of the need for the coming of a Divine Manifestation or Avatar prior to the actual beginning of a new phase of human evolution, and indeed of a new planetary cycle. We may even believe that such a descent of spirit will take the form of a fecundating contact with the humanity of some more evolved planet in this or another solar system. In a sense, the philosopher's task is not to opt for this or that possibility. It is essentially to prepare the ground for a new type of consciousness, whatever be the way that this new type of consciousness can be made truly and definitively operative.

In order to fulfill such a task the philosopher should first

of all investigate the very beginning of independent consciousness in a human being before culture-conditioned interpretations colored the formation of the mind. He should try to
understand afresh the barest facts of human existence
with as few intellectual preconceptions and emotional prejudices as are humanly possible. He should generalize and
interpret these facts, boldly if necessary, yet humbly --
trying above all to define clearly and as simply as possible
the words he uses to express often unexpressible experiences
and the subtle imagery of feelings.

We cannot avoid using words; and by so doing our consciousness is inevitably conditioned by the culture which has
produced and organized these words as collectively accepted
symbols for communication between personal minds and
psyches. Still we can be careful not to make, if at all possible, unwarranted assumptions and not to take for granted
traditional and "moral" judgments. It certainly is not the
true philosopher's function to be an apologist for modern
science or for the European tradition with its religious and
ethical biases.

The trouble with philosophers is that when they write
they are mature persons who build their philosophical systems largely in response to their emotional and intellectual
needs, biases and complexes; and of course the present writer is no exception. What can be attempted however is, I repeat, to start with the beginning of human experience from
an existential point of view unburdened by metaphysical a
prioris -- to try to experience as a newborn child does,
and then to build from this primordial sensing-feeling. The
responses to life and the beliefs of so-called "primitives"
can also be of great value in such an attempt, provided we do
not interject the reactions of our "civilized" minds into these
responses and do not try to "explain" away what does not fit
our preconceptions concerning mind, soul, Self and the experience of subliminal elements.

A fresh, undogmatic, flexible approach liberated from

the familiar patterns of thinking and feeling with which we have been indoctrinated is necessary if we are to provide a "virginal" ground from which may gradually emerge a new open, yet consistent understanding of human existence and a creative evaluation of its meaning and purpose. Such an approach requires that the philosopher has passed through an experience of self-emptying and of what Buddhists and most mystics speak of as the Void (sunya in Sanskrit). An individual must shed the "old mind" conditioned by the culture and the language which moulded and directly or indirectly structured its growth before he can witness within his inner being the emerging consciousness of the New Man. This is the metanoia process, the transforming of the mind or nous. But more than the mind is involved in the emergence of a new philosophy of existence; a repolarization and re-energization of the feelings and of the imagination are just as necessary.

A philosophy is not a matter of concepts only, if by concepts we mean the result of an exclusively intellectual and rational process of cogitation. Psychoanalysis and all that has been derived from it have made it absolutely clear that one can practically never altogether disassociate a concept from some kind of feeling. General Semantics has shown how loaded with emotional contents many words are. To grasp the meaning and impact of words we have to try to perceive the images which they convey to the entire psyche of the person using or reacting to these words. That is why it is so essential for the philosopher who stands at the threshold of a potentially new civilization, and indeed perhaps of a new planetary Age, to empty his mind, his feelings, his entire psyche of old concepts, old values and old images; and this means actually to free himself from the ego-structure which rules his personal life; for this ego-structure has been utterly conditioned by the traditions and the inner imagery of his family and class, of his community, his college and his entire culture.

People who are conversant with the mystical traditions of all countries often delude themselves by thinking that, after some critical experience of apparent "self-annihilation" -- perhaps the experience of the much spoken about "night of the soul" -- they have become entirely renewed or reborn. They may have been renewed in a very real p e r s o n a l sense, yet they may nevertheless remain largely bound, far more than they would admit, to the old images, feelings and concepts of the culture which formed their thinking. It is questionable whether when Descartes had his famous experience in which he tried to bare his mind of all that could be eliminated as non-essential, he actually experienced a deep transformation of the mind. He could have come to the conclusion "I f e e l therefore I am," had he not been the product of a culture which held the intellect and its rational processes as the most essential factors in man. The image of the Thinker has been central in our Western culture. It constituted its greatness, yet also its limitations; for by officially glorifying the thinking process, reason and the dualistic ethics of "either-or," it felt compelled to give to the feelings and to all non-rational processes linked with the image-making and intuitive faculties of man a negative, or at least a lower meaning and value.

What needs now to be transformed, if we are to experience globally a basic human "mutation" in consciousness, are the very basic attitudes of both the mind and the feelings. The image-making power of the total being of man -- his capacity to "see" existence differently within a radically new frame of reference (and not only a new i n t e l l e c t u a l frame of reference) and to "feel" existence in a revirginized way -- this image-making power must be given a new and far more consciously creative character.

We can learn a great deal about this from the eminently pragmatic philosophy of old India -- pragmatic in a way which seems transcendental to us yet is, in a basic sense, eminently existential at a higher level of reality. We can, however, ask too much from India, China or Japan. Their ancient philosophies are essential as liberating influences; but to be free from the past of our civilization is only the first step. This can be a cathartic experience which leaves us either floating in some sort of subjective vacuum, or fascinated by some great (or not so great) Personage whose historical as well as spiritual role we may exaggerate in an orgy of blind and immature devotion.

What is expected of individuals who would be "seed men" for the New Age is quite a different attitude. Such men, Fathers of a global tomorrow, should take a step beyond the cathartic and ego-transforming experience -- a creative step. They have to act in terms of objective reality; but should they be chiefly philosophers, this action will operate essen-ially at the level of basic images and symbols -- i. e. of living and creative "seed ideas." This can be a most power-ful and effective action, for without such "seed ideas" the world-culture which should develop next century would have no solid foundation. Any culture can only grow out of basic ideas, images and symbols provided by a few "seed men" who came during the last period of a preceding culture. Even if there seems to be a violent radical breakdown of this pre-ceding culture -- a seeming solution of continuity like the "Dark Ages" following the collapse of the Roman Empire-- nevertheless the new culture must develop at first by incor-porating some of the "seed ideas" and symbols of the past.

So many "seed ideas" have been sown during the past hundred years! I can only hope that those which should be scattered by this book will have in them the power to feed the growth of men and women of the impending "New Age" in a harmonious, beautiful and serene manner and that they will fall upon a soil rich with the manure of tragedies over-come and blessed. I hope and trust that they will belong to the constructive side of the great "mutation" which is taking place, perhaps not only in mankind but even throughout the entire biosphere, and that they will play a significant, even

if small part in the process of unfoldment of a planetary consciousness in the fruitful minds of self-consecrated and radiant human beings.

II. MAN'S PRIMARY EXPERIENCE OF
EXISTENCE AND TIME

The philosophical "world-view" on which this book is based is h o l i s t i c; that is to say, it is founded upon the realization that what we call "existence" is a process operating everywhere in terms of "wholes" constantly in a state of motion and activity. Modern physics has revealed to us, within slowly moving or changing physical entities, a world of whirling molecules, atoms, particles, moving at incredible speeds. Modern astronomy speaks of billions of stars and galaxies also moving at enormous speeds. But whether we deal with atoms, molecules, living bodies, planets or galaxies, we are dealing with existential wholes each of which has a more or less complex structure and acts as a whole of activity. They constitute fields of energies; they radiate or release energies of various kinds. They are interrelated, and they interact.

All these wholes, as far as we are able to experience them, have a beginning and an end. They also constitute limited fields of activity. Their component energies are integrated by some kind of "binding force" or holistic power; they operate in time and in space or, in other words, they have a finite span of existence, and they also have a certain spatial "form." One can speak of their "cycle" of existence -- a cycle lasting perhaps a millionth part of one of our seconds, or billions of our years. We can also refer to them either as macrocosms or microcosms -- i. e. large or small fields of interrelated activities, galaxies or atoms.

The fact that existence is apprehended by us in terms of wholes of interrelated activity limited in time and space does not imply, however, that Existence, conceived in the most general sense, has a beginning and an end. There is no reason to believe that there is only one universe which began at a certain moment and will end in some final state. We can -- and I personally do -- postulate an infinity of existential cycles and an infinite possibility of space-fields defining the boundaries of existential wholes. However while time-cycles and space-fields have a finite character, it seems necessary metaphysically speaking -- and perhaps psychologically as well -- to imagine "beyond" them a state or condition which transcends existence. Philosophers have often spoken of that condition as "non-existence" because no existential concepts or images can describe it; yet we should imagine, inherent in it, the capacity to "pro-duce" space-fields and time-cycles defining forever new universal wholes.

B r a h m a n .in India refers to both the state of existence and that of non-existence. It includes not only the possibility, but also the actualization, through cyclic processes operating within finite cosmic fields, of an infinite variety of modes and forms of existence; and I shall attempt in later chapters to define in more modern terms a similar picture of ultimate "reality."

However, the main purpose of this book is not the development of a detailed and rigorously constructed type of metaphysics. What is intended here is to present only those aspects or elements of such an all-inclusive world-view required to provide a significant and adequate foundation for a creative and future-oriented understanding of the basic problems now confronting mankind.

These problems cannot be adequately faced o n l y in terms of an extrapolation of present technological trends into the future. They have to be solved essentially at the level of a basic change in human consciousness. A holistic philosophy is needed as a frame of reference for the new global activity of mankind, for without such a philosophy the expected world-society of tomorrow will most likely develop along lines representing a betrayal of man's noblest ideals.

Terms such as "philosophy," "existence" and "holistic" should not be misunderstood. They are not used in the intellectualistic spirit which prevails today in most academic circles in America. I have already defined "philosophy" as an enquiry into the basic character and the implications of human existence. As to the term, existence, it is in this book free from any close association with one or the other of the recent schools of thought and feelings covered by the general term, Existentialism. Basically existence is a state of unceasing dynamic adjustment and transformation in which activities of various types are interrelated and more or less permanently integrated within a field of forces, structured by some kind of cohesive power effective within more or less specific limits in space and time. This structuring power operates at various levels and in a variety of ways. Its operation is "holistic" (from the Greek olos, meaning "whole.") Without it there could be no existential wholes but only an undefinable chaos of random motions.

It is a basic fact of human experience that while the state of existence implies unceasing changes and adjustments to some kind of environment, it also reveals indisputable manifestations of order. The awareness of change and the realization that this change is pervaded by structuring factors implying some kind of over-all order and purposefulness indeed constitute the two fundamental facts of human existence. As man seeks to understand the basic character of his existence and to orient his consciousness toward the possibility of increasing his well-being, he has to take into consideration these two aspects of existence: change and order. Everything changes and events follow one another in a perhaps bewildering sequence suggesting pure randomness and meaninglessness; yet man can also discover that underneath this superficial play of unpredictable events and internal transformations a principle of order -- a holistic, structuring power -- is at work. As human beings develop their ability to perceive this principle of order in its multifarious manifestations they gain the capacity to use the knowledge thus obtained and transmitted from generation to generation so as to control their environment to some degree and have a more secure and more fulfilling existence.

The preceding statements are not the result of merely intellectual speculation; nor are they derived from any Eastern or Western religious systems. They are based simply and directly on the most primary facts of human experience. They refer to a direct existential or phenomenological approach to what every infant experiences after he is born out of the protective envelope of his mother's womb and as his consciousness of existence gradually develops and takes a specific form. Such a type of direct, existential approach is necessary today, for we find ourselves at this crucial time of man's evolution in a condition where we are challenged to consider afresh and to carefully and creatively re-think so much of what we have been taking for granted during the now closing Christian era. We need therefore a fresh start. We need to question the very first moments of any existential cycle. We should attempt to grasp what is most primary in human experience; and this means trying to look at existence through the eyes of the newborn child.

THE EXPERIENCES OF CHANGE
AND PERIODICITY

In his most primary awareness of existence the human infant is the passive recipient of a continuous sequence of impacts affecting his senses and of pressures altering whatever feeling he may have of inner organic processes and needs. Sensations and feelings pass by as it were; nothing seems to remain the same. Shocks, sensations, feelings of pain or well-being follow one another. Whatever awareness there is must be diffused through a nervous system and a brain which simply registers and reacts according to primordial reflexes. There is sentiency as in every living organism and probably in the most rudimentary way in every form of existence. But what we call consciousness in a human sense -- what Teilhard de Chardin calls "reflective consciousness" -- will only develop progressively, though at a really amazing rate considering all that is involved in the process. In this sense of the term, consciousness, every cycle of individualized existence begins in a state of at least relative unconsciousness. Still it is evident that every particular cycle of existence is related to the past, whether in an individual "karmic" sense or in terms of heredity. Past cycles bequeathed certain tendencies to the new "existent" and these act as innate structuring factors in the new organism.

The primary fact of existence is an organic field of activity. The organism-as-a-whole reacts to sensations and to the interior needs of its various systems; but these reactions are at first not referred to an even relatively permanent structure or center of awareness. The newborn does not know himself as existing separate from an outer world. He does not differentiate at first between inner and outer. His nervous system only registers happenings, which follow one another as a series of organic states, movements and reactions. If reactions are different in every infant it is simply because every human organism differs in some respect from other human organisms, both in substance and in field-structure.

There comes a moment when something in this organism becomes aware that certain shocks, impressions and feelings which cause him to vibrate and react have already been felt. The reactions following these feeling-sensations also have the character of having been previously experienced.

This awareness of the "already felt" and the "already re-acted to" must at first be vague; but it quickly gains greater precision. Very soon, it seems, the nervous system of the infant organism registers the fact of r e p e t i t i o n.

This feeling of repetition is the very foundation of con-sciousness. It gradually transforms the passive awareness of a constantly changing sequence of sensations and feelings succeeding each other without noticeable relation the one to the other into the consciousness of r e c o g n i z a b l e pat-terns. Certain sequences of actions and reactions become isolated, acquiring a recognizable form and a definite pur-pose at the level of organic needs. As the sequence of day and night, light and shadow, hunger and satisfaction, un-pleasant wetness and pleasurable dryness are understood to repeat themselves -- as the child's brain registers that the release of painful tension in a cry is followed repeatedly by the comforting actions of the mother -- a primitive feeling of o r d e r emerges out of the original chaos of ever-chang-ing sequences of happenings.

If repetition is assured, foresight is possible. The most primitive awareness of the repetition of daily events grad-ually becomes a definite expectation of what one has fore-seen. P r e d i c t a b i l i t y and the order found to be inherent in nature therefore constitutes a second element which enters into human experience. There is constant c h a n g e; but there is also o r d e r, regularity, periodicity and rhythm of existence. These two elements of existential experience are fundamental. All that is human is based on them; and the great problem for the individual, as for society, is to deter-mine the respective values of these two elements in our ex-perience.

One of the main concerns of human society, be it ancient or modern, is to expand, by incessant collective effort, the field in which existential facts present themselves to the mind as ordered and predictable elements in human exper-ience, and by so doing to reduce as much as possible the realm in which chance, unpredictability, the irrational and the traumatic take place. This collective effort is at the base of all that we call culture, religion, science, civilization. Where the sense of order is satisfied and the principle of predictability is given the consistent and dependable form of natural laws and of aesthetic as well as scientific formulas, security reigns.

This feeling of security is as necessary in the psychological sphere as in the physical and social life of man. Man has an essential need to feel himself acting in an environment where he meets more or less constant evidence of a fundamental and reliable order. He also has the need to feel sure of his own reactions, his responses to interior changes which gradually transform him, develop or age him. The ego-sense is, as we shall presently see, a manifestation of the feeling of that inner order which rules the reactions and the conflicts of individual existence.

Conceived in its most ideal and universal state this sense of order is what we call reason. But each person can also have "his reasons," that is, his own intellectual and psychic order. If that state of inner order is threatened, insecurity arises. This insecurity can become a sort of cancer turning the vital forces of the organism into energies of destruction; it can also produce fantasies and illusions which seek to build a fictitious order substituting itself for the disorder of a psychic life deviated or frustrated by situations, unpredictable events or unconscious reactions which were unexpected and shock-producing.

Yet this need for order can become a tyrant. It often gives to the intellect and to the rigid forms of rational thought a power which can destroy the capacity to feel directly and to experience spontaneously, freely, the quickening flow of events, feelings and relationships which constitute the primary substance of human experience. An exaggerated need for exterior order which a culture and a collective tradition satisfy, and for inner order manifesting in the exclusions, the refusals and the fears of an ego more or less rigid and proud of its own structures, can warp, destroy or hinder all interpersonal relations which might seem likely to transform the established order. An existence frozen in a traditional order which leaves no place for any possibility of radical change becomes a parody of existence, because existence is fundamentally movement, flow, spontaneity and creativity.

Above all, existence is relationship. No existent is born isolated. He is born into a vast field of activities which demand his participation. His consciousness is formed through the exercise of his capacity to enter into relationship with others -- and above all with conscious existents, with companions whose individual rhythms can unite with his and thus strengthen, extend and refine this rhythm. Only relationship can actually transform the pattern of an individual existence. And to enter into relationship is not only to react to something or someone who touches you; it is, for the truly conscious human being, to "meet." Consciousness affirms itself and is enlarged by the mysterious grace released by "meetings," total and spontaneous. Such a meeting becomes most difficult, if not impossible, whenever those who meet have been conditioned to depend on some narrow and rigid form of order imposed by their society.

Thus a human being needs to experience deeply w i t h i n h i m s e l f a state of order and security which permits him to meet, consciously and in a condition of positive strength, the ceaseless unfolding of events and the varied encounters with other living beings. Without this profound feeling and a knowledge of the order which these events reveal to the mind which contemplates them objectively, the individual person can indeed become confused, shocked or bewildered. On the other hand, if this sense of order and structure governs his existence in a rigid fashion and jealously controls his responses to all that he encounters in the field of his activity this field inevitably grows narrower, loses its dynamism and becomes ankylosed in formalism and sterile egocentricity.

Such a situation can easily lead to an ambivalent attitude toward all that derives from the need for order in any mode of existence and in social or cultural activity. Thus one of the greatest problems confronting a man or a society is: How much of order or patterned behavior is required for optimum human development? Moreover the basic question is usually not the "quantity" of order and security which is most important, but the "quality" or type of order and security that is truly constructive and essentially fruitful.

Unfortunately the concept of order and security has been presented by hundreds of philosophers and theologians in a manner which, idealistic as it may have seemed, has resulted in a false sense of existential realities. It gave rise to tendencies which very often have destroyed or perverted the deeper sense of integral existence in man. Too often, alas, these "official" leaders of society and religion have conceived the dynamism of the process of change and the principle of structural order as absolute and irreconcilable opposites. What is more, they have presented this principle of order as being external to existence and indeed pre-existent; and this has led to tragic results, socially and psychologically.

Man indeed experiences existence under a double aspect; but the principle of perpetual change and the principle of cosmic order are not opposed to each other. They interpenetrate everywhere and at every moment. Order is inherent in existential change. There is not really, as so many religious thinkers have believed, a world of order (a rational one) and a world of existence in a state of perpetual change (a world of passions and suffering.) Existence is one; and existence is rhythm and melody combined for him who can accept it in its totality. This "rhythm" establishes the type of order of the existential movement; the melody is the substance of the flow of events and inner feelings or "images." This flow proceeds in a constant state of improvisation, yet it also develops the fundamental themes which limit the emergence of existential possibilities without restraining the character and the quality of the relationships between all that takes form within this vast and wonder-full "river of life." Order is not superimposed upon existence by an outside power; it is the very rhythm of the process of existence. And this rhythm, considered as a cosmic principle, is what we call "Time."

EXISTENTIAL TIME

From an existential or phenomenological point of view time is simply an abstraction of the awareness of ceaseless change. Change implies successive modifications of the contents of the feeling-experience of existence. Every human being -- and in a probably far more imprecise manner every organized whole of activity -- has a "sense of time," for the simple reason that his organismic feelings and the impressions which assail him change constantly. This change may seem more or less rapid, or even appear almost to stop if the attention of the organism, and later of the conscious ego, clings for a while to what is happening at that moment; nevertheless the basic fact of human experience is the awareness of a continuous succession of feeling-sensations merging into each other. Existence is a continuum of ever-changing modifications of the contents of the "field of existence;" and the primary sense of time is the awareness of this fact.

Such an awareness has at first a purely p a s s i v e character. The nascent consciousness of primitive men and infants floats, as it were, on the stream of existence. Life "passes by," but at such a stage of awareness man actually does not feel himself separated from this stream; he is identified with it. He reacts to it in an organic (or "organismic") manner; indeed in a passive manner. This means that the primordial experience of change is not a feeling of s u c c e s s i o n of separate and identifiable "events" but rather the sense of a continuous flow. Existence flows not only by the newborn, but all t h r o u g h him.

As time is at first not separated from the experience of change, the most primitive awareness of time can be called the experience of a continuous "passing." In such an experience there can be no differentiated perception of successive "moments"; such a differentiation comes at a second stage of the development of the time-sense. It arises in the nascent consciousness when the infant organism begins to cling to a particularly pleasant feeling and strives to retain it; or else has been so shocked by a painful sensation that the consciousness retains a persisting awareness of the happening. As a result this particular feeling acquires a special character of distinctness, and the nascent time-sense crystallizes, as it were, around this feeling. The impressive "event" is felt to have occurred at a particular "moment."

The French word for now is maintenant; and this word comes from the verb maintenir -- to maintain. The concept of "now" arises out of the fact that the infant seeks to maintain or, as this may not be possible, to remember what occurred at a distinctive moment. When he makes such an effort the baby's passivity toward existence and time begins to be transformed; he ceases to identify himself (unconsciously) with the very process of organic living and of continuous changes in his existential state. He has created a "tension toward" some event which brought him a particular sensation or state of organic well-being -- a state which gave him pleasure or awakened an instinctive sense of danger. He has begun to learn to concentrate and to fix his attention.

The psychological phenomenon of attention actually is the very foundation of what, existentially speaking, develops as the individualized aspect of consciousness. When the human organism fixes its attention upon a particular phase of the continuous "passing" of the stream of sensations and feelings, what was passing at once became past. When moreover the nascent consciousness realizes that certain feeling-sensations have already occurred and that the organism reacted in the same manner to the repeated experience, a category of experiences acquires a specific character, i. e. they belong to "the past." Inevitably the experience of repetition and of past events leads to the development of a symmetrical feeling of "the future" based on the expectation of the return of the pleasurable or painful change of organic state. What has "already" happened several times could occur "again." One awaits the new event "in the future"; it has become a something in the past. It is only when the attention ceases to identify itself with the "passing" and directs itself alternately toward the past and toward the future that the realization of the "present moment" -- the now -- develops in the already somewhat objectivized consciousness of the very young child.

This process of development of the time-sense and of the change from the feeling of the "passing" to the awareness of past-present-future is one which has not been well understood. Yet such an understanding is most essential if we want to evaluate adequately many of the ideas which have been advanced concerning the nature of time, and particularly the glorification of the "now" -- i. e. of "living in the present," and of an "eternal Now." I believe that much confusion has arisen from the failure to realize the character of the most primary feeling of time -- that of the "passing."

To live with a consciousness of this "passing" which does not differentiate between past, present and future is not to live in the Now. The very young child does not "live in the present." His consciousness floats on the stream of "the passing," constantly buffeted by the moving panorama of sensations and the inner alternation of organic states. It is only as the ego-consciousness and the religious and intellectual development of the mind freeze the primary experience of existence and time into set categories -- the past, the present, the future -- that the sense of time becomes strictly objectified and rigidly defined, then measured by collective means, like the bells of medieval churches, and later by individual time-pieces or clocks. Soon all kinds of problems arise which are referred to what is called time; such as "Being on time," "There is no time," "Time is money," "Bondage to time," etc.

The sophisticated concept of "now" arises as the result of a feeling that one refuses to worry about the past and to build conscious expectations of the future. Then also man, feeling himself limited by time and frightened by what seems to him as "the end of time" as far as his body and his personal life are concerned, begins to dream of and aspire toward a state of existence in which time will no longer pose limits to his activity -- thus to a state of immortality; while philosophers imagine and search for a timeless condition of "Being" endowed with a consciousness transcending all existential changes. To such a consciousness all forms of existence are integrated or harmonized into an Eternal Now.

To speak of an Eternal Now is quite evidently to postulate a completely s t a t i c condition of Being beyond all changes. Such a transcendent condition of all-encompassing, static Being is postulated in contrast to the dynamic ever-changing state of universal existence woven on the warp of time; yet the two states are said by most religious thinkers not to be mutually exclusive; "Reality" includes both. It is said, moreover, that man in his ideal and perfect condition can come to experience in consciousness the transcendent timeless state even while, as a physical organism, he operates in the existential condition of unceasing change and under the control of time's ineluctable rhythms.

There is, however, an aspect of time which has not been accepted probably because it has not been understood by the great majority of the thinkers of the Western world. I am referring to the cyclic concept of time, a concept which, had it been accepted by the Christian-European society, would have made impossible the emergence of the most undesirable, and indeed tragic features of our Western civilization. The concept of universal cycles was of course well-known in

India as well as in China. The early leaders of Christianity, particularly at the Council of Constantinople, denied the validity of this concept on which an entire world-view can be based. And this denial, related to the eagerness to present Christ as the "one and only" Son of God and to consider a human life and personality as the "one and only" existential manifestation of a transcendent Soul created by God, has had extraordinarily wide and long-range results which have now reached a "critical state."

HOLISTIC TIME AND DIMENSIONAL TIME

When one speaks of "cycle" to most Western intellectuals one finds that they relate this term either to the empirical study of some natural or social phenomena -- for instance, cycles in the rate of multiplication of certain animal species, and cycles of economic productivity, of the rise and decline of the stock-market--or else they think at once of Nietzsche's concept of the "Eternal Return." The concept of cycle presented here refers to something very different, that is, to what I call a "cyclo-cosmic" concept of existence which applies to every form of organized whole of activity.

The basic premise in such a holistic world-view is that existence manifests at all levels in terms of wholes, that is, of organized fields of interdependent activities made possible by energies of various types. These fields have more or less clearly defined boundaries in space. They begin with a limited release of energy and a definable (however complex it may be) set of potentialities. These potentialities become more or less successfully actualized during the period of effective operation of these fields; and this operation comes to an end after having produced characteristic results, some positive, others negative. That is to say, existential wholes have a limited span of existence during which a process of actualization of potentialities released at the beginning of the existence of this whole operates.

This process contains a series of phases -- a series having a definite structure. It is a whole in time, or better, a t i m e-w h o l e, i.e. a cycle; and it operates within the finite boundaries of a s p a c e-f i e l d. What I call cycle is a "time-whole"; what I call field is a "space-whole." Every existential whole has therefore to be considered a "cyclocosm," vast or small as it may be with reference to man's position in the scale of sizes in o u r universe. Whether it be macrocosm or microcosm, galaxy or atom, it is an existential whole and it displays the essential characteristics of wholeness, i.e. extension, duration and structure or form.

Time and space, thus considered, are basic factors of existence; they can be regarded as "universal principles." T i m e refers to the fact that a particular creative impulse releases into existence a certain q u a n t u m of energy needed to actualize a definite set of potentialities; and that fundamentally the existential process of actualization of these potentialities must end when the energy is exhausted. But Time also refers to the fact that throughout the span of existence of the whole a structural power operates which has inertia, that is, which makes sure that the process-as-a-whole operates, phase after phase, toward the o m e g a-end inherent in the a l p h a-beginning; and this in spite of an opposite factor which tends to alter the structural "purity" of the process.

This other factor is S p a c e. While Time is essentially a unitarian principle controlling in its general outlines the process of existence which began in "unity" -- o n e original creative impulse -- Space refers essentially to the principle of relatedness. It refers to the fact that no existential whole exists alone. It is constantly in relation to other wholes; and relationship "creates" motion and spatial extension. The energies of the space-fields are not only in a state of mutual interrelationship, but their interplay generates some surplus of energy which the field cannot contain and which therefore, normally at least, radiates into an environment filled

with other wholés. Every whole is related, directly or indirectly, to all the other wholes "in its neighborhood"; and
the term neighborhood should be extended to include wholes
in the at least recent past and in the more or less near future, for space and time are related, but not in the sense in
which modern physics speaks of "space-time." They are
related somewhat as Yin and Yang are related in the
Chinese symbol, Tai Chi.

In this holistic conception of Time as a universal principle, Time is an objective element of existence. It is a cyclic factor, not in the sense that a series of events in
time will repeat themselves serially in a succession of
wholes -- be they galactic wholes or individual persons -- but
in the sense that the process of existence passes through a
series of phases, a series which defines the time-structure
of the process of development of this whole from beginning to
end. What Time defines is not the existential events themselves but the structure of the process of which these events constitute the
contents. It represents, in religious terms, the Will of
the Creator -- a Will which can probably best be understood
in terms of inertia, i. e. of resistance to developments which
would alter basically, though not in existential details,
the course of the existential process and impair its end-results, its "seed"-fulfillment.

Again we find here the contrast between the experience
of change and that of order, or structure. The experience
of change is always based upon the factor of relationship. If
the infant experiences pain when he is hungry, this organic
feeling of hunger refers to a metabolic and chemical change
in the relationship between the various cells and organs of
his body; if he falls out of his crib and hurts his head, this
means a change in the external relationship between his body
and surrounding objects. Time, on the other hand, refers
to the internal process of development of his consciousness
of being an existential whole, an organism, and later on an

individual person. This process has a definite rhythm -- a particular speed of unfoldment -- and it may be unwise to accelerate it by providing the child with an overdose of external relationships that bring in problems with which his organism-as-a-whole may not be able successfully to cope with.

Time is also the rhythm of unfoldment of the whole planetary environment in which man is immersed, as an embryo within the mother's womb. In this aspect we find Time expressed as the alternation of day and night, and of seasons, an alternation whose beats define the natural tempo of man's growth and eventually of his disintegration. Time also is expressed in the structuring power of the entire solar system as a field of energies over the planet, Earth, and especially over the biosphere in which man lives, moves and has his being.

Every whole is part of a greater whole, as well as the container of lesser wholes over whose activities it exercises a structural, rhythmic control.

This statement is basic in the holistic philosophy of existence which this book presents. It expresses an incontrovertible fact of human experience -- not a theory. The human body as a whole contains billions of cells which, in turn, contain a myriad of atoms within which whirl at fantastic speeds sub-atomic particles or waves of energy. At the same time a human organism is contained within the planetary field of the Earth, within which mankind-as-a-whole performs a definite quasi-organic function, as we shall see later on. And the Earth is a whole of organized and interdependent activities within the greater whole constituted by the solar system, which is one of billions of stellar fields of organization within the galaxy.

Can we speak further of metagalaxies or finite universes? Is there no end to the relation of lesser wholes to greater wholes? This is not the place to discuss this metaphysical problem except to state again that there seems no logical reason why we should stop anywhere and at any size of wholes, though the fact that the size of the human body appears to be just about mid-way between the smallest and the largest existential unit known to us may indicate that this entire picture of the scale of sizes of existential wholes could be anthropocentric. But even if it is, the fact remains that we are participating in the activities of greater wholes, just as lesser wholes are participating in the activities of our total human organism -- a participation which may produce well-being or illness.

SCIENTIFIC TIME-MEASURE OF MOTION AND DISPLACEMENT

In Bergson's philosophy (cf. CREATIVE EVOLUTION) a sharp distinction is made between what the French philosopher calls la durée (duration) and the kind of time which enters into the equations of modern physics or of science in general. "Duration" refers to the continuum of events experienced by living organisms and by the consciousness inherent in them. This continuum has a definite direction and irreversible movement. Thus the Bergsonian concept of duration is quite similar to that of time experienced by an existential whole as "the passing," that is, before the concept of separate movements -- or we might say, of time-units -- dominates the intellectualized consciousness of the human being.

As soon as one speaks of time-units and of moments having a separate and recallable character, the factor of discontinuity enters the stage of consciousness; and discontinuity permits measurement. A certain number of time-units are seen to occur between the beginning and the end of an existential process. The process therefore acquires a measurable length -- a length of time -- and "dimensional time" becomes substituted for the Bergsonian "duration" — at least in some instances, the number of which is ever-increasing.

What does the concept of measurement imply? It implies a transformation of the primary and subjective (or organismic) awareness of change into an objective sense of something in motion. The concept of motion implies time based on the succession of identifiable states from which a center-of-consciousness is detached enough to observe them -- to measure their progress and their speed. Whatever can be observed objectively and measured has "dimension." Objects have spatial dimensions -- length, breadth, height. When they are seen moving their motion also acquires a particular kind of dimension which is dimensional time. Modern science speaks of it as a fourth dimension.

Scientific time is the substratum of all the operations which refer to the measuring of the displacement of objects in space. As the measuring implies a measurer, the inevitable conclusion is that the results of any kind of measurement must be referred to whatever does the measuring. Thus the values belonging to the realm of dimensional time exist only when considered in terms of a "frame of reference," that is, in relation to the observer as at least potential measurer. From this results the Einsteinian concept of the relativity of all motion, and the establishment of a space-time frame of reference for all scientific measurements.

At first it seemed obvious that in terms of dimensional time any motion could as well go "backward" as "forward" in the time-dimension; that is, past and future appeared to be as interchangeable as right and left, eastward and westward, upward and downward. Thus the fantasy of "traveling in time" became a boon to the imaginative minds of science-fiction writers. However some recent observations and experiments* have suggested that motion in dimensional time is not reversible, and that at least biological processes move in a definite direction and cannot be reversed.

---

*cf. MAIN CURRENTS IN MODERN THOUGHT

The entire picture created by the concept of a purely dimensional time is indeed awkward and confusing, besides contradicting the basic experience and common sense of man. A four-dimensional space-time continuum is not, indeed cannot really be a "continuum," because continuity eludes measurement. One can only measure the discontinuous; and the act of measurement, whether by yardstick or clock, is an intellectual operation. There is however far more to man and man's consciousness than the intellect, its exclusivistic categories and its irrevocable wedlock with quantity and measurements.

However, this is not to belittle the most significant place which the intellect (and the ego, closely associated with it) occupies at a definite stage in the evolution of consciousness. The act of measuring is, of course, indispensable to our present-day world and in terms of the practical necessities referring to this physical and social world and to the development and fulfillment of the ego-consciousness of man. But, as we shall see in greater detail in the following chapters, the ego is not the total man and the intellectual mind is only one particular form which consciousness assumes at a particular stage of human evolution. We are now confronted with the possibility -- nay, the necessity -- of letting a new type of mind develop within us; and this means of discovering a new frame of reference for our capacity for objective measurements. This frame of reference, which is not exactly "new" yet which needs to be formulated in a relatively new way, is the Cycle -- the Eon -- and the true sense of "eternity" which man can reach at a certain stage in the evolution of his consciousness.

ETERNITY AND TIMELESSNESS

One of the most unfortunate events in the history of human thinking may have been the misinterpretation by early

Christian thinkers of the term which we now translate as eternity. The meaning of this word was inevitably altered as a result of the already mentioned insistence of the Christian Fathers on the essentially unique character of God's incarnation into the "Christed" man, Jesus. That event having been endowed with an absolute character, and the individual human person having also been given such a character, the pre-Christian realization of existence as a cyclic process became unacceptable. According to the Christian tradition there is only one God, one universe, one history, one God-man and one arduous rise of man from a sinful state to a glorious condition of heavenly bliss -- and, in the mystic's view, of union with God; or else a totally negative fall into an absolute hell from which there can be no return. The Gnostic schools of the first centuries A.D. sought to reinterpret the concept of the cyclicity of all existence in more or less Christian terms; they referred constantly to Eons, that is, to the divine state of unity of cosmic cycles of existence, a state in which the wholeness of the cycle is, as it were, condensed into a divine Consciousness -- a cosmic Being. But the Gnostics were condemned and their communities eventually died out or were destroyed, though some of the Gnostic traditions and beliefs persisted in various "heretic" movements throughout the Christian era, and have been revived in various ways during the last hundred years.

Eternity has been, in the official thinking of the European and American cultures, opposed to time and conceived as a "timeless" state. The idea of "the Eternal Now" has influenced the dreams, the aspirations and the philosophical statements of many mystically inclined people, especially in recent years. Such an interpretation of the word, eternity, indicates of course a perfectly valid yearning in human beings to transcend their condition of bondage to particular circumstances which often appear unbearable; but it has the same character as all negative concepts; and today the minds of so many forward-thinking and inwardly rebelling individ-

uals are filled with such negative concepts. These are concepts referring to things which are not what they seem to
be, and which operate in ways utterly different from the behavior of our consciously known physical or intellectual environment; thus rouse in us extraordinary feeling-reactions.

The majority of human beings when confronted with such
events or such subjective inner experiences are made most
uncomfortable. They react in fear or with a supercilious
sense of superiority. They simply dismiss what does not fit
either into their "normal" everyday frame of reference or
into their intellectual categories. Yet there is in man a basically ineradicable longing to be more than he is or knows
himself to be. He deeply feels his inferiority face to face
with the powerful energies of the biosphere and of the cosmos; and this feeling impels if, indeed, it does not compel
him to believe in the reality of a transcendent state and a
transcendent Being that possess, as essential characteristics all the powers and qualities which man seems incapable
of manifesting. Because man's consciousness operates in a
realm of finite magnitudes and is constantly frustrated in its
aspirations and its will to achievement and mastery by this
"human condition" which Existentialist thinkers have pictured as being basically somber, tragic, desperate and absurd, this human consciousness has poignantly sought to believe in a "Reality" which is NOT any of the things man
lacks, despises or fears.

Thus because our conscious being is filled with problems
and so often faces inner situations, outward impulses, moods
and cravings which seem alien to our normal consciousness
and desire-nature, the concept of the "Unconscious" has
arisen and has of late gained enormous prominence; and
because in our modern life we seem never "to have any time"
to do what we want to achieve, the concept of a "timeless"
Reality (or state of consciousness) has fascinated people's
minds. God, or Reality, is conceived as possessing all the
attributes that man does not, yet would so much like to pos-

ess.

As there is a widespread revulsion today against the traditional beliefs of the European-American past, the search for that which is not what our forefathers believed to be reality, truth, wisdom is reaching epidemic proportions. But the great mystics, the seers, the "inspired" leaders of thought of nearly all periods of history have always been fascinated by such a search; they had experiences so unusual and supernormal -- we now speak of "peak experiences" in a somewhat more common sense -- that they could not formulate and thus communicate them, through words, to other people. Poets used symbols to suggest the nature of such experiences; but when all symbols failed they were faced with the need to state simply that what they experienced was not anything anyone knew or could know with normal senses or in a normal state of awareness. And so books of mysticism and metaphysics are filled with terms implying negation -- indeed very often total, absolute negation of all existential facts; thus the concepts of nothingness and non-existence, of timelessness and spacelessness, of the Void, etc.

In the fourth chapter of his book, CREATIVE EVOLUTION, Bergson made a very fascinating study of the idea of nothingness, le Néant. What he tried to convey by means of logical arguments is that one cannot actually conceive "nothingness." What this negation of all existence really means is that our mind, having exhausted all possibilities of different forms of existence, covers up its defeat under a convenient mantleword. Thus the term "Non-Existence" does not actually mean what it seems to say -- i.e. the absolute denial of Existence in any possible form or condition. It simply means that there is a state of reality which transcends any conceivable human idea of order and reality.

The great Hindu philosophers -- for instance, Sri Aurobindo, whose work and spiritual influence extend around the globe -- knew well that Brahman did not mean non-existence but rather an inconceivable state in which both non-existence but rather an inconceivable state in which both non-existence and existence were included, much as Yin and Yang are the two poles of That which encompasses them both, TAO, as the symbol of the TAI CHI pictorially describes. Similarly some of our freest philosophical spirits, including many great scientists, are beginning to realize that "order" and "chance" (or randomness) are the two aspects of the all-inclusive fact of existence; so also are negentropy and entropy.

What this means, with reference to our discussion of time, is that time and timelessness are no more real opposites than samsara and nirvana are absolute opposites in philosophical Buddhism. What we call the timeless state is not a state in which time does not operate but a state in which another order of time is experienced. Nirvana is not really the denial of existence and change, but a condition in which existence and change take on a new character and meaning. Nirvana can be experienced in samsara. They are two aspects of existence.

The "timeless experience" arises in a consciousness which reaches it from the condition of existential time, and which will return to this condition. It is an experience which "lightens up" time-conditioned human existence somewhat as, symbolically speaking, the leaven lightens up the substance of the bread. The holes in the bread are not bread; yet they are in the bread. They contribute to its character and quality. It is in this sense that Jesus compared his disciples, and in a broader sense the Kingdom of Heaven, to the leaven. All true mystics are in this sense "holes" in the bread of mankind. The mystic experience is a state of "fermentation"; therefore the Sufis wrote wondrous poems to wine and the intoxication it produced, and Genesis refers to Noah's "vineyards" which, in mystical parlance, symbolize Schools of Initiation into the Mysteries -- Mysteries referring to the primordial Edenic state of mankind, the Golden Age when Man and God were one.

The state of spontaneous child-like "unity" symbolizes

the beginnings of existence. In this primordial state, there is identification between the experiencing total organism and the continuous flow of existence. Time is apprehended as "the passing." Existence, in the condition which we call "life," flows in and through the existent. There is no separation. Neither is "the passing" separated into time-units, i. e. into moments; but neither is there what we normally call at least in the Western world, consciousness. In the river of life, the newborn is not conscious that there are himself and the river. He simply "is" -- as a throbbing overtone within the great melody of human existence.

But the newborn grows up; and his adult mind molded by his particular culture and environment is trained to establish differences in terms of relationship to other living entities, or even objects; to realize the need for patterns of order to control the interplay of interpersonal, social relationships. He becomes conditioned by this principle of order and structure which we call time; and he begins to feel that "there is no time." As a result he may dream of being in a "timeless" condition of existence. However if he has been conditioned, by his culture and the philosophy of life he has adopted, not to follow such a form of "escape" -- escape from time into timelessness -- he may instead strive earnestly to fulfill time.

This ideal of "fulfilling time" implies a cyclic conception of time -- a holistic approach to time and human existence. It implies the realization that existential time begins and ends, just as any process of existence -- any life-span, be if of an atom, a man or a galaxy -- begins and ends. It means that the very nature of time is cyclic. As I previously stated, there are time-wholes (cycles) as there are spatial fields within which a myriad of energies interact within finite boundaries. Every existent is a cyclocosm; and the aim of existence for every cyclocosm is to fulfill time in its omega condition, just as it is to fulfill space through the full, wholesome and (ideally) "holy" development of all the internal relationships and powers which operate within the individual person's "field of existence."

In this state of fulfillment man's consciousness apprehends time in a new way, i. e. as "eternity" in the true sense of this word. Existential consciousness reaches the state of eonic consciousness; which does NOT mean "unconsciousness" but instead a kind of consciousness able to encompass as a whole the entire cycle of existence of the individual person to whom it refers. In this state of eonic consciousness the conscious "I" has become free from the conditioning pressures of local environment, family, race and culture which moulded the ego, as we shall presently see. In a sense man finds himself then identified with the cyclic flow of existence; but this identification is no longer "unconscious." Indeed it is not really "identification"; it is a state of resonance, of fulfillment in a totally and perfectly formed vibratory response to the "fundamental Tone" that sustains the total individual organism -- the individual "field of existence" -- from birth to death, from the alpha to the omega of its existential cycle.

So it is to live in the condition of "eternity" -- not an escape into timelessness, but fulfillment in the wholeness of cyclic being, in the Eon. It is not merely living from moment to moment in a condition of open receptivity to changing influences and of availability in terms of ever-changing relationships, but rather living every moment consciously as well as openly as a particular phase of the process of existence, in as full an awareness as is possible of the function, meaning and purpose of that phase with reference to the whole cycle.

What such living implies is a fundamental change of existential frame of reference, and an essentially different approach to time and existence. Individual consciousness becomes established in the entire existential cycle experienced or felt, as a whole. This represents a great expansion of

consciousness; but the expansion of a f o r m e d consciousness, whereas what so many people today seek and understand as expansion of consciousness refers to a kind of self-
loss in an u n f o r m e d and "ecstatic" feeling-experience of
unity with all there is. This can be a wondrous feeling-experience no doubt but an experience from which one must inevitably return to the everyday world of differences, categories and conflicts.

The character and quality of this "return" often leaves
much to be desired; whereas the man who grows, unspectac-
ularly and simply, into a realization of his "eternity" does
not have to return from anywhere. He is always present.
His feet touch the ground of everyday experience, while his
head encompasses and accepts, with the serenity of the Sage,
the wholeness of his existence from alpha to omega; and his
will is attuned to the constant and fundamental rhythm of the
self within.

What this self actually is, as the basic sustaining power
of the whole field of existence, and its relation to the ego,
will now be discussed.

III. THE EXPERIENCE OF "I":
SELF AND EGO

The old Socratic injunction "Know thyself" is the theme of endless variations in this period of confused searching for new meanings and values, and particularly for an experiential foundation upon which to base such new values. This foundation refers to the question often heard today: "Who am I?" and thus to what is widely called the search for identity. Words and questions can be confusing and indeed meaningless unless they are carefully scrutinized; and one should never forget that the formulation of a question already conditions, if not determines, the kind of answer one will receive. Even scientific researchers in their laboratory experiments are or should be well aware of this fact, for the way you conceive an experiment limits, if not defines, the kind of results which can be expected from that experiment.

"Who am I?" Thus formulated, the question actually takes for granted the more or less consciously expected answer; for that pronoun, who, referring to a person, makes it clear that the answer will deal with the fact that the questioner is a "person," i.e. an entity, an existential whole. What is asked therefore is not what does "I" refer to, imply and signify, but rather what kind of a person am I. Likewise in the search for one's "identity" what one is actually concerned with is what one stands for as an individual person, and what one's true place, function and character are in terms of the social environment in which one lives;

and the reason for such a search is the fact that one feels intensely or acutely that the kind of "self-image" one has of one's own personality has actually been imposed upon one's consciousness by parents, culture, school and all kinds of social pressures. Deeply dissatisfied with and rebelling sharply against the pressures of an ever more complex technological and competitive society, which seems to think of nothing much besides ever greater productivity of goods, the youth of today tragically and confusedly seeks to discover a "self-image" which really fits his or her deepest sense-of-being-alive and his most vivid aspirations. The term, self, in the word "self-image" refers, however, not to what I shall presently call, self, but rather to what the human being is as an individual person; and this seems to me an incorrect and very confusing use of the word because it hides the very nature of the problem involved in the determination of the essential meaning of "I." What am I -- or should we say what is really "I"?

For most people, it is true, the deep feeling "I am" is the most evident and most basic of all realizations; yet does it actually possess such a taken-for-granted character of indisputable evidence? In this subjective statement, two factors are implied: "I" and "am." The "am" is the evident fact for if there were no existence there would be no statement, no activity whatsoever; and in saying this I do not limit the term, existence, to what we usually consider as physical existence, but I mean any conceivable type of organized activity displaying some degree of permanence. However, if the "am" evidently underlies any organized form of complex activity, the "I" is an ambiguous factor. Of course grammatically speaking the "am" presupposes an "I"; and even if we said "is" instead of "am," the objective term "is" implies a subjective entity that is aware of existence, and in some way, first of all, of its own individual existence. Thus there is that which says "I am"; but the question is: What is this entity which uses the term "I" aware of? What does it mean when saying "I"? What kind of entity is it? We should try to find a convincing way to answer these questions, which are the real questions to ask -- and which so few people even think of asking.

The usual way of obtaining knowledge is through the senses, and through the intellect which correlates, organizes and generalizes sense-data, building thus from this data abstract concepts which are expressed through one kind or another of symbols and images -- words being, of course, the most generally used symbols. It is on this type of knowledge that science is built. There is, however, another approach to knowledge which refers to what is usually called introspection, in which the faculty of awareness of the human organism turns itself inward, as it were, in an attempt to observe, elucidate and evaluate the complex processes which in their totality we call our own existence, and which we usually divide into "body" and "psyche." Then there is also, as we shall see in a subsequent chapter, another kind of knowledge which in a sense includes the two just mentioned types, but which cannot be as yet significantly discussed.

Both the "objective" and the "subjective" approach to knowledge can be validly used and interrelated. By using both we shall soon see that there is a basic ambiguity involved in saying "I"; for this small but so basic term will turn out to refer, potentially at least, to two different factors in the human being considered as a complete whole or "field of existence" -- i.e. to ego and self. It is because these two factors are either confused, considered as one, or inaccurately defined, that the psychology of our Western society is today in such a chaotic state. And as long as this state persists the whole fabric of our society and of our collective official mentality will resist or pervert any deeply constructive and spiritual attempt at building a "New Age" civilization.

THE OBJECTIVE AND "HISTORICAL" APPROACH

The basic problem to be solved when one uses an objective approach is to ascertain whether the "I-feeling" is a primary feeling-experience, a "given" in the philosophical sense of this term, or the result of a process unfolding after birth and in relation to the environment of the newborn. If it is not a feeling-experience inherent in the organism of this newborn, how does it develop and what purpose does this development serve?

It is impossible of course to be certain of what a newborn baby feels; but as this is an "objective" approach we can look for evidence of this I-feeling experience. As far as I know there are no such pieces of evidence, or at least the feeling does not manifest in any reaction or mode of behavior which would tend to show that the newborn is definitely c o n s c i o u s of being "I," i. e. of being a distinct unit of existence with a more or less permanent individual character. He may be aware, in a subconscious and organismic sense, of something else; and we shall presently discuss this "something."

As the infant grows during the first months of his existence, he is surrounded by parents, siblings, nurse perhaps, who respond in different ways to the fact of his existence as a newborn human organism. They feed him, talk to him, play with him, and address him by a certain name -- perhaps it is only "baby," or it may be Paul or Jane. These grownups t h i n k of the infant as a baby, as a little person; and they look eagerly for signs of particular reactions to the feeding, cleaning, sleeping processes this tiny organism is experiencing. The o r g a n i s m is undoubtedly experiencing these and other biological processes; but this is something quite different from a consciousness of being a distinct "I."

This infant-organism, named by his parents Paul or Jane according to their personal preferences (or the wishes of grandparents, or some accepted social-religious tradition) very soon must be aware of the difference between inner organic feelings (like hunger, wetness, cold) and outer sense-impressions or shocks; yet this difference is no doubt at first most imprecise. As he comes to be aware of the fact that some changes of feeling are repetitive, having already happened and later on occurring again, so must he be aware that these changes are met by other events which constitute reactions to the former and which also repeat themselves. Nevertheless a clear distinction between inner and outer events -- between the mother who satisfies the feeling of hunger and this hungry body that reacts with contentment to the feeding -- takes quite some time to take form.

Soon the child begins to talk; that is, he imitates and responds to vocal sounds he hears and that are associated with other sensations of warmth, shape, color and probably of "love" (whatever love may mean then to the infant's feelings). Then, if he wants to refer to his needs and his feelings, he uses the name by which he has come to realize these "presences" around him call him. He says: "Paul wants -- or "Baby wants." Only at a later date does he say "I want"; and when he says "I" he almost certainly does so because people around him are heard to say "I" on a great number of occasions, the meaning of which only progressively reaches his nascent consciousness.

We shall discuss the term "consciousness" in the following chapters, but we certainly should realize that while we may philosophically and theoretically say with Teilhard de Chardin, as well as with Hindu philosophers, that every existential whole has some degree of "consciousness" (in the most universal sense of this term), nevertheless the word consciousness, at the strictly biological level, refers to some diffuse kind of awareness and sentiency, plus the capacity to express a few basic emotions, but not to what Teilhard calls "reflective consciousness." Reflective consciousness is awareness focused and defined (or definable)

in terms of a particular frame of reference. It is awareness turning back upon itself, after rebounding (as it were)
from some sort of mirroring surface or boundaries. Indeed
this kind of consciousness, which may only be possible to
man, presupposes an awareness of "boundaries," that is,
the awareness that this organism that reacts to external impacts is a whole distinct from other wholes, each whole having somehow a relatively separate field of activity --
a distinct, isolatable field of activity; "my" field.

This fact the child begins to realize; and, as he realizes
it, twin feelings arise at the same time within the patterning
process that goes on within his brain, and perhaps within
other nerve-plexuses as well: "this is mine" and "therefore I am." This "I" that "possesses" a certain characteristic, distinguishable set of reactions and a particular "quality of feeling" which seems different from the quality of feeling of other human existents (judging from the way they act,
speak and radiate feelings) -- this "I" is the initial manifestation of what I call the ego.

The term "possesses" does not refer here, at least not at
first, to physical possessions; or it does so only to the extent that this new consciousness of the infant does not yet
differentiate too clearly between his own organism and play-
things or objects (or even persons, like his mother) which
he calls "mine." "My" mother, "my" dad, they are part of
"me"; so feels-thinks the infant. And soon the term "my"
increases in scope; and with it the sense of "I" -- the ego-I
that possesses whatever he can include within his field of
activity, his "own."

A study of this ego-sense and of the phases of its development would cover much interesting data. All that can be
said here is that this ego-sense operates as a function of the
development of consciousness; it represents a primary fact
of this development of consciousness, but NOT a primary
fact of organismic existence. One must distinguish very
clearly between what refers to the fact of existing as an or-

ganic whole -- and what belongs to the realm of the human consciousness. Consciousness appears within the holistic field of activity of the human organism; but it represents another level of activity, and this new level can acquire a definite independence from the organismic field, once its characteristic operations have become stabilized, structured and formed into a mind. A mind is an organized field of conscious activity operating according to functional principles of its own; but these principles have inevitably at first a social-cultural character. The society and the culture constitute a kind of "matrix" which is needed for the early development of a mind, just as a material womb is required (at least under natural conditions!) for the growth of the embryo into a viable organism, a baby.

The ego is that which structures the operation of the mind and, through the mind at its most instinctual level, the conscious feeling-responses of the person. (There are, of course, also compulsive organismic feeling-responses, like instincts and unconscious types of fears, complexes produced by the frustration of organic drives, etc.) The formation and development of the ego have been conditioned and often almost entirely determined by family and social pressures, by school education, by imitative behavior often strengthened by a sense of dependence upon exemplars -- the parents, friends, etc. -- and a feeling of social or personal inferiority. Thus the ego has been called a "social construct." It remains bound to local factors of race, climate, culture, as long as mankind has not reached a global state of operation. It is probably that even in this state ethnic-geographical differences will remain vividly impressed upon the development of the ego and the mind of the child until, becoming an adult, the human individual is able to emerge deliberately (and most likely under some special influences) from this socio-cultural womb, and to be born (i.e. "reborn") as a truly individualized person -- as a "free individual." And by free, I mean here, free to enter into some new type of allegiance which he has selected in (theoretically !) full consciousness of what he is as an individual.

When most people today speak of self -- of myself and yourself, of "the self in transformation" (title of a book by Dr. Fingarette) -- they are referring to the individual person whose consciousness is structured, i.e. defined and limited by an ego. When a person says "I was beside myself" he implies that whatever acted as "I" was really alien to the conscious field within which his ego normally rules, rejecting into the abyss of the subconscious (or personal unconscious, according to Carl Jung) feelings, thoughts and motivations that do not fit into this ego-controlled field of consciousness. The "I" of the normal human being speaks from the throne of the ego.

What I call self is something entirely different; though without the presence of the self vibrating through the total field of activity which constitutes the person-as-a-whole there could be no ego -- simply because there would be no living organism. The self is the center of power in the whole organism; the ego is a structure of consciousness which is made possible by the integrating power of the self. But the ego is not the self. The self is an organismic fact; the ego is a product of the development of consciousness under the pressure of external factors, but also within the individual range of possibilities of response to life and society defined by the individual rhythm and character of the self. When we are dealing with the self and the ego we are dealing with two levels of activity and integration.

Perhaps a more "subjective" approach will help us to see more clearly what these two levels represent.

THE INWARD QUEST

The process of "introspection" is arduous as well as ambiguous. It contains many pitfalls and through it one must constantly be alert to the possibility of meandering and losing one's way, attracted by what has been impressed so forcibly upon our consciousness during childhood and by education that it has come to be completely taken for granted. It should be obvious that if I can be expected to reach a fundamental awareness of what is at the very root of my existence, I will have to discard all that is but surface-activity and whatever does not belong to this essential "I," the nature of which I am seeking to fathom, but belongs instead to the images which my family and my culture in general have made of it.

In India, and in recent years in a Western world increasingly influenced by Asiatic philosophies and techniques of "spiritual development," the inward quest for the self (the atman) begins with a No-saying to whatever the mind normally considers as subjects for attention. Neti! Neti!... not this, not this. As the procedure is taught today, the first thing for the searcher to do is to try to dissolve or repudiate identification with his body. He will say: "I am not this body and its wants"; then, "I am not my feelings and emotions -- my desires, my fears, my reactions to love, hate or resentment -- not even my longings for beauty, sharing, comfort, peace, salvation." Lastly the concentrated consciousness, fixed one-pointedly upon its most interior processes and activities, will try to dis-identify itself from the forms of the mind, the habits of thought, the ambitions of the thinker, until an inner quietude and silence is reached in which everything having "form and name" (in Sanskrit, rupa and nama) has fallen away. What remains is said to be the pure, unconditioned "I" -- the supreme identity which transcends the forms in which it manifests in terms of body, emotions and mental processes.

There is, however, something in that approach -- in this process of rejection and denudation -- which is quite questionable because illogical and semantically confusing. What is discarding the non-essentials of consciousness and stilling the voices of the senses and the feelings, the wandering thoughts? What is saying "No" to them, if not the very factor which the seeker is claiming to discover at the end of the quest? Is not this factor the very same "I" that is there at the beginning of the process?

We might say that it is this "I" which is seeking all the while to free itself from what was not its essential nature. But if so the end of the process simply reveals to us in its purity not only what was there at the start, but what desired or willed this process to take place. What the end reveals is that an abstracted awareness, feeling or "realization" of existence remains after everything dealing with the c o n - t e n t s of consciousness has been discarded; but if there had not been in the beginning a living organism with all its bio-psychic activities and its mind (developed by a particu- lar language, culture and social environment) could there have been a process of ab-straction and rejection?

The resulting experience of residual "I"-awareness at the end of this Neti! Neti! process does not tell us anything about how the body and the mind came to exist in the first place nor how this total organism maintains its structural identity through unceasing changes. It does not reveal to us the primary fact of existence, the root of our being. Even if it is true that, once a newborn baby reaches a sufficient degree of maturity in a sufficiently developed culture, an "I" exists within this human organism able to disengage it- self from the accumulated contents of its everyday conscious- ness, this does not mean that such an I-feeling is primary and fundamental.

As already mentioned, the infant when loudly proclaim- ing his wants does not begin by saying "I want," but rather "baby wants," or "Peter wants." Likewise a primitive man in New Guinea has certainly not the same kind of I-feeling as the present-day English or French person. Lecturing on "The myth of the self," Dr. Fingarette (of the University of California in Santa Barbara) claimed, on the basis of an analysis of early Greek writings, that the Greeks of Homer's time had no really similar sense of self; and that in ancient

China it was essentially based on social relationships. In India when the Forest-Philosophers of old proclaimed the concept of at man and its identity with the universal B r a h- m a n, it is questionable indeed that they meant by at man what modern psychologists of the Jungian or the Transpersonal school mean by a capitalized Self. We must not forget that the term, at m a n, referred originally to the breath, and that the yogi's attempt to detach his consciousness from the perceptions of the body and the images-concepts of the mind was always preceded by some process of control or harmonizing of the rhythm of breathing.

What this means is that this supposedly essential realization of being "I" as a distinct self has been and is in man an evolving realization. It is not an a p r i o r i unquestionable fact of existence. Behind it, at the root of it, some other more fundamental fact should be discovered if the "inward quest" is pursued relentlessly and honestly.

Let us say that, speaking as an enquirer, I have been able to relax completely and still the wandering thoughts of my mind as well as physical sensations and inner feelings. What I reach then may be called a state of consciousness "without contents." In that state it is said that consciousness exists in a pure, focused condition as "I," that is, I have become the "I" that perceived and thought thoughts, the "subject" in all feeling-emotions, the transcendent self that manifests through the body, the emotions, the mind, but without being affected by their incessantly changing states -- unconditioned, free, as the true "I" timelessly is and ever was before "having" a body and a mind.

But is this assumption not actually reversing the roles? Let us think, by analogy, of the process by means of which attar is extracted from the rose petals, or of any process of abstraction, i. e. of drawing out some essential product from a complex living organism. Such a process of extraction (or abstraction) removes what appear as superficial elements in order to obtain the desired product -- the "quintessence."

But is the perfume the basis of the rose's existence? Is it not rather some element which is drawn out of the more superficial manifestations of the rose's total living organism, from root to flower? Likewise the state that is reached at the end of the successful process of denudation of all that is felt to be externals of existence is a state of consciousness which may very well be a "quintessence of consciousness"; but this state does not necessarily refer to that without which there could be no consciousness, simply because without it there would be no living organism, no human being.

At the end of the introspective Neti! Neti! process as usually practiced in our modern society, we may have reached a state of consciousness without contents; but even if this consciousness is entirely "withdrawn" from body, feelings and mind, nevertheless the basic activities of the body (and perhaps of an even larger field of activity surrounding the body) are still operating. If the withdrawn consciousness experiences a pure, undifferentiated realization of "I," it is because this "I" actually exists in terms of consciousness. But there are elements of existence which do not enter into this "I" realization, because they do not belong to the field of consciousness. Thus the "I" that is experienced does not include all that is unconscious. It refers to a sublimated form of the ego.

It was the ego which, because it was spurred by existential pressures, crises, suffering, anxiety, or perhaps stimulated by contact with a "spiritual Teacher" or even a psychotherapist, started this inward quest. It was thus driven to attempt a search for a solid, primordial, ineradicable foundation for its existence. And at the end of the quest this ego-"I" may find itself in a tranquil condition, free from the conflicts and the traumas of everyday mundane consciousness. It may see itself as a pure, unattached, undismayed, unaffected unit of consciousness. Because this ego-"I" has repudiated and overcome by an exercise of its will what distorted, blurred and perverted its approach to all the facets of existence and particularly all its reactions and responses to interpersonal relationships, it now exists as a purified and "free" quintessence of consciousness. But this type of consciousness does not refer to the whole of existence. The bare fact of existence remains unrealized and indeed unsought as long as the "I" that started the process of introspection and abstraction remains in control, even while it is disentangling itself from all that to which it has been attached. The king may throw away all the signs of his royalty, all his possessions; yet he may still know himself as "king by divine right"! Can the king really inwardly abdicate? Can he accept a new status of existence in which his position acquires a new meaning because it is no longer identified with traditional quasi-absolute power, but rather with an ideal of service without special privileges-- service to every existent within his kingdom?

The basic problem here is not the emptying of what the normal ego-consciousness holds -- its emotional and mental contents -- but the transformation and indeed the dissolution of the container itself, viz. the consciousness in its formed, ego-structured condition as "mind." What should start the quest is not the will or desire to "reach" the pure condition of "I," but a readiness to do what Jung graphically called "relaxing the cramp in the conscious" -- a readiness without expectation, and especially without the expectation of remaining conscious, at least not in the sense in which the ego has been conscious until then. The true inward quest should begin not only with the willingness to surrender the contents of the normal everyday ego-consciousness but in an attitude of non-attachment to the container of these contents.

This adventurous quest should not resemble our recent moon-landing expedition in which every move was prepared in advance and minutely rehearsed, with the astronauts hanging by the unsubstantial umbilical cord of radio-communication to a directing mother-control on earth, exercised in the name of national, military and business interests -- and only secondarily of so-called scientific research. It should really be an adventure in which the adventurer not only gives up all connection with his point of departure, but is ready to burn his ship when reaching the unknown land; otherwise this is no real adventure but merely a technical feat, and the adventurer can hardly be called a "hero" but rather a well-trained technician.

Let us try to indicate what such an inward quest might mean and lead to, if undertaken in such a spirit of t o t a l surrender -- of container as well as of contents.

I am the adventurer. I close my eyes. I try to quiet down and still the surface-waves of sense-impressions, the emotional eddies and the currents of thought which affect my consciousness. Then I try to l e t g o entirely, to forget that "I" exist, that anything exists. All is void. And yet... a heart beats, lungs expand and contract, motions are dimly felt. Through whatever is now sensed, there is a great peace -- the silence of a calm ocean unmoved by winds. Within this silence, as it deepens, an awareness of quiet, rhythmic activity seems to arise. It may best be spoken of as a soundless "tone," a vibration of definite pitch, though it seems also to contain a myriad of overtones. What is this "tone"? It is so pure, so simple. It i s; it so definitely, irrevocably "is"! It seems to spread t h r o u g h that great peace of which I am aware; but is there an "I" that is aware? Whatever is aware is implied in this "is-ness," in that undeniable fact -- that tone, that peace, that no-whereness and nothingness that spreads everywhere. Yet it is centered. It is rhythmic, unperturbable movement; but so still, so pure! It is perhaps what men call "existence." W h o s e existence?

If the thought of such a question enters the consciousness, something changes. The feeling-experience is no longer the same. It becomes somehow limited, a little awkward, indeed "self-conscious" in the colloquial sense of this term. The conscious "I" has taken hold of the feeling and made it a conscious fact; it is then almost impossible to avoid comparing it with other experiences, formulating it in words -- thus m e n t a l i z i n g it according to the language and the traditional concepts of my culture (or in terms of my revolt against these concepts and of my search for a more satisfying culture).

This is, of course, what I am doing now as I write about it. Yet in the very background of my unavoidably unsatisfactory effort at making the experience not only conscious but formulatable, there remains a residual feeling (an imageless "feel") of a "happening" that did not belong either to "me" as "I"-ego or to what in any precise and communicable (because rational) sense I am able to speak of as "consciousness." It did not belong to this field of consciousness because, though there was indeed a feeling-awareness of this all-pervasive vibration or tone, it was nothing "I" could hold in the framework of my consciousness. There was no thought implied in this feeling-awareness, no emotion or desire to hold it. It simply w a s t h e r e. But there was in this "being there" finality -- I might say an "absoluteness," though I dislike the word, absolute. There was strength, yet simplicity, purity, quietude; and when the processes of consciousness and thought returned, it seemed in memory, as I remembered what had occurred, that it must be called a "transcendent" experience in contrast to more familiar happenings.

Yet whatever was experienced was n o t transcendent for it seemed to pervade space itself -- the space of my existence, I have to say, if I want to make sense. It was -- I felt a f t e r w a r d, but not at the time -- the foundation of this existential whole out of which, or within which, sensations, feelings, thoughts form themselves and reach the condition of "contents of my consciousness." It is "my" consciousness because these sensations, feelings, thoughts have a more or less definite character; they are arranged so that they react and respond to everyday life in a particular way. T h i s p a r t i c u l a r w a y i s m y s e l f. It is the Law of my consciousness.

This consciousness is, as it were, managed by a power -- which is what the term, ego, really means. This managing power is like the Executive in the American political system. The Executive-"I" sits in the White House of consciousness; and he may be powerful, or impotent; but he is not the nation-as-a-whole. Neither is the Electorate -- the people who vote -- the nation-as-a-whole. The nation-as-a-whole is not only the sum-total of every person living in the United States; it is also the soil and the resources, the climate and the air, the lakes and rivers, the harbors, the mountains, the trees and the animals of this part of the North American continent. All of it must be included in the existential wholeness of the nation. And more still must be included: the collective mind of the people, the ideals and urges which integrate all these existential factors into a national entity occupying a place in the vast planetary mind-field of international consciousness and interplay of activities. Of all this multitude of activities integrated into a vast existential whole much emerges into the consciousness of mankind to produce the conscious image of the United States as a nation with a particular character, a trend of historical development, a political life of its own centered in a Government; but much of it also remains unconscious in terms of world-history and everyday world-events -- for what really and totally is "America"?

Likewise what is, really and totally, this individual person who knows himself consciously and is known officially by a particular name -- who displays a particular temperament and character -- who eats and sleeps, feels and thinks, suffers and enjoys, loves, is loved or rejected -- that is full of conflicts, problems, concerns, anxieties over which presides an executive "I"? Is this executive "I" the real ruler? Or is he dominated by set traditions and fears (complexes) and pressure groups (instinctual urges, emotional desires and mental ambitions)? How can I validly refer what I am not conscious of to this "I"-Executive? Will I say like Louis XIV in Versailles: "The state, it is I"? Is existence limited to consciousness?

Three and a half centuries ago the French philosopher, Descartes, made a courageous attempt at questioning every opinion, doctrine and prejudice which he had inherited from his culture and environment. He had come to doubt the validity of everything he knew; and he sought to discover one thing only that would appear to him certain and indisputable. He then came to the realization expressed in the famous sentence "I think therefore I am." But this young man of 23 was not actually searching for the basis of his existence; he was trying to find a basis for his consciousness. He told us that he had three visions or dreams accompanied by lightning and thunder (a Biblical reminiscence?) and indeed whatever happened had a strong feeling-content besides producing an intellectual realization. It was an "immediate and irrefragable experience." But the result was interpreted by his consciousness as the clearest and most distinct idea he could have. It was an idea, extracted or abstracted from all the previous experiences of his mind and formulated in terms of his cultural and genetic background.

Consciousness develops when there emerges out of the total activities of an existential whole a sense of structural order in the reactions and responses of this whole to the challenges of everyday life. This sense of structural order establishes more or less steady as well as more or less definite boundaries to all the sensations and feelings that are projected by the nervous system of the human organism upon the "screen" (a figure of speech, of course) of consciousness. This center, and this sense of structural control gradually emerging from it, is the ego. It is the "I" to which everybody refers when he or she speaks of his feelings, desires, thoughts, aims, etc.

Normally it is an "I" as busy with contacts with the outer world as the President of the United States is busy -- and no doubt worried -- in the White House. Remove the busy-ness; let all contacts, pressures and problems be forgotten -- and the "I" may well relax into a state of peace and quietude. Perhaps this "I" may then be able to transcend all responsibilities and pressures; this "I" may pray to an equally transcendent God. In such a state of openness the President in the White House of consciousness may dream or daydream of "America," of the pulsating multitudinous life of the nation-as-a-whole. He may then consider himself only as a central agent through whom the life of this national whole seeks to attain within and through him the level of consciousness and to demand a decision on some grave matter. But if he says "I am America," woe to America! If on the other hand he quietly listens and simply remains open and aware, forgetting his executive position and prestige, just feeling the pulse of this America with all that its existential wholeness encompasses, then he should "know," beyond or through any conscious form of knowing, the real existence of what he has been called to represent at the level of the consciousness of humanity.

The President in the White House is not the existential whole that is the American continent within the boundaries of the United States -- the continent with all it encompasses. The ego-"I" in every man and woman is not the human person-as-a-whole but only the characteristic structure and the center of gravity of the consciousness of the person. The human person is an existential whole, an organized system of activities. Activity is the basis of existence; but existence implies wholes of existence; it implies not only activity, but structured and integrated systems of interrelated and interdependent activities. What is primary in existence is the fact that it is the state of "wholes of activities." Within and through every whole a Principle of Wholeness operates. I call this Principle ONE. It could as well be called SELF -- not a personal, or superpersonal, or cosmic Self, but a principle and as well a power of integration.

THE INTERPLAY OF POWER
AND CONSCIOUSNESS

The basic organismic fact in man's existence is that a myriad of cellular activities and periodical rhythms constitute a whole; and that this whole originated in one cell -- or more exactly in the combination of two cells (male and female) into one. Unity is at the root of all cyclocosms. All existence begins in a condition of unity and with the activation of a particular unitarian rhythm of existence-- a particular vibration or tone. This rhythm is the expression of an integrating power which I call SELF. Any form of integral existence which has individual characteristics that can be maintained through a complete life-cycle displays selfhood. In the lower kingdoms of life this capacity for self-maintained integral existence and the particular rhythm and "tone" which express it are characterized, not at the level of the particular plant or animal, but at that of the entire species to which this particular living organism belongs. We can speak then of "generic selfhood."

When man makes his appearance in the evolutionary process, to this generic selfhood -- that which constitutes his "humanhood" -- is added the potentiality of individualized selfhood. SELF operates therefore in man at two levels of existence: at the strictly biological level as the fundamental rhythm of the body-organism, and at the level of the "individual person" as the (at least latent) individuality of this person. This individuality may not be effectively actualized during the person's lifespan for it is only at first a potentiality. Various factors may assist or block the process of actualization of this potentiality, the most obvious factor being the combined influence of family, community, culture, religion and national events. Physical illness may impair this process; but it may as well stimulate it powerfully as a compensation for biological inadequacy.

The generic and the individual levels of selfhood are closely related, but to each belongs a specific type of con-

sciousness. There is a diffuse type of organismic awareness which refers to the body functions and to what happens
to them during the person's lifespan. Such an awareness is
directly involved in the rhythm of the basic self, i. e. in all
that refers, first to man's common humanity, and secondly
to the individual genetic particularities which make every
human body different in some manner from every other body.
Thus all men have the same "fundamental Tone," different
from the Tones of other living organisms; but every man also
has his own somewhat different i n d i v i d u a l tone, which
is, one might say, a particular modification or modulation
of the one basic Tone of mankind.

The normal individual person of our day is not conscious
that there are such tones as expressions of the principle and
power of SELF. He is not conscious of that deep-rooted
power that vibrates through and sustains his whole organism.
He is no more conscious of it than is the youth who has always
displayed an exuberant vitality and experienced no real illness conscious of "health." He takes that power for granted
and may hear it referred to as vitality or life-energy. He
does not experience this self at the root of his total being as
a definite or definable "presence," for not only does it not
speak to him in intelligible terms, but it has been so covered
up by the many images and forms of control stamped upon
him by family, school and society at large, that the tone of
the self no longer can be heard or sensed as a directing and
integrating power. The self simply i s; it acts by its very
presence. Its vibrations sustain by their integrating power
-- quietly, steadily, without any change of pitch or character -- the vast and complex interplay of all the activities operating within the "field of existence" which we call a "person." The self is structuring power, not consciousness.

However, the essential purpose of the process of development of every human person is to build a type of reflective consciousness which, when it is truly mature, will not
only be able to perceive the existence of the self within his

total organism, but to bring to a conscious state all that refers to the integrative power of the self. What we call ego
is, when seen in the light of such an ultimate consummation,
the instrumentality by means of which an existential consciousness can be formed and effectually structured as a
mind which will serve as the indispensable container for ever
more complex, but also ever more basic (and eventually
"self"-oriented) contents of the truly individualized consciousness. The process of formation of the ego is therefore a
very necessary feature in the full development of man's potentialities; but the ego is a means to an end, and not the
end in itself.

To develop fully as an individualized consciousness man
needs a broad, inclusive, steady mind. He needs a steady
and effectual frame of reference for the development
of what we call "values"; that is, in order to exercise his
capacity to discover significant relationships between all
factors which contribute, positively or negatively, to his existence. He needs a formed, but resilient and flexible mind
in order to emerge from the state of passive subservience to
environmental influences of a "local" type to one of deliberate responsible and eventually creative activity -- an activity
able to reach ever more inclusive environments and an ever
broader consciousness of universal patterns of order. The
ego is the means to a steady actualization of the human potentiality, of individual selfhood in terms of a fully
conscious and autonomous existence, free to
choose its own type of allegiance to a greater whole.

The role of the ego could be at least partially illustrated
by considering this ego as the "scaffolding" needed to build,
say, a soaring temple. This scaffolding is necessary for
the adequate, timely and efficient transportation of the building materials to where they belong; it supports the masons in
their work, etc. But once the temple is completed, the scaffolding should be dismantled and its materials used for other

purposes. Alas, most men become so involved in the appearances and the safety of the scaffolding that they identify themselves with it, rather than with the slowly rising temple which is hidden behind it.

Such an illustration is far from perfect and does not take into account many important features of the human situation, but at least it should serve to emphasize the fact that the ego is only a means to an end, a transitory phase in the total development of man's consciousness within a mind fully open to the power and light of the self. Within that mind the symbolic marriage of power and consciousness can be accomplished; and the constant interplay of power and consciousness is the fulfillment of all cycles of conscious existence.

IV. SELFHOOD AND RELATEDNESS

No existent is born alone. He takes form within, or he emerges out of something that is already existing in a particular environment, and he is born in the midst of numerous existing wholes that, directly or indirectly, react to his appearance into the world. This most basic fact of existence implies that the moment any new entity is formed and occupies a place in space it is inevitably in relationship -- potential if not actual relationship -- with other entities. As an existential whole he is powered and sustained by a self; he is a unit of existence because in and through him the integrative power of ONE (or SELF) operates. But his original selfhood is challenged, or assisted, in the actualization of its potential of existence by what a great many relationships bring to his growth.

Thus we can easily see that two basic factors are operating in the process of existence: one factor refers to the selfhood of the existent -- the other, to the inevitable fact that he finds himself related to other selves. Selfhood and relatedness are indeed like the two foci of an ellipse. The curve of existence is shaped by the interaction of these two factors, which constitute two centers of attraction, each exerting a very basic pull. The two pulls may often appear to act in opposite directions; yet both are necessary for the full development of the process of existence.

We shall come back in a moment to this interaction; but first of all we have to recognize another basic fact: the ex-

istence of two types of relationship, which we will call matricial and associative.

Before the child can be born as a relatively independent
organism able to operate in the environment of the Earth's
biosphere and to develop as a conscious person, this organism has to pass through a prenatal process of embryonic
growth. This process is made possible and sustained by the
assimilation of chemicals drawn from the surrounding mem-
branes in the mother's womb. Such a process of assimilation represents the working out of a specific type of relationship between the growing embryo and the body of the mother
within which this growth occurs. We can call such a
relationship a "matricial" kind of relationship so as to differentiate it from another category of relationships which occur only after birth. In this matricial type of relationship
the mother's body is the positive, active factor; the embryo,
the passive and receptive pole.

Normally the relationship is smooth, unconscious or instinctual, and completely under the control of (1) the formative forces of the human species and (2) the particular genetic "code-script" determining the more individual characteristics of the organism-to-be. As this matricial relationship reaches its natural and preordained fulfillment -- provided, of course, no destructive impact has disturbed the
relationship -- what was, just after impregnation, "seed potential of existence" is actualized as a human organism capable of a relatively autonomous kind of existence after it
leaves the womb and starts breathing.

Once the baby breathes, he becomes relatively independent as a biological organism. He soon requires food -- normally the mother's milk. But milk, or even some substitute
food, can be given by some other person, or by an animal.
The baby becomes an "existent" with a gradually increasing
degree of autonomy. As this occurs, he finds himself confronted by (and no longer "enveloped in" as in the pre-

natal stage) other existents. With these existents (other human beings, animals, etc.) he must establish relationships of a new type -- associative relationships. What characterizes these associative relationships is essentially that they imply at least some degree of mutuality; that is, they lead to a more or less conscious interplay of actions, reactions, more actions and further reactions between the participants in the relationships. Also they imply some sort of "challenge" to the newborn; and these challenges normally increase in intensity, acuity, extension and complexity as the baby grows into a child, an adolescent, an adult.

However, the fact that the child is confronted with the need to associate with other existents does not mean that he no longer experiences "matricial" relationships. These take another form; they are transferred to the level of the psyche, i.e. of the mind and the feelings. The child after birth is still enveloped in a kind of "womb," but this is a psychic matrix constituted by the social, cultural and religious body of collective traditions which have structured and which permeate through and through his family, then his school environment. Thus, while he meets other persons and living things in terms of associative relationships, there are still some of these persons to whom he is related in a "matricial" sense, because it is through them that the power of the enfolding social-cultural environment manifests in a most focalized manner; it is these persons who are "feeding" his developing consciousness with psychic and mental "foodstuffs."

The mother is the most important among these persons, because not only does she take care of the baby's physiological needs -- thus continuing in a more complex and diversified manner to play the role once performed by her own body during gestation -- but after birth she also in a sense holds the child within the warm psychic embrace of her love. The whole family is at first much like a psychic womb to the growing baby. The father is not just another person but he, too, in an indirect way, "feeds" the growth of the child by (normally) gaining the social power -- money -- which provides food and the satisfaction of other primary needs. Thus the mother focuses upon the infant the capacity for love and care which is inherent in all biological matrices -- i. e. in all females who have given birth to a progeny; and the father focuses upon his child the male power to provide food by the exercise of his strength, his skill and his cunning, and, at the human level, his intelligence. The relationship of the child to his mother and father is thus of the matricial type. Yet there is in such a relationship a basic ambiguity, for the parents are not only "providers" of what the child needs biologically and at the most primary psychic level of his unfoldment, they are also individual persons. In the first role they exemplify what the psychologist may call "archetypal figures"; that is, they do not appear to the very young child as individual persons but as essential aspects of the life-process directed toward him; they fulfill a direct function in the formation of the generic human being.

Yet sooner or later the developing mind and ego of the child will perceive through the "mask" of the archetypal figures also human persons. Once the archetypal character of the parents vanishes, or at least becomes transparent, the child can enter into associative relationship with them. But this transition from one type of relationship to another is often confusing to the child, and in some cases, traumatic.

The difference between matricial and associative relationships is that the former operates largely as an unconscious and compulsive factor, while the latter refers to the conscious level of the gradually building ego. Any environmental influence which moulds the development of the child's personality in a way analogous to that in which the mother's body fed the embryo in the womb has, at least to some extent, an unconscious and compulsive character. The child unconsciously absorbs group-feelings and collective mental images. They feed his consciousness. Something in him may already want to react negatively and rebelliously against them, much as a mother's milk may in some cases poison the baby's organism. But the young child is not conscious of what it is within him that forces such a negative reaction; it may be an organismic reaction, rooted in the vibratory character of his "self." The child will in most cases push such reactions out of his growing and as yet unsteady field of consciousness; and in this manner complexes are gradually formed -- complexes which probably always arise at first from a negative reaction to a matricial relationship.

The child indeed feeds on the contents of such matricial relationships; and his ego-formation can be poisoned by them. It is not only a question of imitation, though children do seek to imitate their elders and the friends who impress them particularly. The child unconsciously absorbs the substance -- psychic and mental -- of his family, social and cultural environment, and later on of his school environment. Here too the child's relation to the teacher has an archetypal and matricial character. This relationship can also become ambiguous, if largely undeveloped and unconscious emotional or sexual factors enter into the relationship. Indeed associative and matricial relationships constantly affect each other during the process of ego-building. Conscious responses to associative relationships interact with unconscious (or semi-conscious) reactions to the psychological-mental materials which pass, in a kind of psychic osmosis, from the social-cultural womb of community and tradition to the psyche or inner life of the youth. These collective psychic materials often interfere with the conscious responses of the growing ego; and thus a rebellious trend may develop, or the ego may collapse, defeated.

The building of an ego which structures and integrates the diverse contents of the field of consciousness is essential; the more so the greater the variety and intensity of images and experiences which affect the senses and the capacity to give feeling-responses to encounters with other human ings, or even with other non-human living organisms, like pets or plants and in general, Nature. Matricial relationships should provide not only a sustaining, but also a selective power during the development of the child. Perhaps the greatest problem facing young children in our technological society is the abundance of impressions, images, and the variety of relationships with heterogeneous types of human beings which confront the nascent organism and consciousness of these children. This problem becomes even more crucial as a result of the loss of the archetypal character of the parents -- and of most teachers during the school years.

Matricial relationships operating at the psycho-social level are needed to provide a secure container within which the consciousness of the child can develop steadily and without an unassimilable abundance of images and adjustments. The field of consciousness must have boundaries or else consciousness develops in a chaotic manner and without the ability to give a definite value to all the impacts and contacts with which it is bombarded. It needs examples of order, harmony and steadiness in order to gain an appreciation of structural factors. It needs archetypes as principles of order. However, in our human world in a state of radical crisis of transformation, it is difficult for parents and even teachers to be exemplars of order and steadiness and to perform archetypal roles. A fantastic and probably unwholesome stress is placed upon "personal" relationships, upon personal spontaneity, permissiveness, and individualism at any age and under any conditions -- though in fact, or perhaps because of this fact, our modern technological society leads, perhaps inevitably, to a depersonalization of human existence.

It is certainly true that the "individuality" of the child should be allowed to express itself; but one essential question is rarely asked because of the psychological confusion between ego and self: Is the child actually born as an "individual?" He is potentially an individual person, but not actually. He has his own rhythm of existence. Within and throughout his "field of existence" the tone of the self vibrates, sustaining the entire organism. However, this organism is at first generically "human"; it does not constitute an individualized person. Consciousness exists only in a latent condition because the infinitely complex network of the child's nervous system and brain is not yet efficiently operating. Connections have to be built; even the capacity to feel individual emotions is still to be developed. How can it develop wholesomely if the child is at once thrown into a chaotic world of conflicts, emotional tensions and incessant challenges?

The answer to such a problem -- the problem of "bringing up" children from the generic condition to the individual state of formed consciousness -- has been in the past to provide for the newborn a family and social-cultural-religious environment (a "matrix") securely and steadily structured by principles of behavior and collective norms and a traditional value-system. According to the ancient Hindu ideal, the family and the society were strictly ordered in a manner that was believed to reflect the very order of the universe. The same situation existed in old China, and indeed more or less implicitly everywhere on the globe. This social-psychological order moulded the early development of the child, restricting his experiences, but also providing a secure basis, great images and steady examples for his growth.

The trouble was, of course, that in the great majority of cases this precluded the rise of truly individual behavior and thinking; yet certainly not in every case. "Individuals" did emerge from the archetypal and traditional patterns. These were "reborn" persons, liberated from matricial relationships, in whom the power of their true "self" was able to express itself in conscious acts, in really "autonomous" deeds and creative thoughts. In Christian Europe and early America, a greater but different emphasis was placed upon

the individual person than in India. The power of social-
cultural and family matrices was still most effectual, and in
some ways even more rigid than in Asiatic countries, but
with more possibilities to escape from the power of the collective Images and archetypes. However, did the men (and
the few women) who broke away from, or somehow overcame
the power of the matricial relationships which had dominated
their formative years, emerge as true individual s e l v e s --
or did they emerge as e g o s whose wills had become temp-
ered by the very effort they had to make to become "free"?

This is always a difficult question to answer in any particular case. Rebellion against the rigid power of socio-cultural matrices and family archetypes can generate a hard-
ened strength of character; such a strength was often considered, perhaps especially in the America of frontier-days,
as very desirable. However, the type of individual produced
under such conditions is highly competitive and aggressive
and perhaps anti-social, if not more or less overtly criminal. What mankind is facing today is another kind of situation
produced by the fact that the socio-cultural matricial power
of society has almost entirely broken down in most countries.
Now the parents' ideal for bringing up children is to be
"chums" with them at a personal level. The children have
become involved in their parents' conflicts and emotional
scenes. They are allowed a completely unstructured manner of conduct, perhaps because their parents are too busy
or too concerned with their own ego-problems and/or their
jobs to have time to exemplify any wholesome Mother-image
or Father-image. The child growing up in a climate of permissiveness is constantly a witness to television's chaotic
images of what human existence is. He is "free," he is "op-
en"; but what can he do with this freedom and his unformed,
traditionless mind?

Surely the child develops precociously; but what does
precociousness really imply? A nervous system and emotional responses which are often confused by unassimilated

emotional-mental "food." The child may well have longed for structuring guidance; but not finding any steady and relevant guidance from his parents or his teachers -- and as well from examples of behavior brought to his immature consciousness by his environment (including T. V.) -- the child had no other possibility left to him but to develop an aggressive or defeatist ego. Aggressiveness is usually but a screen to hide basic insecurity and deep-seated fear, a feeling of isolation and alienation -- in short a fundamental inability to enter into associative relationships that are steady and creative, and not merely the product of chance encounters and of a yearning to forget both his ego and his society in turmoil.

Yet everything depends upon relationships. If individuality is one of the two poles of existence, relationship is the other pole. We are dealing here with a dualism which is the most fundamental fact of existence. Selfhood and relatedness are just as inseparable and necessary to any form of existence as time and space are required as the substratum of any manifestation of existential activity.

Selfhood, as I have defined the term, is the permanent factor which constitutes the basic rhythm and structuring power at the root of existential wholes; while relatedness refers to the factor of unceasing change which, as we have already seen, is the most primary fact of human experience. Every change is the result of some kind of relationship being altered. Every transformation in the consciousness of a human being can be traced to some relationship which triggered the need and the desire for transformation. Within any cycle of existence, self is the permanent factor, the changeless rhythm and essential character of the field of existence; but it is through relationship that changes occur, over and above this fundamental rhythm. It is through the energy released by associative relationships that the human person is able to grow and to actualize the inherent potentiality of conscious fulfillment in selfhood. The progress --

or it can also be "regress" -- of every existent depends on the character and the quality of these associative relationships, and on the energy they release.

This is why an exaggerated and over-idealized kind of individualism is unwholesome; and indeed why our present-day Western society is breaking down. Man-the-individual is not the final solution to the problem of human existence. It represents only an ideal of transition -- an antithesis which must lead to a synthesis. A new image of man must be developed, indeed is being developed, under the pressure of an impending global catastrophy -- or at least of the possibility of it. It is the image of Man-in-relationship; man as an individual who freely seeks his associates and companions, and whose consciousness becomes attuned to the harmonic interweavings of a group of minds drawn together by a common purpose. The most basic of such purposes is to participate in the building of a new society no longer based on "local" conditions and social, cultural and religions exclusiveness, but on a global realization of the organic wholeness of mankind and of the Earth.

TOWARD A NEW IMAGE OF MAN

A kind of dialectical process operates in the evolution of man's consciousness and indeed of man's approach to himself as well as to other men. What is evolving is basically the manner in which his sense of being a person (or, as psychologists would say now, his "self-image") is related to his desire and ability to enter into relationships with other persons. As a self, Man is; but he needs to be, and indeed cannot avoid being, in a constant state of relationship with other human beings. In the manner in which he experiences himself, in the same manner does he experience -- and give value and meaning to -- his relationships.

Some of these relationships, as we have already seen, are primary facts of life; they are matricial relationships. He is born out of a biological womb, only to find himself striving to build mental and emotional capacities enabling him to operate successfully within various types of matrices. At the tribal stage of human evolution the tribe is a most effective and binding matrix; and so is the land on which the tribesmen work and which feeds them. A tribesman actually has only the rudiment or rather the potentiality, of individual selfhood. Selfhood for him has a generic character defined by race, land and rigid traditions and rituals.

The rudimentary individuality of primitive man did not develop for long ages, but this is not the place to study in historical-cultural detail various phases of the development of man's consciousness of himself as an individual. All that it is necessary to say is that in the archaic tribal state matricial relationships have an overwhelming power. The human being is in a prenatal state so far as his sense of individuality is concerned. The tribal "we" does not allow much freedom of development to the individual "I." This development can only come through relationships of an associative type. But the tribesman's associative relationships operate exclusively at first within a matricial frame of reference, i.e. within the tribal whole of activities.

Through intertribal exchanges of needed goods and through marriage, through wars of conquest and the making of slaves who are incorporated into the tribe, new associative relationships are made. The tribe grows into a kingdom, and in cities men can relate to each other in freer ways, while trading and the ambition for power on an individualistic basis develop mental cunning and intellectual capacities. All these new factors tend to isolate man from the matrices which had so closely bound him; and the process of individualization proceeds.

Man, by then, has developed an ego which is based no longer on the particular function he fulfills in the tribal organism but on a new ability to take a stand, exclusively his own. It is on that basis -- also on the basis of what he possesses and of his social station in the city or kingdom--that

he enters into relationship with other men, in terms of strictly associative relationships. The original "we" has changed
into a possessive, and perhaps blatantly expressed "I." This
ego-"I" in many cases no longer feels a relationship of identification with Nature in general. His relationship to a house
or a field is more likely to be a possessive one: they belong
to him. The matricial power of the land loses its intensity,
though it remains as a sometimes unconscious compulsion, a
kind of instinctual and even irrational bio-psychic bondage;
and today we still see such a bond very widespread all over
the world.

The glorification of individualism came in the Mosaic
revelation of the greatest Name of God: "I am that I am" --
which I believe really means: I am the absolute fact of being "I" -- "I" without any attribute -- just "I." For Western
man individuality is God's signature within him. He is an individual "by divine right"; a king in his own kingdom. But it
soon becomes a lonely kingdom disturbed by constant feudal
conflicts. Moses was perhaps the first "rugged individual-
ist"; he also spoke with God "face to face as a man speaketh
unto his friend." Then began what became known as a "dialogue" between God and man, between the personal I and the
absolute Thou (cf. Buber's writings). Indeed the individual
must be able to communicate with a divine absolutely and
always reliable Thou, because he is no longer able to enter
into relationship in the depths of his existence with other individuals -- so alone and alienated from his fellowman has
he become. Today LSD is taken by even more alienated
young people in order to exorcise their sense of ego, and to
re-enter the lost Edenic state of unity with all -- a return
to Paradise, but alas artificial and dangerous paradises that
present only relief perhaps, but no lasting ultimate solution
to the tragic tensions of individual existence.

If the communal, unconscious and compulsive identification of tribesmen with the living and psychic wholeness of the
tribe constituted the thesis of a dialectical process, and

the pure, quasi-absolute individualism which has been an abstract ideal for many men in our theoretically "democratic" Western world is the antithesis, what kind of a synthesis can we then expect will emerge from our historical "Age of conflicts" when, or if, a New Age begins?

The phrase "unity in diversity" has been used by a number of thinkers working toward the ushering in of such a New Age whose motto would indeed be "synthesis." But such a phrase, however beautiful and hopeful it sounds, needs explanation; above all, it fails to take into consideration the most essential element in the situation. What is needed is a clear realization of the fact that unless men participating in this postulated New Age enter it as conscious "selves" and not only as "egos," there will be no New Age. The final WE-realization which represents the state of synthesis cannot emerge from human minds whose consciousness is structured by a rigid and closed ego, but only from human persons who have clearly realized that the very source and sustaining power of their total "field of existence" is the self, and whose egos have become utterly dedicated servants of the self -- and therefore of humanity as a whole.

Such statements require amplification and explanation; and once more we must return to a consideration of the essential difference between self and ego. We shall soon discuss more specifically what is meant here by SELF (or ONE) as a universal Principle. What has already been stated is that this all-capitalized term refers to the power of integration which is inherent in every form of existence -- in every whole, every organized system or field of activity. SELF, according to this holistic approach to existence, is the principle of wholeness in every whole; and it is the power that integrates all the component parts of such wholes.

As we shall see in the next chapter, this power of integration operates at several levels of existential activity. Just now we are concerned with two of these levels, the one that we call "life," and the other "mind" -- using this term in a somewhat special sense.

Integration at the level of LIFE has a g e n e r i c character. We deal at that level not only with living organisms but with collectivities of organisms -- with species and genera. The principle of selfhood operates n o t in terms of a particular existent, but in terms of an entire species. An entire species encompassing a myriad of living organisms is structured by the same formative and integrative power. The self or individuality resides in the species, not in any one particular specimen -- for instance, in wheathood, but not in any one stalk of wheat (mutants and domesticated animals represent special cases which we cannot discuss here.)

At the level of MIND, or more precisely of what we shall call in the next chapter "ideity," we are dealing with processes of integration which are not only very complex but which have not yet produced, at the present stage of human evolution, completely stabilized results -- at least not as far as the normal state of human beings is concerned. A mind r e p r e s e n t s c o n s c i o u s n e s s in a f o r m e d c o n d i t i o n. What gives to the consciousness a p a r t i c u-l a r form, i. e. what "individualizes" a human being's consciousness, is the ego. And as we have already seen, the ego is an ambivalent factor. On the one hand it reflects u n c o n-s c i o u s l y the presence of the root-self of the human organism, without which there would be indeed no organism and no consciousness referring to that particular organism; on the other hand it is powerfully influenced by family and socio-cultural pressures, which in turn are conditioned by race and local geographical conditions. Moreover the ego is profoundly affected by the vital energies and urges of the body in which it operates (mostly through the brain and the cerebro-spinal nervous system); it is affected by them, but it can also affect them through the operation of its will, or u n w i l-l i n g l y through the effect of its own tensions and stresses.

What could not be made clear enough in the preceding chapter is the fact that the ego actually is the instrument through which the g e n e r i c s e l f centered at the root of the human organism is being refocused at a higher level, at which it becomes the i n d i v i d u a l s e l f. Stating the matter in such a way may be confusing, because there are not, in a basic sense at least, t w o selves. What we are discussing now is a process by means of which the power of integration, SELF, establishes a new center of operation without thereby ceasing to operate at the former level. This process can be called the process of "individualization" -- not to be confused with Jung's process of "individuation," though the latter is related to the former. This process of individualization could be likened symbolically to that which raises the root-energy of a plant in order to produce a flower. The root still exists while the plant blooms -- it remains the "fundamental" factor in the plant -- but a new center of integration has been established at the level of the flower which has the power to begin a new process of integration resulting in the seed.

This illustration is not to be taken literally, for there are essential differences between man and plant; it is only a symbol -- one used often by yogis and occultists in the past, though usually not well understood. What is symbolized in this illustration by the process of formation of the seed is, in man, a process which should produce, when brought to the final stage, a "mind-organism" able to operate in a condition freed from the pressures of both instinctual drives or biological urges (sex included) and social-cultural traditions and collective images.

The real purpose of all true "occult" techniques everywhere is to bring to birth, as it were, such a mind-organism, which indeed can be likened to the seed of a plant. The seed is transferable; it leaves the old plant and m a y become in due time the starting point of a new plant; in this sense, it has gained a kind of "immortality." The mind-organism of which we speak is also a transferable factor in that as the body disintegrates the integrative power of the root-self of this body is transferred to the new center, the center of i n d i v i d u a l (and no longer g e n e r i c) selfhood. This mind-organism retains therefore the particular vibration, rhythm and essential character of the original biological organism (the human person) within which it was formed. It retains it after the death of the body and thus achieves an at least relative kind of immortality. To this "mind-organism" various names have been given; for instance, the "Diamond body" or "Christ-body" -- or in India, s v a r u p a, the "form of selfhood."

This process of transfer from a biological center of integration (generic self) to a mental, or "ideistic," center (individual self) constitutes a repolarization of the consciousness. In biological-generic man consciousness is related to life-function and the goals of life-preservation and life-expansion. In a truly individualized man consciousness is centered in the "mind," but it is NOT a mind identified with intellectual processes and autocratically ruled by the usual kind of ego found today in most human beings. It is NOT a mind the contents of which are still conditioned by both biological drives and a local culture with its set traditional patterns and its exclusivism.

Symbolically -- and also perhaps in some actual yet not obvious sense -- this "new mind," free from compulsive life-urges and social-cultural patterns, is centered in the "heart" rather than in the cortical parts of the brain. However, what is mean in this connection by the "heart" (according to many old occult religious traditions) is not the physical organ itself, but the heart as a symbol of the individual rhythm of the entire "field of existence"which constitutes a person. This occult heart is the power that makes the physical organ pulsate according to a basic rhythm or vibratory quality; it refers to the "timbre" of these pulsations (using the term, timbre, in its musical meaning). And very likely this heart-power can be located -- in the electro-magnetic force-field (aura?) which, in dynamic terms, constitutes the

real individual person -- at the place where the vertical axis
of the spine corsses the horizontal line of the extended arms.
At this place, according to Rosicrucian symbolism, the divine Rose blooms at the center of the Cross of existence.

This symbolism refers to the fact that the transfer of the
power of the self from the g e n e r i c center at the base of
the spine -- the M u l a d h a r a C h a k r a in Hindu yoga --
to the i n d i v i d u a l center at the level of the heart requires
in most cases some kind of "crucifixion." But it may be that
the final crucifixion, the most pervasive and indeed total crisis, has to be related to a process which occurs within the
skull -- "Golgotha" means the place of the skull. At the end
of this new process man truly becomes "more-than-man,"
reaching the state of h o l i n e s s, which means indeed the
perfection of wholeness at the new level of selfhood. At that
level individuality itself is transcended and man has the spiritual right no longer to say "I," but WE.

MAN, IN THE "PLEROMA" STATE

These crises which may be called "crucifixions" actually
always occur as the result of one kind or another of relationship. They are powered by the energy released by relationships -- released either within a state of joyful exaltation or at the core of ego-annihilating tragedy or shock.

The relationship between a g u r u and his (or her) c h e -
l a s, strongly featured in the tradition of India, can be such
a transforming and, always to some degree at some stages
of the process, crucifying relationship. It is in a sense a
revolution which unseats the autocratic king-ego and radically upsets the legal and institutional structures of the society (the conscious personality) over which he rules. In our
present-day Western world the psychoanalyst or psychiatrist
tends to replace the old-time guru, or the Catholic "direct-
or of conscience." But back of the authority of the true Hindu
stands a spiritual-cosmic realization, if not actual Power,

which differs from the religious kind of background invested in the priest -- and which the psychologist of our day is sadly lacking.

What our Western type of psychology aims for in the majority of cases is simply to make of a disturbed and perhaps anti-social person one who can function smoothly and more or less contentedly or (as we say now) "creatively" in our society -- a society of egos organized for the welfare and aggrandizement of egos. The modern psychologist seeks to cure the neuroses produced by the cultural emphasis placed on the ego and its competitive-aggressive drives by relieving the tensions produced by a long series of unresolved conflicts and making the disturbed person face more objectively what is now called "reality" -- a biological and social kind of reality. The patient, if the cure is effective, becomes much better "adjusted" to his society. But this so-called adjustment may actually mean spiritual defeat for the individual person; for the crises he had been experiencing were perhaps means to bring about a radical repolarization of his consciousness -- a repolarization requiring a repudiation of the values forced upon him by a society ambiguously mixing worship of aggressive individualism with the cult of conformism to set patterns of productivity-at-all-cost.

Relationships able to intensify, and perhaps to generate, the process of repolarization of selfhood to which we have just referred must be relationships which challenge the obstinate power of the ego-will, and also the person's subservience to the intellectual traditions of his family and culture. The Hindu guru was, ideally at least, a man who had overcome his ego-state of consciousness and who had become free from bondage to his caste and to all social patterns. He was an asocial individual in terms of the society of his environment and his time; but his allegiance had been transferred to a higher, far more inclusive type of spiritual community, an "eternal" (i.e. eonic) type of community.

I call such a community the "Pleroma of Man" -- the

"Seed-consummation" of the evolution of humanity on this planet, Earth. When the Catholic Church speaks of the Communion of Saints and the "Church triumphant," or when Teilhard de Chardin describes the Omega state before the close of the human cycle, it is to such a spiritual community that they refer. The modern Theosophist speaks of this state of synthesis of consciousness as the "White Lodge," but unfortunately very often materializes the concept, which has given rise to a variety of misinterpretations due to a lack of philosophical understanding of the whole cyclocosmic process of evolution, and in some instances caused by a too devotional and sensationalistic approach to so-called spiritual facts.

The main difficulty in approaching such concepts or inner realizations is that the approach will be perverted to the extent to which the person's consciousness is still dominated by the twin powers of a social-cultural-religious tradition, and of an ego conditioned by this local, exclusivistic culture. What is needed to break such a two-fold bondage is either a relationship in which one of the two or more participants is an individual who is indeed "free" from it, or one in which two or more egos generate by their interplay a kind of "fire by friction" which can burn their exclusivism and release new realizations -- either in joyful exaltation or in tragic conflict. In the great majority of cases such a "fire" can only be generated when the relationship brings together two human organisms, rather than two egos. And it is because this fact is more or less clearly realized today by many people that contacts between human bodies are often emphasized as a basic requirement for self-repolarization. Such contacts obviously lead most of the time to sexual union; but they are also glorified, short of actual sex contacts, in the many "encounter groups" which have sprung up of late in America, and in the nudity cult.

The essential point here is the distinction between the ego-ruled, socially and culturally conditioned individual person, and the human organism considered in its broadest and deepest implications as what could be called a "field of existence." The term, field -- so basic now in modern physics -- is used here to indicate that an individual person, considered in his totality, is indeed a force-field -- that is, a complex, structured network of interdependent activities operating at several levels of vibratory frequencies. He is a dynamic whole sustained by the fundamental tone of the self -- a whole in which lesser wholes operate in a state of unceasing relatedness (cells, organs and, at the level of a still more intense rate of motion and changes, molecules, atoms, electrons, etc.)

Internal cellular and organic interrelationships generate excess energy through the interplay of anabolic and catabolic processes, conditioned by definite structural laws and the genetic codes regulating the functional behavior of every unit within the whole field, i.e. the total organism. This field includes so-called "psychic" as well as "physical" processes. The external relationships in which two or more human "fields of existence" interact and affect each other are also to some extent structured. They have been structured so far in nearly all cases in the past of human evolution by a particular culture and religion, and by social-political laws and regulations.

What is now at stake is the need to change the character and quality of this structuring power, i.e. the power of a socially, culturally and religiously organized collectivity, whether it be a small tribe or a large nation like the U.S.A. or the U.S.S.R. This implies nothing less than a radical revolution in the social-cultural-religious order according to which human beings are living today -- "radical" in the sense that it involves the root-power within man, i.e. the self.

I spoke, a few pages back, of the process of repolarization of the self from the generic to the individual level of activity, feelings and consciousness. This repolarization requires the development of the ego-function, that is, of a power integrating the results of everyday individual experiences into a structured set of responses -- this "set" constituting what we call the "character" of the individual person. But the ego at first can only operate in terms of structural models which are forcibly impressed upon the growing child and later upon most adults by the family, school and social environment; and this environment, alas, has so far been operating historically on the basis of relatively narrow local conditions and a more or less rigid traditional "way of life." This way of life, until recently at least, was always conditioned by the principle of scarcity and the struggle for material goods and often for adequate "living space" -- and the geopoliticians of a few decades ago, especially in Germany, stressed and overstressed this fact.

As a result the type of order which the ordinary ego imposes upon the inner life of a person (i. e. upon his mental, emotional and behavioral values) is of a type which cannot accomplish the purpose that originally called for its existence, that is, the fulfillment of individual selfhood in an organism of consciousness -- in a "mind" free from generic urges and inadequate social-cultural drives. These drives are inadequate, and now obsolescent, because they are based on a primitive type of relationship of man to his environment -- a relationship founded on scarcity, anxiety, fears and unceasing conflicts. And so the mentality of most men is likewise totally inadequate to face the opportunity which awaits mankind at the threshold of a New Age. The hour for the beginning of this New Age should strike soon -- next century, I believe (cf. my book BIRTH PATTERNS FOR A NEW HUMANITY, 1969); but how many human beings will be ready for it? How transformed will be man's social environment -- and, what is the essential question, transformed in what way? The way of the technocrats, already controlling most of mankind today, East and West -- or the way which the project for an ideal city-community near Pondicherry, India,

AUROVILLE, is foreshadowing? The way of police-based power -- or the way of integral love and harmony?

Men speak today of democracy and individualism. These words sound well; they can be the most deceptive screens to hide the failure to cope constructively with new human possibilities and to achieve what individualism was meant to accomplish as a means to an end. As the French writer, St. Exupery, wrote in his beautiful book, FLIGHT TO ARRAS: "The individual is a path. Man only matters, who takes that path." As already stated, the individual, in terms of the evolution of consciousness, represents the phase of antithesis. We need the antithesis. Mankind has needed and still needs, in many places, the negation of the thesis of unconscious tribal unity -- the emergence of power-hungry individuals proud of their isolation, proud of being "self-made" -- which in fact means rather, formed by the energy of their revolt against the "binding force" of obsolete because narrow and exclusivistic traditions. But that stage of evolution is now passing. Men must become widely open to the new phase -- the phase of synthesis, the phase which must gradually witness an ever more significant, valid and effectual "planetarization of consciousness."

What this means is that, to the internal order which human "fields of existence" display, an external ordering of mankind-as-a-whole will have to answer. Humanity must develop as a planetary organism -- or, even more accurately, as a complex "organ" operating within the planetary organism of the Earth; for the Earth is that vast body within which we live, move and have our being as whole persons (i.e. as individualized "fields of existence").

Why has it been so difficult to think of the Earth as such a global organism in which mankind performs a specific function -- as every life-kingdom, and oceanic currents and winds and van Allen belts also perform their specific functions? Simply because -- especially since the dawn of Christianity, perhaps as early as the Greek and Hebraic cultures and even in Asia for different reasons -- man has striven to separate his consciousness and his sense of value from the level of biological and telluric facts of existence in order either to center his consciousness at the level of the rational intellect, or else to dissassociate and free this consciousness entirely from the values essential to the tribal stage of human development.

I repeat this was a necessary phase -- the phase of the antithesis -- the Neti! Neti! aspect of man's effort at reaching toward the Unknown, and indeed the Unknowable, the Timeless, the Absolute, or else toward the Rational, the Law of laws, the Supreme Mind of the Great Architect of the Universe. But now man should be ready to take a new step. This step does NOT deny the validity of either the thesis (tribal unanimity in terms of compulsive drives) or the antithesis (the individualism of the great Rebels, adventurers in search of gold, or ascetics and saints in search of God). It includes something of both, indeed what is essential in either approach to "value." The new evolutionary goal is a planetary super-tribal community, a community of fully conscious, inwardly free but whole individuals, each of whom will bring to the global Whole his own self-realized "truth of existence," that is, his ability to fulfill effectually whatever his place and functions call for within this Earth-community.

This is the ideal of what Sri Aurobindo calls "the gnostic society," and many of the more aware "hippies" of our day are intuitively orienting their groping, and most often confused steps toward such a goal. We may smile patronizingly and call such visions "Utopia"; according to our cyclocosmic picture they announce a super-social condition of human existence which is the inevitable end of human evolution. It is the true Omega state when freed from the Catholic imagery in which Teilhard de Chardin clothed that state. It is symbolically the "seed"-state -- the Pleroma.

How can we reach such a human state? This must be done

individually and at the same time collectively. It must be done by transforming the image which an individual person has of himself, and of Man in general. It must also be done by changing the quality of one's relationships to other men, and by providing new concepts and ideals of relationship for small groups of persons at first, then for the whole human society -- a very arduous program which often indeed seems impossible of attainment. It cannot be realized miraculously or all at once. Seeds must be sown, which in due time and season will germinate; and thus a new society will emerge.

The first step is the realization that the process is not only possible, but inevitable. No man ever sacrificed the present for the future unless either this present had become totally dark and empty, or the individual believed with absolute one-pointedness that the end of the process was inevitable -- and so was his participation in it, simply because nothing else really mattered. The first alternative is rooted in despair; the second in faith. Both are valid at some time and in some places. The second is the most constructive because it knows what is ahead out of a knowledge which is beyond reason and argumentation. The call is heard in such a manner that the individual's response is inevitable -- irrational, yes; but creative of future tomorrows. In some particularly dynamic and creative minds this "call" becomes formulated into a philosophy. A new vision of what the ultimate values of existence are in essential reality is then translatable in terms of a new way of life, of new relationships.

Without a holistic philosophy such as I am presenting here it seems very difficult to formulate this new way of life, to bring new relationships perhaps intuitively longed for and sought to a truly conscious state of realization and effectiveness. Such a philosophy is needed. It can only be accepted by the mind that has realized that "I" is a limiting concept as long as it is bound to a traditional cultural environment and as long as this I-sense is not integrated with, nay more the servant of, a realization of WE.

But what kind of WE-thinking, even more than WE-saying? This is where discrimination is greatly needed, for the pull toward the old thesis is always strongly felt at times of great crisis and deep disappointment with at least temporary failures. The unconscious "we" of the tribal community with its utterly dominant psychism and its subservience to rituals and leaders endowed with some mysterious mana or magical power is a lovely and restful refuge for the weary or the confused. "The group" summons to its safe harbor the battered egos that feel helpless before the storm. But this is not the way to the true "Seed of Man." The Pleroma can only accept into its radiant wholeness the strong and daring individual who has won repeated victories over the down-pull of our "Dark Age" (Kali Yuga). Thus all the "tests" mentioned in old books referring to the process of Initiation -- which is, indeed, the process that leads to the Pleroma-state. These tests no doubt were symbolical, but very real to the candidate for Initiation.

Today the process, especially for the strongly ego-conscious Western man, very likely takes on a rather different character. Life itself is the Tester for him who has the strength of character not to refuse being tested by it -- as so many people do, lured by easy escapes into the unformed or the archaic, or so clever at rationalizing the importance of by-paths which avoid head-on confrontations with the great enemy, the ego, and its magic wand that makes of every relationship either a footstool to reach the throne of self-glorification, or the deep couch of self-indulgence.

The real "Path" is lonely. It seems to force upon him who treads it, isolation; but it is easy to misunderstand the meaning which old Indian sages and yogis gave to this term, isolation, at a time when society was utterly ritualized and men, women and children all had rigidly defined and mostly hereditary roles to play in it according to a divinely ordained pattern of collective existence. Isolation then was meant to dis-collectivize man, to force him to face his transcendent self -- and so also were meant many practices of "meditation." Today man is (in a sense) individualized and living in a chaotic ego-worshipping society; but this is a false kind of individualization. How can it be transformed into the true one, if not through the magic power of relationships fully lived, whether in happiness or tragedy?

The way therefore is to live a life of full relationship under whatever conditions and circumstances it might be -- to develop a sense of openness to relationships, of non-possessiveness and humility in relationship -- to be truly "available" wherever and whenever needed and to overcome fear and the lure of easy escapes -- and even the tendency to be proud of one's humility and wisdom. Above all, it is to take nothing for granted and to question every claim to special privilege or revelation. It is to have faith when there is nothing one can even "believe" to be true -- faith in the inevitable; but open, willing, ready, able to meet the inevitable under any form and disguise, while remaining firm and steady in one's truth and one's sense of destiny.

The self and the Other are the two eternal polarities of all existence. They are the Yang and Yin of the cycle of change and of the process of growth. In relatedness man discovers his true self; and in that discovery he at last understands the essential meaning of the Principle of relatedness which is the ultimate secret of all existence. To him who passes through the threshold which opens into the Pleroma-state this secret is revealed -- revealed within his holistic consciousness that embraces now the entire sweep of existential cycles, from the alpha to the omega. Because he partakes of the symbolic character of the seed, he realizes himself as end-consummation, but as well and at the same time, as germinal beginning. He thus partakes of the consciousness of the Eon. He becomes the Eon -- the fullness of Time, Eternity -- in an "instant" of supreme clarity. He understands the world; and the weight of the world presses upon his illumined mind that is one with the Mind of the Whole. A man has become Man; and "I" has become WE.

Part Two

IN THE METAPHYSICAL MODE

Chapter V: FOUNDATIONS FOR A
              METAPHYSICS OF WHOLENESS

The philosopher as interpreter (118); Piercing through facts and un-
covering principles (119); A world of interacting wholes in ordered
motion (120); The Principle of Wholeness, ONE, as an integrative power, as SELF (121); Potential and kinetic energy (122); God as the Unity aspect and "Source" of cycles (123-124); Potentiality and possibility - The transcendent God in Hindu theism (124-125); The cyclic relationship between the world of existence and the Ocean of infinite potentiality (126); Yin and Yang (127); The cyclic rhythm in a man's life,
and the development of consciousness (128); Power and consciousness
(129); Consciousness as relatedness (130); As the aura of wholeness
(131); The relationship between the Infinite Potential and finite wholes
(132); The end results of a universal cycle: "success" and "failure"
(133); The dualism inherent in Form (134); Absolute Compassion - The
Pleroma envisions the new universe to give the failures of the old a
second chance (135); Conscious and unconscious love, and the expansion of consciousness (136); The cyclic relationship between potentiality and actuality (137); Success and failure in the great cycles - The
seed man (138-139); Condensation of the chapter (139-141); The need
for an image of God, and the realization of ultimate Principles (142).

Chapter VI: THE CYCLIC PROCESS

The beginning of a cosmic cycle of existence (145); Two poles: Unity
and Multiplicity (146); Fear as the original sin (147); The Creative
Word -- a formula of cosmic integration - The Eternal Virgin, and the
Pleroma as a fecundant force (148); The Divine World: existence without past, totally future-oriented (149); The Divine Child and the hidden
Father (150); Ishvara, the Son-aspect - The Two Creations: Genesis I
and II (151); Ananda, Lila and the child Krishna (152); Matter and Life
in evolution (153); Regressive phases (154); The involutionary factor
in mutations (155); The operation of ONE at the level of Life (156);
The individual's emergence from the tribal matrix (157); The two symmetrical movements of the cosmic process - Structural patterns and
ever more differentiated modes of energy (158-159); Involution of form
and energy, and evolution of material wholes (160-161); How the two
processes interact - The planetary Life-field and the unity of mankind
(162); Soul-fields, generic and individual (163); Man's "Living Soul" -
The tragic process of "individualization" and its crises (164-165); The
transfiguration of the individual by the Divine (166); Avatars and creative Impulses (167); Buddha, Christ, Mohammed, Baha'u'llah - Three

categories of men, as cycles begin (168); The crucial choice: the way of the seed or the way of the leaves (169); Transmutation and its shadow (170); The Omega state and Aurobindo's Gnostic Society - A Humanity of Christs and Buddhas on a transubstantiated Earth (171).

Chapter VII: SOUL-FIELD, MIND AND REINCARNATION

The cyclocosmic vs. the modern scientific world-picture (172-173); The ever-present potentiality of change vs. causal determinism (174); Permanent selfhood and the indeterminacy of relationships (175); Definition of mind (176); Mind and time -- Mind and the physical brain (177); Mind at the levels of Materiality, of Life and of Ideity (178); The Soul Image and Soul-field - Mind, a formative power (179); Consciousness as a feed-back process and the field-of-existence (180); The one-to-one relationship between Soul-field and living organism (181-182); The fundamental Tone of selfhood and its overtones (183); The raising of Kundalini (184); Tantrik rituals (185); "Modulation" of Life into Ideity through the individualization of consciousness (186); Building of the "link" and transcending the ego (187); Western and Asiatic techniques (188); "Wars in Heaven" and the origin of evil (189); The "image of Man": Theme and variations (191); The Auric Egg (192); The operation of karma (193); What is it that cyclically reappears? (194); Success and failure: the action of ONE (195); Individual Adepts and the White Lodge - The monad and the Ideity-field (196); The model of the atom: wave vs. particle (197); New Age symbols - The dawn of eonic consciousness (198); Reincarnation (199); The rhythmic activation and inactivation of the Ideity-field (200); Mind as a creative power of consciousness - The higher and lower mind (201); Personal immortality - Memories of past lives (202); Spiritualism and its "proofs" (203); Predecessor and successor in a serial process (204); The process of rebirth (205); Development of a human person (206); The "time-binding" and "personality-binding" fourth and fifth dimensions of activity and consciousness - The Divine Marriage (207); The Soul: a quality of beingness (208); The Soul-Image as an Office (209); Does the Presidency choose the President? (210); The Man of Plenitude and the process of planetarization (211); Field of energies vs. personalized entities - Dangers ahead (212); The great need: Faith in Man -- and acting it out (213).

V. FOUNDATIONS FOR
A METAPHYSICS OF WHOLENESS

As we approach a metaphysical formulation of what we may call "ultimates" of existence so as to present a consistent and understandable picture of atoms, men, universes and of what has to be implied as a transcendent background or foundation for such a formulation, it may be well to state that what I shall be doing is not "inventing" intellectually a "new model" of the universe, but simply trying to extract from the very facts of human experience their most universal implications.

If man is confronted in his earliest and most basic experiences with the fact of unceasing change and (what seems to him, rightly or not) randomness or chance happening, and also with the realization that within that change there are order, periodicity and cyclic patterns of unfoldment, then we can use this dualism, generalizing and interpreting it so as to reach certain universal and "metaphysical" conclusions. As we are aware everywhere of motion and activity, we have to deduce from this activity the release of something we call energy. All around us we observe the birth, development and decay of living organisms and of various kinds of "wholes of activity"; we therefore deduce from this the operation of some integrative power which establishes and maintains or transforms the identifiable characteristics of these organisms or organized systems of activity.

The true philosopher is not an inventor, but rather an interpreter. His aim is to provide man with a world-picture which gives meaning, consistency, direction and purposefulness to human existence at all levels. He therefore should begin with "facts" generally experienced or at least experienceable by those to whom he addresses himself; but he cannot, should not stop at facts; nor should he lose himself in analyzing and dissecting them for the ambitious purpose of eventually controlling them, for that is the task of the scientist and engineer. He must pierce through the facts as if they were gates to greater wisdom. He must try to "see," symbolically speaking, the full grown oak within the acorn -- the pattern of universal cycles within illumined moments of consciousness in which his entire being "resonates" to the rhythm of the universe in whose being he participates, alas most often unconsciously. He must pass from the contemplation of a living organism to the feeling-intuition of "life" within him as within the whole biosphere of our Earth.

He can, if he knows how to persist in his flight toward an ever wider knowledge, feel the pulse of the universe -- its in and out breathings. And because there are always spheres beyond spheres which he can perceive or intuitively apprehend, he should be able to reach a still more essential state of abstract understanding -- in, through and beyond dimensional wholes and processes of emerging and disintegrating -- in which he will come to grasp the meaning of "ultimate principles" which are both transcendent and immanent, nowhere to be seen in strictly existential terms, but whose "presence" and influence can be felt intuitively everywhere.

The chapters which follow are the result of a man's long striving after understanding and wisdom. They may seem at first abstract and metaphysical; yet their contents are of the greatest importance in the development of consciousness today, with our society in a state of radical crisis. The world-pattern they present is evidently not essentially "new." It has many antecedents; but it is formulated in quite a new way, and I believe that this way has a great deal of practical bearing on our present-day problems and especially on the protests of our youth against the obsolescent, if not obsolete, world-outlook of our traditional religions and our social-cultural Establishment. Thus these forthcoming pages should not be considered as an intellectual exercise based on some flight of world-transcending imagination; instead they should be read and pondered carefully as a possible key to the discovery of a new world of "reality" -- a world of great rhythms and profound peace, a world freed from anxiety and religious fears or guilt.

ULTIMATES OF EXISTENCE

The picture of the world which modern science presents is one of universal and unceasing motion. But this motion is not chaotic and haphazard even though it includes an element of randomness; it is ordered motion -- motion within boundaries, within more or less clearly defined and relatively permanent "fields." Existence implies the fact of wholes of existence -- wholes which are composed of parts and at the same time are themselves functioning parts of greater wholes. Because a whole is composed of a multiplicity of parts or elements in a state of ordered interrelatedness and interdependence, there must be operating within this whole some kind of structuring power -- or, more abstractly, a Principle of Wholeness endowed with the power to integrate disparate elements and to maintain effectively the pattern of their organization within the field of their operation and throughout the span of existence of the whole.

I have called this Principle of Wholeness ONE, because such a simple all-capitalized term avoids the mythological, religious and emotional implications of most other available terms. When written in capital letters the word, SELF, is used in the same sense. It refers to the integrating principle and power which establishes the fundamental rhythm,

tone and individuality of a whole, i.e. its relatively permanent "identity" in the midst of constant changes, internal as
well as external. When I speak of the self of a particular
man or of a particular universe, I am referring to the "un-
ity-aspect" of that entire human person, or of that universe.
The "multiplicity aspect" of these wholes -- human and cosmic -- would then refer to the myriad parts or component
lesser wholes (cells and stars) contained within and active
within these wholes.

Every whole has thus as its foundation a self; this self is
however only an existential expression of the abstract, and
we might say super-cosmic Principle of Wholeness, SELF
or ONE. This Principle is not an entity. It operates everywhere, at all times, wherever and whenever there are existential wholes of any and all sizes. Existence can only be
conceived in terms of existents, that is, in terms of relatively individual fields of activity with more or less definite
boundaries and with a basic rhythm of their own upon which
certain individual or generic characteristics are based.

Motion with reference to wholes should be conceived as
"activity"; thus I have spoken of atoms, men or solar systems as "fields of activities." Every existent constitutes a
field of activities; these activities are (in the broadest sense
of the term) "functional" because they are interrelated, interdependent, and structured by an integrative power. We
will see presently that this integrative power operates in two
ways or at two levels. In its most abstract sense it is what
has been called the Principle of Wholeness, ONE; but it is
also that Power which structures or gives "form," abstractly speaking, to the existential field of activities. We shall
see that this Power is one of the two basic aspects of what
we will have to call, for lack of better terms, "consciousness" and "mind" -- but not the aspect usually associated
in the West with these confusing words.

Activity presupposes a release of energy; but here again
we have to deal with terms which can be understood in many

ways, and therefore which need to be defined. Energy is usually defined in elementary physics as "the capacity to perform work." It is difficult however for the mind of the ordinary man not to refer this capacity and this performance of work to some "entity" which is able to perform. "Performing" means acting through (p e r) a form. The human mind finds it hard not to take for granted that activity requires an actor, and performance a performer using a form exterior to himself.

Energy can be conceived in two aspects: potential and kinetic. A pianist ready to perform a composition or an improvisation using the form of a piano has potential energy which he releases as he plays. From this fact, man in most cases has deduced that as existence is a release of potential energy through existential forms -- cosmic, biological, atomic, personal-human -- there must also be a Releaser, a super-existential Performer, God. This God, as external to the universe as the pianist is to his piano, "desires" to create an existential universe in order to "enjoy" the realization of His infinite power and capacity for self-expression through a multitude of forms. He is essentially transcendent to the universe, even though as performer he is also immanent in the performance. He is, from the Hindu point of view, the One Player -- the One Actor in all existential activities. To the follower of the Hebraic-Christian tradition, this God made man in His image, and therefore man as a God-created Soul is transcendent to his body. Man expresses himself in his life-performance according to his unique character and his "free" will; and his performance may be wonderful or awful leading him eventually to Heaven or to Hell.

According to this anthropomorphic picture of existence and of what is beyond and above existence, God is THE One, the Supreme Being -- for the Vedantist He is "One without a second." He is absolute Unity. But the difficulty -- indeed the basic impossibility -- evident in all purely "monistic" metaphysics, is how to pass from this "One without a second" to the world of a multitude of individual existents, which includes the individual person who is speaking about this One without a second -- a rather awkward situation! If there is in God a "desire to be many," as is often stated by religious metaphysicians, then this desire is actually the seed of multiplicity. A unity in which multiplicity is latent is no longer really an absolute unity; and calling the world of multiplicity an "illusion" is merely intellectual prestidigitation.

The term, unity, is therefore not to be considered as an absolute. What we are speaking of is the state of wholeness rather than that of unity. The pianist who wants to express his emotions or who seeks satisfaction, money or fame through his performance is a w h o l e of drives, thoughts, desires, emotions and bodily activities -- not a unity. In his performance the potential energy related to s o m e of these components of his total personality becomes kinetic energy, i. e. released energy. But he is not alone in the world, and the release of his energy is motivated by some kind of n e e d, even if it is only the need to release a surplus of energy in the activity of playing or, as we say, "just for the fun of it."

When I speak of ONE, I do not mean a One, a Supreme Being; but rather a Principle of Wholeness which operates without essential differentiation equally in e v e r y w h o l e, be it an atom, a man or a galaxy. Without the operation -- or should we rather say the catalytic "presence"? --of ONE there would be no existent, no "whole of activities," no limited field of existence, and no finite cycle of time -- only a diffuse flow or an explosive release of energy.

However, this ONE, this Principle of Wholeness, is not responsible for the existential fact of motion, of energy being released. It is only responsible for the fact that all releases of energy occur in "u n i t s of energy," i. e., in the terminology of modern science, as "quanta" of energy. A universe is "born" in the release of a tremendous quantum of energy. Any existential cycle (or any process of exist-

ence) begins in a single release of energy. Where does this
kinetic energy come from? The theistic conception is that it
comes from God, the cosmic Performer Whose infinite, omnipotent Being contains an infinite potentiality of energy-
release, i.e. of creative activity.

According to the cyclocosmic and holistic world-picture
presented here, the process of release is different, and more
understandable. The concept of God is retained, but not as
an absolute. God can still be considered as the "source" of
the energy-flow released "in the beginning" of a universal
cycle of existence; but a source is (strictly speaking) a place
at which water emerges into visibility; from some deep underground current or lake water flows through the source.
The vocal sounds which a man utters are released through
his throat and lips; but the energy and the emotional (or intellectual) contents of the vocal sounds come from the whole
human organism.

Such illustrations are evidently not to be taken literally.
They are simply meant to show by familiar image-symbols
that the energy released into the field of activity of a cosmos
-- be it macrocosm or microcosm -- "emerges" into existence in a single act and THROUGH a One, but FROM what
we may conceive figuratively as an infinite Ocean of potential
energy. I refer to this "Ocean" as the Infinite Potential.

POTENTIALITY AND ACTUALITY

The words "potential" and "potentiality" are very important in our philosophy. Their relation to "actual" and "actuality" should be clearly understood; for in a very real sense
nearly everything else depends upon this relation and the way
in which it is conceived. If I use the term "potentiality" instead of "possibility" it is because while what is possible
may or may not manifest in terms of actual existential fact,
what is potential, as I use this word, will inevitably be
actualized at some time and in some field of space.

This distinction between possibility and potentiality is of the utmost importance, metaphysically speaking, especially insofar as the character of God or ultimate Reality is concerned. According to the theistic concept, of which the Bhagavad Gita is perhaps the earliest expression, God is essentially transcendent to the universe He has created, and this universe actualizes only a few of the infinite number of possibilities which God's infinite imagination could conceive and His omnipotent will could actualize. In the Gita, Krishna says: "Having produced this universe with a part of myself, I remain separate and undiminished." Such a concept is anthropomorphic, for it is a deification of what takes place when a creative artist, who has produced a work of art, in a sense withdraws from it, yet remains in possession of immense possibilities of future creations. For such an artist these future creations constitute only possibilities, because he can just as well not concretely actualize them as realize them.

According to our cyclocosmic world-picture, what is potential will be actualized. The Ocean of infinite potentialities not only contains in latency every possible mode of existence -- or we might say every possible solution to the infinitely complex problem of existence -- but all these possibilities have been, are or will be actualized as an infinity of universes in infinite Duration and infinite Spatiality.

This means that there is a fundamental relationship between the Infinite Potential and the multiplicity of modes of existence. If on the other hand one thinks of God as "separate" from the universe, and this universe actualizing only some of the possibilities in His divine Consciousness when it pleases Him, there is then no essential relationship between this transcendent God and the realm of existence. He may "desire" such a relationship and create a universe, but on the other hand He as well may not. If moreover His creativity remains, as it were, "within" Himself and only a Play (in Sanskrit, Lila) of His imagination, so that he is truly the One Actor and the world is an "illusion" (m a y a), then existence is indeed a dreamlike play of shadows on the screen of God's Mind; which is perhaps what the Javanese W a j a n g shadow-plays were meant to suggest.

When however the Infinite Potential is figuratively conceived as an infinite "womb" out of which all possible modes and forms of existence m u s t "emerge" into actuality -- and this they do, as we shall presently see, when the n e e d for them is realized at the end-stage of the cyclic development of consciousness (the Pleroma, or o m e g a state of consciousness) -- then the metaphysical-cosmic picture is indeed basically different. As already stated, this picture establishes a fundamental relationship between the Infinite Potential and the condition of existence, i. e. the many universes and all the cyclocosmic wholes they enfold. It is t h i s r e l a t i o n s h i p which is the most fundamental fact. It is a relationship between potentiality and actuality, and therefore between the as-yet-not-manifested and the to-be-manifested, which includes also the already-manifested but no-longer-existent.

Such a relationship, conceived in terms of infinite Duration, must have a cyclic character or else we could not speak of an ordered universe whose fundamental keynotes are Rhythm and Harmony. We can think of it in terms of a periodical alternation of states of "manifestation" and "non-manifestation"; and this is the picture presented by traditional Hinduism which tells of an infinite succession of m a n v a n t a r a s (periods of cosmic existence) and of p r a l a y a s (periods of total non-existence or "divine rest") -- each period lasting many trillions of our human years.

It is questionable however whether this picture of a quasi-absolute alternation of periods of manifestation and non-manifestation is the deepest one that the subtle Hindu mentality conceived; it may be only a popular or exoteric image suggested by the process of breathing -- exhalation and inhalation. We may find a more convincing and more fruitful picture in the ancient philosophy of China; for there we find that two cosmic Principles, Yin and Yang, are constantly interrelated, one waxing in intensity as the other wanes, then vice versa. If these two Principles are equated with the conditions of non-manifestation and of manifestation (i. e. with potentiality and actuality) we see that the manifested and the unmanifested states are always present but in cyclically varying degrees of strength. If this is the case then the whole picture of existence changes; and it changes in a way that is probably more comprehensible to the modern mind and more productive of constructive results.

In the Chinese picture -- represented by the well-known Tai Chi symbol -- Yin and Yang are enclosed within a circle. Their relationship is at every point a dynamic one; it leaves no room for any static rest-period. It changes at every moment. But there is That which encompasses all phases of the forever cyclically changing relationship between the two Principles. "That" is TAO; and this TAO is the changeless Harmony of the bi-polar Wholeness of "Reality." We say "Wholeness" because TAO cannot be conceived as "unity," but rather as Harmony, as the polyphonic interplay of two principles of existence.

The Chinese concept of TAO and of the cyclic process of Yang and Yin can be applied to a particular cyclocosm -- a universe, a man, or an atom. It can refer to the cycle of the year, of a man's life, or of a universe's life -- a cycle having a beginning and an end. But in this present discussion I am not only thinking of existence as a dynamic process starting with the release of a quantum of energy and a particular set of defined potentialities which will become actualized in the omega condition at the end of the cycle. I am dealing with the relationship between the actual fact of existence with all it implies and the infinite potentiality of existence -- that is, this Ocean of potentiality which to our minds can only appear to be "non-existence." Such a relationship is therefore to be considered as a purely metaphysical concept. Yet we will see that this concept, abstract as it may seem at first, can be seen to apply to man's most basic approach to what we call "spirituality."

It can be so applied because if existence and non-existence -- or actuality and potentiality -- are in a state of constant relatedness n o w and at all times, then our approach to existence itself becomes radically transformed. To put it more simply, this would mean that an individual person -- a human cyclocosm -- can experience at all times both existence and non-existence; that it is no longer a simple matter for him to pass through the successive phases of his existential cycle from birth to death, but that he is at all times partially living and partially dying. He is unceasingly balanced between states of actualization and states of potentiality -- perhaps of "re-potentialization." As a baby, the potentiality-polarity is dominant; he is more potential than actual. As the human being matures and performs his work he increasingly actualizes his innate birth-potential, and therefore the "potentiality factor" in him decreases. In old age, especially if he has lived a very full life, the accumulation of what he has actualized weighs upon his consciousness; his thought and feeling-patterns lose their potentiality for change and readjustment, and sclerosis or senility may gradually lead to physical death -- or to what the physicist might call the victory of "entropy" and an eventual return to chemical undifferentiation.

But this is only one side of the picture. The aging human organism loses its "potency," i.e. its capacity to release power in terms of energy-consuming activities. But an opposite process also takes place, or at least could take place, and this in a most significant manner. C o n s c i o u s n e s s can develop, just as the body gradually loses its potency. The aging man may grow into radiant wisdom, and a process of re-potentialization can take place in polar opposition to the process of physical out-wearing and disintegration. "Power" and "consciousness" constitute another basic dualism in the process of existence; and through consciousness, existence itself can, in a sense at least, become transcended.

The term "consciousness," however, is one with varied meanings, and it is indeed a most confusing word. It is particularly confusing because of its association with "mind" -- another term which can be and has been interpreted in many ways. Let us try to clarify the meanings of these words according to the cyclocosmic and holistic approach.

CONSCIOUSNESS, WHOLENESS AND RELATEDNESS

Every existential whole sufficiently integrated to possess an individual rhythm of existence structuring a consistent interplay of "functional" activities is conscious; but there are many grades of consciousness just as there are levels of integration. What we usually call consciousness in the human sense is what Teilhard de Chardin calls "reflective consciousness." It is consciousness turning back upon itself and becoming both centered and structured by a collective, social cultural set of patterns of responses to existence as well as by an individual ego -- what scientists would probably call a "feedback" process. But every existential whole has some kind of consciousness, however vague and diffuse it may be. In its primary form and at the biological level of organization consciousness is more like "sentiency"; at a higher level we can speak of "feeling-responses" and sensitivity -- and recent experiments have shown how amazingly sensitive plants are, a sensitivity which seems to include even most definite feeling-responses to human thinking*. But there is

---

*cf. the experiments conducted by Clive Backster and reported by Thorn Bacon in NATIONAL WILDLIFE for February-March 1969 which imply that not only plants, but cells as well "resonate" or react to whatever happens to living

no reason to deny a kind of consciousness even to what we call "inorganic" matter -- to atoms and molecules.

Consciousness is wholeness in operation. It is the most basic expression of relatedness. Consciousness, in existential wholes, is indeed relatedness referred to any relatively steady and organized system of interdependent activities. It grows in complexity, intensity and quality during the process of evolution of such wholes of activities. The more complex and lasting the patterns of interrelatedness and interacting changes, the more developed consciousness is within the whole.

The component parts of a whole are related to each other and are in constant functional interplay; and out of these interactions an internal consciousness is produced which has a basically systemic or organismic character. This kind of consciousness in the human being of today is actually below the threshold of what we usually call consciousness, even though it has repercussions upon and indeed affects "subconsciously" the development of the ego-consciousness. This ego-consciousness is mainly based upon external relationships -- i.e. relationships to the person's environment, to the people and the culture which surround the child's development from the time of and even before his birth. In the preceding chapter I spoke of matricial and associative relationships; to each type refers also a definite type of consciousness, even though the ego usually has a remarkable way of jumbling and misinterpreting these two modes of consciousness, producing complexes as a result.

The character of both the relationships and the consciousness implied in and formalized by these relationships de-

---

organisms in their neighborhood; which in turn seems to indicate that the entire biosphere somehow constitutes an integrated field (cf. also MAIN CURRENTS IN MODERN THOUGHT May-June, 1969, page 143).

pends on the level of integration at which the conscious whole operates. The principle of integration, ONE, is in itself without character and qualification. It simply is an ever-present constantly effective "force" inherent in all releases of energy originating a definite cycle of existence. We may think of ONE also as the basic "Law" of existence; but these terms "force" and "law," or even "catalytic Presence," are obviously inadequate. Perhaps gravitation can be considered as the basic aspect of ONE at the level of materiality. At the level of what we call "living organisms" able to maintain, heal, reproduce and transform themselves ONE operates as "Life." It may be thought of as universal "Love" at the level of relatedness corresponding to "feelings." It is also that which brings consciousness to a formed focus as "mind."

The important point however is to realize that as we use this term here, ONE does not mean a One, a mysterious Supreme Being active everywhere. In a sense it is similar to and probably identical with the Hindu concept of atman. From our modern point of view it may really be called the Principle of Existence, in as much as existence can only be conceived in terms of wholes of existence, and ONE is the Principle of Wholeness in every whole, in every cyclocosm.

Consciousness therefore may be thought of as the "aura of wholeness." Just as wholeness implies relatedness in all forms and at all levels of existential activity, it likewise implies consciousness. However, one can conceive of a type of consciousness which in a sense transcends the state of wholeness, though it is still implied in relatedness. It refers to the relationship already mentioned between Existence and Non-Existence -- which is more precisely the relationship between actual existence and the infinite potentiality of existence.

When we speak of "infinite potentiality" we transcend, as it were, the level at which ONE is operative within any and all wholes, whether it be atom, man or universe. That which is infinite is not whole. When we speak of time in terms of cycles of immensely varied length, time belongs to the realm of wholes; and so do spatial fields of force within whose boundaries the activities inherent in these wholes take place. When however we associate the concept of time with that of infinity we should speak of "infinite Duration." Likewise we should not speak of infinitely extended space-fields, but rather of Spatiality, or (in a most abstract and transcendent sense) of SPACE as the infinite potentiality of emergence of finite fields. This infinite potentiality can become actualized in cosmic wholes of many dimensions but as well in the dimensionless mathematical point. Infinite Duration also transcends all concepts of length of cycle; it is the potentiality of the vastest eon of time, but also of the most mystical concept of the "instant," the timeless moment.

The essential point in our philosophy is however that there is a relationship between, on the one hand the Infinite Potential, and on the other all conceivable forms of existence. This of course is a transcendent type of relationship in as much as one of the poles of it, the Infinite Potential, has a transcendent character. It is not a relationship between wholes existing at the same level (so-called "horizontal" relationship); or one between a lesser whole and the greater whole of which it is also a component part ("vertical" relationship). It is a relationship between the Infinite and any-and-all finite wholes. We cannot say that the Infinite really "contains" the finite; neither would it be exact to say that the Infinite Potential "gives birth" to a finite whole, a universe -- except as a symbolic figure of speech. We have used the symbolic expression of an "emergence" of a universal whole out of the infinite Ocean of potentialities; but this, we must stress, is only symbolic. The traditional symbol of all creative beginnings is the appearance of a dot at the center of a circle; but before the dot appears there is really no circle -- only "nothingness." Yet in our philosophy this nothingness is to be understood as the Infinite Potentiality of every imaginable thing.

The most important fact is that existence takes form in relation to this nothingness which is the potentiality of everything. We should not say that something "emerges" out of this nothing; for "nothing" is not a place. But something -- the germ of the cosmos and in a sense any germinal beginning -- begins to exist in relation to the infinite Potential...which "is-not." We should therefore try to understand this relation; and the only way we can understand it with any degree of rationality and consistency is to realize that it operates in several modes. It is operating in the process which leads from the Infinite Potential to actual existence, secondly, during cycles of existence, and thirdly, in the process which constitutes the transition from a closing cycle of existence to the Infinite Potential. If the picture we make of this relationship is to be symmetrical we have also to imagine this relationship in its most transcendent character when Existence seems to be entirely absorbed in Non-Existence. Existence however can no more be entirely absorbed in Non-Existence than the polarity Yang can ever be entirely overcome by the power of Yin; and this is what the Hindu world-picture fails to show.

The end-results of a universal cycle of existence, at least in a figurative sense, "return to" the infinite Ocean of potentiality, but they do not utterly vanish into it. They "are" in it in two opposite conditions because, as I shall presently explain, every cycle of existence ends in a state of extreme duality. This duality is opposed to ONE, and this opposition compels the emergence of a future universe -- a future cycle of time and a cosmic field of existence.

Why this state of duality at the end of a cycle of existence? Because -- and this is a fact which we experience in so many ways -- the release of any potentiality of existence leads to both positive and negative results; or, in human terms, to "success" and "failure." Thus every universal cycle of existence ends with (1) a unified group of existents in whom the potential purpose inherent in the initial creative Impulse (or creative WORD) that gave birth to the cycle finds perfect fulfillment, and (2) a mass of waste material, the disintegrated remains of the existential wholes and minds which failed to actualize the functional purpose for the fulfillment of which they were produced. *

We may put this in other words by saying that the problem of existence can always have two opposite kinds of solution. The very fact of existence in terms of wholes, i.e. finite fields of activity having a particular "form," implies both an "inside" and an "outside"; it implies the need to relate the inside to the outside, and vice versa. Wholeness, relatedness, consciousness are terms, I repeat, the meanings of which are rooted in the same fact of existence. In man the refusal to be related -- born essentially of fear -- leads to a negative type of wholeness, i.e. to the utter isolation of the individual from his surroundings. The relationship of this individual to the greater whole of which he is a part as a result turns negative; and we have then the great symbol of c a n c e r -- the cell or group of cells proliferating in a negative, isolationistic relationship to the whole organism.

The refusal to relate and the refusal to love produce a type of consciousness which crystallizes into a mind-struc-

---

*A third possibility undoubtedly has to be considered, i.e. only partial success at the end of the cycle; but I shall not discuss it here in order not to complicate the picture. Of course the student of Christianity will not fail to relate these situations to Heaven, Hell and Purgatory. Such religious concepts, however valuable they may have been at some historical period, can at best be considered only as symbolical representations of the states of fulfillment and non-fulfillment to which I am referring, and which can be related, as we shall see, to actual existential facts in the realm of life.

ture -- a form of consciousness -- which operates destructively under the power of a tyrannical ego. This ego has cut itself off from sustaining relationships to the greater whole within which the individual person was born to function. It may manage to survive for a time -- perhaps for a long time at the level of mind -- through predatory acts and a process of vampirizing; but sooner or later it must disintegrate and reach a condition of chaos.

This condition is also a condition of potentiality; for instance the chemicals in the soil resulting from the disintegration of autumnal leaves can be assimilated by any plant. Manure constitutes the potentiality of food for the growth of almost any future plant. But it represents potentiality in a condition of inertness or, one might say, of total indifference to existence. On the contrary, the unified host of perfect Beings (the Pleroma) who "return" to the state of potentiality at the close of a planetary or cosmic cycle, reach that state as a positive, arousing factor. They have reached an all-encompassing consciousness -- an "eonic" consciousness -- to which nothing that existed throughout the vast cycle during which they achieved "success" could possibly be alien or of no concern. They have become, in their togetherness and unanimity, the cycle itself, the Eon; and because of this fact, wholeness, relatedness and consciousness in them operate as absolute "Compassion."

Back of, within and through this Compassion, ONE operates. It is at that supreme level, the compulsion of relatedness which must seek a way to bring together in a new universe the successful Ones and the disintegrated failures. This way must be found by the successful Ones, the Pleroma. They envision the Image of a new universe in which the failures of the old cycle will have a "second chance," as it were, to experience wholeness, consciousness and relatedness within organic wholes.

Success and failure are two inevitable polarities of existence. Every release of potentiality as power to be used poses a problem, a crucial dilemma: Will the power be used constructively or destructively? Will it mean success or failure to the entities using it? The answer depends on the capacity for relationship of the user. At the level of human beings who have reached a state of conscious individualization we can equate the capacity to enter into positive relationships with other human beings with "love"; but love here means the capacity not merely to relate emotionally and/or possessively with someone else, particularly of the opposite sex, but to relate with that person in terms of what this relationship of love will bring to a "greater whole" -- whatever be the type of "greater whole" within which the lovers can c o n s c i o u s l y feel themselves participants.

C o n s c i o u s n e s s here is the crucial factor, because unconscious love and indeed all forms of unconscious relationships can mean for man, at the truly individualized stage of his evolution, a negative, passive return to some sort of prenatal condition. The French speak of l'égoisme a deux, where a man and a woman become so involved in one another as to reconstitute, as it were, the bi-polar state which occult traditions claim to have been the condition of man in the beginning -- the condition symbolized in Genesis by Adam b e f o r e Eve appeared, before the principle of duality superseded the passive, reflective condition of unity. "Conscious love" is love dedicated to an ever greater sense of wholeness, to a quality of relatedness which increasingly forgets the exclusiveness and egocentric limitations of instinctual, biological and emotional, thus actually unconscious love.

The progressive development and expansion of consciousness is the one essential factor when man has emerged from his dependence upon matricial relationships -- when mankind as a whole, or an individual person, has reached the state of real maturity. This theoretically occurs at the "mid-point" of the life-cycle -- a fact which Dante used as the starting point of his mystical adventure in "The Divine

Comedy." But this need not be the exactly chronological mid-point. What is implied in the concept of this "mid-point" is that at that time a new type of relationship between potentiality and actuality is theoretically possible.

I have said a few paragraphs back that the relationship between potentiality and actuality operates in several modes or conditions, that is, (1) in the process which leads from the Infinite Potential to actual existence, (2) as it exists during the cycle of existence, (3) as it operates during the transition from the ending cycle to a "return" to the state of potentiality, and also (4) during the condition of pure, but not absolute potentiality which is a state of relative non-existence. Man reaches the "bottom" of his cycle of existence when the power released at the beginning of the cycle reaches a point of relative equilibrium before the waning phase begins and organismic vitality starts to decrease. In a sense this cyclic moment resembles somewhat the fall equinox when day and night are of equal length and, most important symbolically speaking, when the seed is formed within the fruit. The formation of the seed marks the beginning of the dying process in the yearly plant. Something happens within the plant; the species-as-a-whole is being focused in the seed; and this means that the potentiality for a resurgent life begins to manifest in that seed, just as the power which operated within the parent-plant begins to wane.

This potentiality for a future cycle is expressed not in terms of a release of energy or power, as was the case at the beginning of the cycle (Phase One of the relationship between potentiality and actuality), but in terms of a rise of consciousness. The first half of the cycle saw a most basic expression of power through activity; the second half witnesses, in the vegetable kingdom, the growth of the seed and its liberation from the dying plant, and in the human kingdom -- if man is really man, i.e. a conscious individual person -- the development of a gradually more independent consciousness able to operate in a mind which no longer should reflect, more or less passively, the collective mentality of a culture and social-religious tradition. Instead it should become consciously aware of and should respond to the fundamental rhythm of the self, i.e. of the man's true individuality (in Sanskrit, his d h a r m a -- his "truth of being").

By the term "mind" is not meant here a composite mass of intellectual information and operative formulas more or less well-organized by a type of traditional thinking process, or a computer-like kind of brain-mechanism. The true or authentic mind is an o r g a n i s m   o f   c o n s c i o u s n e s s attuned to the rhythm of the self, and with an increasing capacity for being unaffected by and free from bio-social drives or compulsions -- as a seed becomes increasingly free from the plant and either falls to the soil, or is carried to new land by the wind of a new destiny.

It is the potentiality of such a gradually freer, more independent and authentic "mind" which is impressed upon the individual's consciousness at the theoretical mid-period of the life-cycle; and the last "half" of this life-cycle should be essentially consecrated to the actualization of this potentiality of such a "seed-mind" in individualized man. The ultimate end of this process of actualization in so far as humanity-as-a-whole is concerned is the perfect state of "multiunity" of the Pleroma of Man -- the host of Perfected Soul-Minds who in their unanimous togetherness represent the "success"-aspect of the o m e g a phase of the human-planetary cycle. As this phase is reached the purpose of the existential process is fulfilled in actual concrete fact. The o m e g a has realized what the a l p h a had projected into existence as what has been called "the Word of Power."

This, nevertheless, is only the "success" aspect. The "failure" aspect is the mass of waste-products and disintegrating human mental stuff reaching, in unconsciousness, the condition of chaos -- chaos which polarizes the "divine" state of Pleroma-consciousness. The autumnal leaves decay into pungent humus after a brief glowing phase of golden or red splendor; they polarize in chemical death the immortality of the seeds. This immortality is only relative, for the seed will die into the future plant; but nevertheless the seed will have become the focal point for the creative action of a whole species of earthly life, and indeed an "agent" for the vast life of the greater Whole, the planet Earth.

Likewise the "seed man" in whom the potentiality of an eventual fulfillment of Pleroma-consciousness has become actualized, at least to some degree, also reaches what may be called immortality in mind. This "mind" may have become in some cases an independent "organism of consciousness" whose individual identity is not destroyed by death. Conscious immortality so understood is the goal sought after by all truly occult disciplines; but it is quite evidently not the type of so-called "soul survival" to which spiritualistic groups refer rather unconvincingly, considering the type of "message" usually conveyed by these "surviving souls."

CONCLUSION

We shall attempt in the next chapter to outline, as briefly as is consistent with clarity of thought, the pattern of unfoldment of a cosmic cycle of existence. Now in concluding this chapter dealing with the fundamentals of a metaphysics of wholeness, I would like to present the following remarks which may elucidate some of the basic concepts we have been discussing, by re-stating their inter-relationship in a more condensed manner.

The process of existence can never be really understood on the basis of an absolute kind of monism, with One God as solely responsible for every activity in it -- as the sole "Reality" -- and everything else as more or less an "illusion" moving in an illusory freedom. Neither can existence be validly interpreted on a purely pluralistic basis featuring a kind of spiritual individualism somehow functioning in the midst of a material universe in which operate more or less rigid laws of Nature without any understandable origin. Everywhere, at all times, indeed even beyond existential time and space-fields, the principle of polarity operates. Two trends of opposite polarities are recognizable, directly or intuitively. But within these two trends a third factor is always present, though its presence operates in several different ways, at different levels.

I have called this "presence" ONE. We cannot define it precisely because of the different ways in which it manifests, but it can best be understood as the Principle of Wholeness; for wholeness is the all-inclusive Fact. It is the fact which all existents explicit. It is implicit in the potentiality of existence, beyond any finite existents, beyond any cycle of time and limited space-fields.

To speak of a "trinitarian" view of reality would nevertheless be rather misleading: ONE does not belong to the realm of number. It is a Principle that is effective above, yet within numeration. It is not to be confused with number one. It is implied as well in number two -- in any number. It is even implied in the concept of infinity, just because it is a "concept" formulated by the minds of existents who are wholes of existence. It is implied in every word I am writing now, because I exist -- "I" whose power-of-existence is a self -- and selfhood is an aspect of ONE just as life or materiality, or what I call "ideity," is the principle of operation of consciousness within an integrated mind.

At the beginning of any cycle of existence ONE manifests within "the One" that is the creative Impulse of existence during that cycle -- the originating WORD or Logos. ONE manifests in the quantum of energy released as a unit of the power that will differentiate into the varied modes of energies necessary for the unfoldment of this process of existence. ONE manifests in every existential whole, every cyclocosm. It manifests in the atom and the molecule at the level of materiality -- in the cell and the organism at the level of life -- in the consciousness of man (and of whatever may exist as "more-than-man" in terms of what we may call with Sri Aurobindo "super-mind") at the level of ideity. ONE manifests in the Pleroma of perfected Beings (which is for the Catholic believer, the Communion of Saints, and for the Theosophist, the White Lodge) at the level of divinity. It manifests as that all-encompassing Compassion which is aroused within the infinite Ocean of potentiality and is, within the state which men tend to call Non-Existence, the seed of future cycles of existence.

To speak of ONE as "God" and then of God as "He" makes no philosophical sense. It is quite probable, however, that a mystic like Meister Eckhardt had a real intuition of the ubiquitous presence of ONE when he spoke of the Godhead as a mystical reality beyond God. The Hindu concept of Parabrahman might also be interpreted in a similar sense, with Mulaprakriti somehow referring to what I call the Infinite Potential; but it would seem that the tendency in the Hindu mind was to think of Parabrahman as transcendentally superior to Mulaprakriti, or (as in Sri Aurobindo's metaphysics) to speak of one absolute Brahman in two aspects -- manifested and unmanifested. The human mind seems overeager to think of any ultimate Reality or Essence as a Something, even if it is implied that this Something is also Nothing. The Chinese intuition of Tao is more like what I am attempting to picture intuitively as ONE; and in India we have also the concept of TAT which, while it is often equated with Brahman, should really be considered in a different light, that is, as a Principle.

In the Chinese symbol of the Tai Chi, the two comma-like figures of Yin and Yang (black and white, non-manifestation and manifestation, night and day, etc.) are enclosed within a circle which they totally fill; and the tendency is to say that Tao is represented by the circle. But while Tao is represented symbolically by the circle, it is not the circle, and especially not the circumference binding, as it were, the interplay of the two polarities; or it is so only when these polarities, Yin and Yang, are seen operating within an existential whole, though this whole be the entire cosmos. Tao -- at least if seen as identical to what I call ONE -- does not include Yin and Yang (as Existence and Non-Existence). It is implied in both Existence and Non-Existence. It inheres in their relationship. It is the rhythm of the relationship between actuality-of-existence and potentiality-of-existence. It is "present" everywhere -- in the circle of the most extensive cosmic field of existence, but also in the dimensionless mathematical point which symbolizes spatiality in its condition of non-manifestation. It is present throughout the vastest cycle of cosmic existence which one can conceive, but just as much in the mystical "instant" in which cyclic time is apprehended in a flash of eonic consciousness in a state of all-inclusive condensation; and the Buddhist philosopher refers to such a flash of eonic consciousness as Sammasambuddhi, the instant of total lucidity which immediately preceded the realization of the Nirvana state by Gautama the Buddha.

All that I have just said concerning ONE is, of course, only symbolic. It deals with the manifestations of ONE at levels about which I am able to project some kind of concept with inevitably inadequate words. "Nothing" or "the Void" is also a concept. To speak of "Imagelessness" is still to present an Image; just as the "anti-novel" of vanguard authors is still a form of novel. I hope nevertheless that what I have said may awaken or arouse in at least some minds an intuitive consciousness which transcends, though it certainly should not exclude, the Image of an all-powerful, all-loving God Who is "He," Who created the universe and the souls of every human being, and Who is to be adored. The need for such a God-image is psychologically obvious; this Image is deeply rooted in the collective Unconscious of mankind. It has power, the power to arouse intense feeling, transforming faith and indeed, it seems evident, to perform what we call miracles. It is a channel through which a human being in distress and in need can relate himself effectually to at least a wavelet of the infinite Ocean of potentiality. No one in his senses would want to deprive humanity of such a channel; and to assert that there is no God is just as absurd as to claim that God is a person with a beard sitting on a throne, Whose judgments send immortal souls to everlasting states of paradisical bliss or torturing hell.

However, if we believe in a progressive evolution and expansion of consciousness, we should also believe in the possibility, and indeed in due time the inevitability, of reaching ever more inclusive Image-concepts of a "Reality" the infinite potentialities of which must always remain incompletely fathomed by any mind, human or divine. What I have tried to convey is this infinitude of potentialities of existence and of consciousness -- consciousness being but an expression of the fact of wholeness. Infinite Potentiality reaches, nevertheless, ever beyond the vastest expanse of consciousness, as infinite Spatiality is ever beyond the most extended field of space, and infinite Duration ever beyond the lengthiest cosmic cycle. Likewise ONE is to be conceived as that Principle that inheres in all "ones," in all units of existence, in all cyclocosms, in all men and all "gods." It is SELF in all selves, root-power in all existential wholes. If Motion is never ceasing, ONE is within all movements as their fundamental Rhythm.

We cannot avoid, if we are metaphysically inclined, to postulate such Ultimates. They should be not only ultimates of existence but ultimates which include the most fundamental of all relationships, that of potentiality-of-existence to actuality-of-existence. If there is an "absolute," this relationship is such an absolute, for within it we find implied ONE as the basic Fact of existence, Motion in terms of Rhythm, Duration and Spatiality. This relationship -- how could we imagine it more effectively than in terms of all-encompassing and all-transcending HARMONY?

VI. THE CYCLIC PROCESS

From Beginning to End to Re-Beginning

A cycle of existence begins with a release of power; a certain quantum of undifferentiated energy is actualized. Two unavoidable questions therefore arise: W h e r e does this energy come from?-- and W h y was it actualized as kinetic energy able to produce existential results?

As we have seen in the previous chapter any released quantum of energy or unit of power is the actualization of a finite amount (an awkward term!) of potentiality. Some factor acting within the infinite Ocean of potentiality has been able to transform potentiality into actuality -- or we might say potency into power. This factor is "consciousness" -- the kind of consciousness which has developed at the end of a previous cycle of existence, Pleroma-consciousness.

We have already seen that this Pleroma-consciousness is, symbolically speaking, the "seed" of a universe -- the o m e g a aspect of the cyclocosmic process manifesting as this universe. We also saw that the last stages of such a cosmic cycle produced not only such a Pleroma (i. e. the unanimous group of perfected Beings who successfully actualized the initial potential of their own cosmic cycle), but also a chaotic mass of decaying elements which constitute the end-results of the many "failures" in this universe. Thus a cycle ends in a condition of duality which, if we are permitted the use of such an emotion-laden word, is "intolerable" to ONE and to the Compassion inherent in the all-inclusive Pleroma-state of consciousness. In the omega state of the cosmic cycle, the two poles of existence, unity and multiplicity, are as far apart as they can be. They must once more be brought into relationship; and this means that the disintegrated remains of the past universe must be given a "second chance" to experience the state of wholeness and to "feel one" in organismic togetherness.

Abstractly speaking, the Seed Pleroma represents the pole of unity, as it has reached a condition of supermental, "divine" unanimity in consciousness. All the potentialities implied in the Logos -- the One-in-the-beginning -- are actualized; and the "presence" of ONE is all-powerful. However I prefer to speak here of "multi-unity"; for in that unanimity of consciousness of the Pleroma, there nevertheless remains residual memory of the individual paths which every perfected Being participating in this Pleroma has taken to reach unity. It is therefore a state of unity which includes as it were the quintessence of a multiplicity of existential experiences; and for this reason I speak of "multi-unity" and of the multi-une Pleroma.

The pole of multiplicity is represented by the disintegrated and atomized remains of the failures of the universal cycle. Each of the entities which had utterly failed to reach the Pleroma state and dropped by the wayside at each phase of the process of evolution was eventually reduced to a completely insulated unity of materiality in a condition of nearly absolute non-relatedness and indifference or inertia. This is the condition to which modern scientists refer as the end-state of the trend toward undifferentiation, i. e. "entropy." The term entropy, however, should be applied to any kind of activity which fails to respond to an opposite process -- a process which produces a gradual expansion not only of consciousness but of the capacity for relationship and integration (i. e. love and wholeness). Such a process, now called "negentropy," is an expression of the power of

ONE.

Entropy at any level results from a lack of response of the existent to ONE. It implies the opposite of love, that is, hatred. And hatred is essentially the product of fear -- the fear experienced by a man confronted with a new phase of the process of existence. It is such a fear that is the only real "original sin," for every frightened refusal to move one step ahead in the process of evolution -- the Hindu would say in the performance of one's d h a r m a -- generates a force that runs in a direction opposite to this evolutionary process.*

Fear cuts one off from the flow of power which is available to the existential whole in whom the process of consciousness-unfoldment has begun to operate. The small unit, when it refuses to relate and, through relationship, to increase in consciousness, becomes blind to the presence of ONE in the new phase or at the new level of his growth. He clings to his egocentric response to ONE, i. e. to a lesser form of integration. He gradually builds around his ego-consciousness a fortified wall within which the consciousness eventually will die, suffocated, and the wall itself will in time disintegrate and become dust -- the dust of a failure.

At the end of a universal cycle (and to a lesser extent, or in a purely relative sense, of a n y existential cycle) we find, therefore, a sharp opposition between the two polarities, unity and multiplicity. As a result the "need" to once more

---

*cf. my book FIRE OUT OF THE STONE. The real "sin" of Adam and Eve occurred a f t e r they had eaten of the fruit of the Tree of good and evil which had given them a new and discriminatory consciousness of the dual power in all life-experiences. They had taken a positive evolutionary step, but became frightened by its implications and by their new responsibility. Thus they tried to "hide" the symbol of the new power. They had failed the test, and had to face the karmic results of this failure.

provide a formula of integration (a logos or creative Word) on the basis of which a new process of relationship between the One and the Many can start, is the ineradicable feature of this omega situation. It can only be met by what constitutes the positive, dynamic pole of the situation, the Pleroma of perfect Beings, "seed" of the ending universe. The Pleroma therefore "visualizes" the Image-formula of a new universe. It must be a new Image-formula, because the conditions of existence are different in every universe -- the conditions and character of the pole, success, as well as those of the pole, failure. There are an infinite number of possible ways of solving the eternal problem of existence; the Ocean of potentiality is infinite. Duration and Spatiality are infinite, rhythmic Motion is unceasing, even in the state we call Non-existence, though in a different mode -- we might say an almost purely subjective mode.

The divine Host of Perfect Beings, acting as a unanimous "divine" Mind, at the end of the universal cycle "enters" as it were the infinite Ocean of Potentiality -- often symbolized in past traditions as "the Eternal Virgin." Acting as a fecundant force, this divine Mind brings to the infinite Matrix a realization of the need as well as the Image of the new universe which It has envisioned. This fecundant act arouses in the Eternal Virgin the "desire" to exteriorize some of the potential required to substantiate and energize the Image impressed upon "Her" by the Pleroma-Mind. Thus the logos or divine Plan for a new universe is "conceived"; but it is conception in potentiality and not yet an actual fact. The cycle of concrete existence has not yet begun. There is still "nothing" to be seen. But within the infinite Ocean of potentiality a formative process is unfolding, held within abstract boundaries by the catalytic presence of ONE. The Formula for the universe-to-be is being "imagined" in its broad developmental lines by the divine Pleroma-Mind, and with each aspect of this Formula, Image or Archetype, a measure of potency adequate for its actualization is being integrated.

It is to such a process that many occult books of the past referred when they spoke of a "divine World" above and beyond our world of concrete existence. It is the "ideal" world in which what is divinely conceived by the union of a visualized Image and the potentiality for its manifestation unfolds in ideal outlines but without any relationship to actual substantial existence, except in the sense that the concrete reality which is to take place within a finite space-field and equally limited time-cycle is an answer to a cosmic need -- or as some would say, to Karma, which means essentially to the "unfinished business" of the past cycle.

During this ideal phase of unfoldment of the Image impressed upon the Infinite Potential by the Pleroma-Mind one can presumably not even speak of the "memory" of a cosmic need. The Pleroma has become absorbed into the Ocean of Potentiality. The past is forgotten or almost forgotten. Potentiality is supreme -- and potentiality means, in human terms, that which will become actualized sooner or later in infinite Duration. The Infinite Potential we might say always looks to the future, or to what we can only interpret as "future" with our time-sense. For any mind it is the future; because mind is a formative agency.

A mind obsessed with potentiality is utterly future-oriented; it operates within a time which has no past, which is an unceasing surge of new possibilities unrelated to the need of any past. It is, in this sense, the child's mind, a mind that plays with ever-changing, ever-renewed possibilities unconcerned with their relationship to the facts of existence. Yet these possibilities are nevertheless conditioned and structured by the capacities of the child's organism. Even the divine Child is held within the framework of the Mind of His Father Who has projected Itself into the Mother's womb as the organic structure of the Child; but the Child is not aware of these conditioning limitations. He goes on playing with

possibilities in a never-ceasing game (in Sanskrit, lila).
He does so as long as He operates in the divine World, in the
world of pure imagination; as long as the real confrontation
with actual existential relationships has not begun or at least
not in earnest at a definitely concrete level; as long as His
consciousness is still mostly plunged in the Ocean of potentiality.

The concrete world of existence begins when a cosmic
unit of power is released which whirls at fantastic speed
through the as yet unstructured field of space. Concrete existence begins because, into its whirling spirals, the chaotic
remains of the past universe, the dust of the cyclocosm that
was, are drawn at once -- unconscious remains, inert, utterly indifferent to the possibility of renewed existence but now
caught in a maelstrom of motion, subjected to immense impacts which are reiterated for incalculable periods of time.
This is the level of existence at which ONE operates in terms
of materiality. Potence has been released from the infinite Ocean of potentiality as cosmic power. It has been released because the Pleroma-Mind, the divine form of consciousness, did "fecundate" the infinite Potential, the Eternal Virgin. It is always consciousness that
transforms potency into power.

The Pleroma-Mind is now the effective "Father" of the
new universe; but as occult traditions always state, this Father remains "hidden" behind or beyond the created world.
Actually He did not "create"this world. He only "e-manat-
ed," that is, he projected in "mind" (in Sanskrit, manas)
the essential Image of the entire new process of existence
or more accurately the structure of the process, the
fundamental formula or genetic pattern, in the cosmic sense,
defining the basic patterns of relationship between the essential factors in the existential process that is to be. The original Impulse which began the cosmic cycle of existence
surged through this basic structure, but from the Infinite Potential, somewhat as the light of the projector in a

motion picture theatre surges through the film and then is projected upon the screen. The cosmic screen is in this illustration the new Space-field whose boundaries are defined by the need of the process for space adequate to the type of cosmic relationships which will be interplaying -- a cosmic "living space."

What we call in the Christian tradition "the WORD that was in the beginning" (the Logos), and what the Hindu philosopher calls Ishvara, is not the "hidden Father" but the Son. It is the "new God," the divine Child -- in contrast to the "old God," the Seed-Pleroma of the past universe, the Father. This Father, in the first chapter of Genesis, is called ELOHIM, a plural noun. It is the Pleroma-Host of the past universe now acting as Father, because the "new God," Ishvara, has been "born." The divine FIAT LUX (the projection of "Light") does not however refer to the actual Creation of the concrete cosmos but to the "fecundation" of the Infinite Potential by the seed-Pleroma; and the entire first chapter of Genesis deals with the projection of Archetypal Images into the womb of the Eternal Virgin, thus to the "divine World" already mentioned.

It is only in the second chapter of Genesis that the formation of the world of concrete existence is dealt with, and this only in terms of our planet and humanity. At this stage God is Yahveh Elohim (or in Hebrew Yod-He-Vau-He). He is only "one of the Elohim" and as we shall see, the Ruler of the realm of Life.

In more mystical and more complete cosmologies the "new God" (the Son, Ishvara) is the divine expression of the original release of power which is the Source of the new cycle of cosmic existence. He is "the One." He is the AUM Tone of the new cosmos, the Self of the universe; nevertheless He must not be considered as ONE or SELF. He is existence in the alpha condition of unity. He is the one Power that differentiates into many modes of energy, each mode being required to energize a basic function in the universal whole. He is the one stream of white Light which breaks into the several colored Rays and their immense number of sub-rays. He is the Power within the cosmic Word "imaged forth" by the Father ELOHIM, the Word, that contains an immense yet finite number of Letters; and each of these Letters is a potential "Soul" -- each an aspect of the Word that resounds, unchanging, throughout the cycle of Time.

In the beginning the divine Child is still infused with potentiality. He dreams his life in a mostly subjective state of imagination, filled with what in India is called A n a n d a, the pure, unconstrained joy of existence. He is the Player of an infinity of games, but these games are mostly imaginary. For this divine Child existence is indeed a play, Lila, in which He is acting all the parts. It is mainly to this state of divine Being that the great Hindu tradition refers when it speaks of God--God-Ishvara, God as the child Krishna playing with the g o p i s, symbols of the many energies of the spiritual world of Soul, each Soul a divine r a g a, or melody.

This is a beautiful, joy-filled vision of existence. It represents the i d e a l of existence in the childhood stage -- the stage in which potentiality dominates; and in a sense we may consider this stage as the most "spiritual"; for, being so close to the Infinite Potential, which is then symbolized as the Divine Mother, it partakes of the character of "infinity." But actuality and its finiteness, or Karma, sooner or later will in turn dominate the stage on which the drama of existence is performed. The lovely, joyous Play of the Child becomes indeed increasingly like a drama.

Why a drama? Because the moment the factor of relationship in terms of concrete living personalities comes to be the focus of attention of the evolving existential wholes, conflicts must inevitably arise. They arise when the energies of Life begin to operate at full strength. This is the symbolic crisis of puberty. The world of the child becomes that of the adolescent.

Life, in the most basic sense of the word, characterizes a particular level of integration and therefore a level of relatedness and consciousness. ONE operates at that level as Life, just as before in the world-process It operated as Materiality.

What we call "matter" is rarely understood in its most basic sense. It constitutes the first condition of existence, a condition in which potentiality is still most dominant. Occultists and even scientists of the last century have often spoken of "proto-matter"; and today physicists are beginning to postulate "particles" which are even more primary than electrons, protons, mesons, neutrinos and the like. Whether what they are looking for is really to be conceived as "particles" is questionable; it is probably not really "physical" in the usual sense of the term. It belongs presumably to a "sub-quantum" realm. Whatever it be, it is far more an expression of potentiality than of actuality. In it the Yin of potentiality dominates the Yang of actuality.

As this Yang of actuality increases in strength we reach the stage of atoms, then of molecules. We pass from the realm of stars in which enormous heat prevails to the realm of planets which, as they presumably cool down (though the term "cooling" could be misleading), become the stage for the evolution of the most primary forms of Life -- perhaps what we now call "viruses." These viruses today are thought to be intermediaries between crystals and the large molecules which constitute the foundation of living cells. But it is questionable whether they are evolutionary links between what we call the inanimate and the animate, between the level of Materiality and that of Life. They may instead perhaps represent the "return" of some of the earliest living structures to the mineral-crystalline stage -- somewhat as there are mammals who, though born on land, have returned to the sea.

Evolution in other words contains regressive phases. Some of the new developments prove too difficult and too frightening to the entities born at the very onset of these "mutations"; perhaps the mutation was premature -- the new release of potentiality came before the capacity developed in the new organisms to actualize in a steady manner this unfamiliar potentiality. And a regressive step occurs -- a return to the old condition.

Whether or not viruses represent such a regression, the fact seems evident that from time to time the evolutionary process does witness such backward steps; and this may be a very important fact to consider today because the extraordinarily rapid development of intellectual powers in Western mankind may have become so dangerous, and indeed so destructive, that a "calculated withdrawal" to safer human conditions of existence may prove imperative in the long run. This does not need to be a really regressive step provided its purpose is well understood. It is always possible for man to realize that he has made a false start; or at least that in order to make this start he has dropped values and ideals for the lack of which the start, as it develops, will lead into paths of destruction. Such a process of withdrawal in order to go back to the original starting point and then start again with a more inclusive consciousness of all that is needed to make the new lines of progress really constructive -- this can be most valuable and indeed most indispensable. And mankind may be now facing the necessity to make such a withdrawal if it is not to experience a far more catastrophic situation -- a new "Deluge" crisis which could be, however, not destruction by "water" but by atomic or sub-atomic "fire."

The originators and contemporary proponents of the modern evolutionary concept have been so eager, for obvious reasons, to utterly abandon the ideal of "special creations" by a transcendent divine Creator, that they may well have become blind to the possibility that evolution is not merely a one-directional process "upward," but that it also includes what I might call directed mutations. I do not mean by these terms what the religious mind would interpret as "divine interventions" in the usual theological sense. I refer rather to the existence of several levels of integration; which means several "modes of operation" (and these may be very inadequate terms) of the Principle of Wholeness, ONE.

The transition from one level to another may have to be considered, not strictly as an evolutionary process, but rather as the result of a new phase in the balance between potentiality and actuality. That is to say, when a further step in the actualization of a new type of potentiality is taken -- a type of potentiality which was inherent in the originating Creative Word -- this step implies two factors: (1) the readiness of the evolutionary developments up to that phase of the existential process to accept the new development, and (2) a new release of power, that is, a decisive action transforming potency into power. I refer to this action as an "involutionary" factor.

The source of this action is in a sense the "hidden Father," the ELOHIM. But this "hidden Father" is not hidden in some transcendent Heaven. He is hidden within. Potentiality is not "outside of" or "above" actuality. It is, within the already-actualized, the to-be-actualized. In a basic mutation, that is, in the process of transition from one level of integration to the next, the future acts upon the present. The future acts when the present is ready to accept the mutation; when, in a deep sense, the present "needs" the action of the future in order to become the new present.

Yet as we have just said, the present may not be quite ready; the change may be somewhat premature; thus trouble is expectable, which may be called a "calculated risk." The Initiator -- in terms of occult processes -- may have to take the risk that the Initiate may not be entirely able to adjust to the new type of life and consciousness resulting from the initiation. But the risk has to be taken if by not taking it a destructive force may operate in the vacuum created by some radical life-crisis, or the opportunity might be delayed for too long a period, as such an opportunity depends upon the rhythm of the evolutionary process of humanity as a whole.

But let us return to the transition from the level of integration, called Materiality, to that which is named Life. In matter immense power is locked by what science today calls the "binding force" operating in atomic structures. This binding force sets boundaries to the atoms. The atom is a whole of activity. In this whole, the Principle of wholeness, ONE, operates; it operates at the level of Materiality.

At the level of Life ONE operates in a new way, in terms not only of the maintenance of the wholeness of the whole, but in terms also of the capacity within this whole to reproduce itself. The first way in which this capacity operates is through cell-division, mitosis: the one becomes two, the two become four, etc. -- a process operating according to a "geometric progression." Then (ignoring in this brief outline other possible reproductive processes) the sexual form of reproduction establishes itself and with it a tremendous increase in the possibility of new genetic combinations, which in turn means an ever indreasing possibility of ever more complex relationships between living organisms.

In Biblical symbolism, Yahveh Elohim, Who appears at the beginning of the second chapter of Genesis, is the Ruler of the realm of Life. The "soul" with which he animates the material structure, Adam, made according to the divine Archetype mentioned in chapter one of Genesis, is the "living soul," Nephesh Hayyak.

I cannot go here into the whole Biblical story which I have studied and interpreted, step by step, in my book FIRE OUT OF THE STONE: A Reinterpretation of the Basic Images of the Christian Tradition. All I need say is that the Bible, when properly understood, expresses in terms of a symbolical narrative the entire evolutionary development of humanity in its relationship with a divine Power guiding this development and presenting to man new, gradually more individualized possibilities of growth. The series of "Covenants" between God and man is simply a symbolical expression of the progressive development of the relationship between the archetypal potentiality, which we may call MAN, and actual types of human beings who are able to attain gradually "higher" states of consciousness.

The entire Mosaic episode and Moses' contact with a God Who declares Himself to be "I am," refer rather obviously to the appearance of a new type of human consciousness -- individualized consciousness.

At the tribal level of life man is not truly conscious and does not act, except in superficial personal instances, as an "individual." The tribe is the real unit of existence; and its power and its dictates operate at a psychic subconscious level, not too different from the level of animal instincts. At that level Life rules in a compulsive and basically unconscious manner. Life is indeed a jealous and autocratic god, who relentlessly chastizes the men and groups who disobey its directives. Tribal taboos are the human-social equivalents of animal instincts; they cannot be disobeyed. When man is able to disengage his consciousness from the autocratic power of the tribal organism, disobedience to the taboos means at first almost certain death, or exile (which at the psychological level means very much the same thing for tribal man, for exile cuts him off from the land, the culture and the rituals which were the sources of his strength).

A time comes however when man is able to free himself from the tribal matrix. He emerges as an individual. Potentiality henceforth operates within him as the Individual Soul. This step represents the great turning point in evolution; and in order to thoroughly understand its implications, we have to discuss more fully the concept of "Soul" as I use this so confusing, yet apparently indispensable term.

TWO COSMIC MOVEMENTS

We have already seen that the Creative Word released at the alpha state of the cycle is an immensely complex formula which constitutes, metaphysically speaking, the potential solution of the cosmic problem of existence in the new universe -- a problem inherited from the old universe. The Seed-Pleroma of the old universe visualized and emanated the basic principle of this "solution" into the Matrix of the Eternal Virgin -- the Infinite Potential. The result, as the new universe begins, is a tremendous release of at first undifferentiated energy which whirls through the "newly opened" space-field; but this cosmic quantum of energy is released through a kind of "film" -- the Creative Word -- which stamps upon this energy the pattern, blueprint or archetype of what is to be essentially the end-result of the whole cosmic process of existence.

This cosmic Archetype represents only a potentiality of development. We may speak of it as a factor in a divine World of Formation; but it is not an existential fact. It is not "real" (a word which comes from the Latin root, res, a "thing!"). To conceive this pattern differently is to confuse potentiality and actuality, a confusion so much in evidence in occult or religious doctrines. The architect's blueprints may be "real" in one sense of course; but they are not the concrete thing, the house. The house alone should be called "real" if we want to avoid semantic misunderstandings.

The cosmic Archetype constitutes a "structural" potentiality of developments in the existential world in which the power released "in the beginning" acts upon the chaotic remains of the past universe. Potentiality is not consciousness. The blueprints are not conscious; but the architect who made them is conscious. This Great Architect of the Universe (as Free Masonry speaks of Him) is the Biblical ELOHIM: and He is also, I repeat, the seed-Pleroma of the past universe.

He is the "hidden" Father, because once the new world-process begins, the responsibility for the "management" of the process rests upon various cosmic Agencies.

At the level of Materiality, the Gnostics spoke of a Demiurge and of Cosmocratores, Builders of the material foundations of the cosmos. These Builders represent the first stage in the relationship between the structural potentiality of the cosmos, the logos-pattern, and the primary actual facts of existence. Pattern-plus-energy operate upon inert substance and the results are proto-atoms and atoms of various types.

However, we have to consider the manner in which these atoms are produced. They are produced it would seem by fantastically powerful and speedy whirling motions. These whorls of cosmic energy define the character of the space-fields within which galaxies and probably solar systems will progressively take form. We must assume that there were at the origin of the universe -- and in a relative sense of any kind of cyclocosm -- whirling motions of various types. These basic types of motion are the primary differentiation of the Power released in the original creative surge in which the universe began at the level of existence. But what is implied in such a differentiation is not only a differentiation of the character of the performing energy, but of the "form" through which the energy operates (per-forms).

When an old-time painter started drawing a human face, he would first draw, in broad strokes, the general outline of the face. In some cases (if he followed the rules of "dynamic symmetry" on which ancient Greek art was based) he would divide the space of the sheet of paper or canvas into geometrical patterns which would constitute the "hidden" structural foundation for the drawing.

This can be taken as a relatively valid illustration of the cosmic process according to both ancient esoteric traditions and to logical (or cosmo-logical!) types of thought. In other words the cosmic process includes three basic factors: basic structural patterns which become pro-

gressively more complex and differentiated -- definite r h y-
t h m s   o f   e n e r g y   a t   w o r k   which also become more
differentiated as they per-form through these differentiating
structural patterns -- and the at first inert and undifferentiated u n i v e r s a l "d u s t , " remains of the universe-that-
was, gradually becoming integrated into atoms of different
types by the whorls of cosmic energy acting upon this primordial stuff of existence.

If this is understood then it should be clear that the cosmic process of existence operates in two opposite and symmetrical ways, even though both refer to one process of gradual complexification and differentiation. As we consider the
earliest structural patterns we find them to be very broad
spatial outlines defining only primary forms, like the spiral
form of the galaxies and other types of stellar organizations;
and the cosmic energy performing through or according to
them is also broadly differentiated into a few basic types.
These cosmic forms become ever more restricted as the
process of differentiation and complexification goes on; and
the cosmic energies as a result become more specialized.
Both, as they progress, occupy l e s s   s p a c e .

On the other hand if we are looking at the world-process
from the point of view of the proto-atom and the atom, we
see at work a process of agglomeration and integration of
simple units into more complex existential wholes which encompass m o r e   s p a c e . It is to this process that Ian Smuts
gave the name of "Holism" in his book HOLISM AND EVOL-
UTION (Viking Press, New York, N. Y.) We may speak of it
as a process of integration of smaller into larger wholes.

To distinguish clearly between these two movements,
which nevertheless constitute only o n e process of existence, I speak of the i n v o l u t i o n   o f   f o r m   a n d   e n-
e r g y and the e v o l u t i o n   o f   m a t e r i a l   w h o l e s . These
are symmetrical and interdependent movements; but the
former is the positive a g e n t , the second refers to what is
a c t e d   u p o n .*

These two movements should not be thought of as separate or as constituting two realms of existence. There is actually only one realm of existence; but within it the two basic movements should be distinguished. One might speak symbolically of a "descending" and an "ascending" progression. The forms come down into matter; the existential wholes ascend or evolve through progressive stages of refinement and of ever more subtle integration. The "forms" define the fields within which the atoms, the molecules, the cells, then living organisms, etc. are integrated by increasingly differentiated energies; and over this integration ONE, as it were, presides. These forms however are not the outcome of chance contacts between atoms; and this is where our philosophy of operative wholeness is in basic contrast to the attitude still generally taken by modern scientists, exceptions notwithstanding -- exceptions which seemingly are becoming ever more numerous and articulate.

Also to say that these forms are pre-existent is only partially true; for both these forms and the chaotic materials which are becoming integrated within them can be said to have been "before" the present cycle of existence begins. They were enfolded within the infinite Ocean of potentiality -- the forms, as potentialities within the Pleroma-Mind that visualized them in their fundamental character (but not in their existential details); and the remains of the failures of the past, as "chaos" (chaos being also potentiality in a negative or passive mode).

---

*Medieval Alchemists spoke of natura naturans (active Nature) and natura naturata (the natural materials being acted upon), but in a more restricted sense. The Hindu philosophers spoke of the Causal level (karana sharira) and the Existential level, the level of material realities upon which "astral" energies play.

In other words, the cosmic structural forms and the material elements which give concrete substantiality to these forms constitute two polar aspects of the one all-encompassing process of existence. I believe that one could establish definite correspondences between the galactic form and whatever primary type of material stuff was drawn into this immense galactic whirlpool billions of years ago; correspondences also between star-fields and atoms, between planetary fields and molecules and single cells. We would then realize that there is a "Life-field" which is the structural reality of the biosphere not only of our planet, Earth, but of any life-bearing planet.

Within this Life-field all living organisms operate obeying some over-all, general directives which refer to the types of integration which we define as Life. Then the planetary Life-field differentiates into biological species and genera, each of which represents a generically operative type of structure according to which energies of Life act and interact within a multitude of organisms. At this stage of the process mankind (the human species -- homo sapiens now) is also to be considered as a structural form with which are associated certain types of differentiated energies; and because of this the "unity of mankind" is a planetary fact which defines a special potentiality of planetary consciousness.

This one basic structure, mankind, differentiates into several races each of which is probably definitely related, at least in its condition of origin, to a particular continent. As a result of this relation to the geological and climatic conditions of a continent or of some local section of it, each develops a certain type of characteristic response to life and eventually a specific culture and collective institution.

Up to this last stage a particular form was seen to define and structure a field of existence within which a vast number of material entities operated in a more or less identical manner, regardless of superficial existential differences.

All the trees or the tigers belonging to the same species have fundamentally similar characteristics and features. The species is the unit-form of existence -- and also of consciousness: one basic form for many particular organisms. And to a lesser extent, as we have seen, the men of an archaic tribe are also to be considered not as true "individuals" but as particular "specimens" of a common racial-cultural type. This is so until the process of individualization begins to operate at the very core of the human being. Then something momentuous occurs; a one-to-one relationship is established between a structural form and a human organism.

SOUL-FIELDS AND INDIVIDUAL PERSONS

Now we should realize that what has been called "structural forms" could as well and should indeed be called Souls. When I spoke of "fields" structured by these forms I meant Soul-fields. The creative Word which is the fundamental pattern or blueprint for the cosmic process of unfoldment of potentiality into actuality is indeed the "Universal Soul," Anima mundi. It is, in association with the original release of cosmic Power (an essential point never to be forgotten), God, the Logos, This is the "new God" -- the Son -- heir to the Karma of "unfinished business" left by the universe-that-was. He is the One, the unity aspect of the entire universal cycle -- its Alpha condition. Within Him the presence of ONE operates. He is a Whole; but divine as this Whole is, it is not the Principle of Wholeness, ONE.

The Universal Soul differentiates into cosmic "Soul-fields" -- galactic, solar, planetary. Within the planetary Soul-field every life-species has its own Soul-field. Every tribe also has its more limited Soul-field; and projecting upon this Soul-field the deep sense of wholeness and life-integration felt by the entire community, the tribesman worships this projection as the tribal God and, in a partly divine, partly human sense, as the Great Ancestor. A time comes when man-the-individual is able to emerge out of the tribal womb. Then what was in him until then only a potentiality of "individual Soul" becomes an actuality -- misty and remote though it must remain for a more or less long period of time.

When I spoke of man's "living Soul," as mentioned in Genesis II, I meant a Soul still subservient to the dictates of Life and of Yahveh, God of the Life-sphere. In this living Soul the potentiality of "individualization" already exists -- symbolically because, Biblically speaking, Yahveh is one of the Elohim. This potentiality begins to stir within man when the Serpent, symbol of time and of potential eonic fulfillment, appears as number 3 to the Adam-Eve duality. But the Two are afraid and tragedy ensues. When the Sons of God, Ben Elohim, "marry the daughters of men" (cf. Genesis VI:2) the potentiality of the process of individualization takes another step, a more definite one; yet this event opens only a condition of potential individualization for mankind.

These Sons of God constitute what is symbolized in Greek mythology by Prometheus who gives the fire of self-consciousness to man. In India's esotericism this evolutionary event is pictured as the coming to Earth of the Kumaras, who are said symbolically or literally to come from Venus. The result of this coming is also a tragedy. It causes, according to the old traditions, the differentiation between black and white magic which eventually brings the Deluge. This may refer also to a geological event, the division of one vast continent, including most, though probably not all, of the land-masses, into two -- the separation being the curved mountainous under-sea ridge running north-south in the midst of the Atlantic Ocean.

The Mosaic episode, I repeat, symbolizes the definite formation of the "individual Soul." A one-to-one relationship is established between a Soul-field so structurally differentiated that it may, in principle at least, become closely associated with one particular human person. But here again,

while this potentiality is now definitely a c t u a l i z a b l e, it
is still extremely difficult to bring this about; and again the
initial result of that event is to a very great extent negative.
The result is egocentricity. It is a period of conflicts between "proud and stiff-necked" egos. Greed, which until the
event of individualization was expressed in terms of tribal
and bio-psychic acquisitiveness and possessiveness, now becomes exacerbated and intellectualized by the personal ambitions of virulent egos. Lust, too, and anger become increasingly mentalized and individualized. Competitiveness
replaces cooperation and tribal sharing. And eventually we
have the rise of technology at the service of greed -- and the
tragic state of mankind today.

When I speak of the "event" of individualization I have no
especially definite existential happening in mind. But one
may accept the date of the beginning of the Hindu K a l i Y u-
g a, i.e. 3102 B.C., as marking the start of the process of
individualization at the planetary level; and let us not forget
that K a l i is also the divine Mother and that while Kali Yuga is the "Iron Age" or Age of Darkness, it is also the long
period during which a new humanity is in the state of gestation. This is the date of the close of the more or less mythical Great War which supposedly marked the total destruction of the Warrior Caste, engineered by the divine Manifestation, Krishna, whose teachings are recorded in the
BHAGAVAD GITA. As a result of the famous battle of Kur-
ukshetra, the Age of Philosophy began in India under the
domination of the Brahmin caste.

The BHAGAVAD GITA is probably the source or first
manifestation of what is now called "theism"; and on the basis of its teachings the Bhakti movement later developed, paralleled in the West by the intense Christian devotionalism of
the post-Greco-Latin period. In the life of Christ we see
symbolically expressed -- which does n o t mean that Jesus
was not an actual and "Christed" personage -- the final stage
in the process of integration of Soul and human organism.

The one-to-one relationship between the Soul-field and the human body-mind which at first, and still in an immense majority of individual instances, was distant, imprecise and u n f o c u s e d, became in the person of Jesus totally focused and effectual. Whereas in most human beings today one can only say that the Soul "overshadows" the personality -- which means that integration is still only a potentiality -- in Jesus, Soul (the divine Nature) and body-mind (the human nature) came to be completely interpenetrating and united. The result of such a "divine Marriage," that is of the total and perfect actualization of potentiality, is the formation of the "divine Soul" and of its Pleroma-type of consciousness.

I have stated in my book FIRE OUT OF THE STONE that this divine Marriage occurred at the Transfiguration of Jesus in the presence of his three closest disciples, Peter, John and James; and this event as narrated in the Gospels is filled with revealing symbolism (cf. chapter 9: "Christ-love: The Covenant with Individuals.") I have also spoken of the whole life of Jesus as embodying and/or being "mythified" into the "Christ-event." Jesus, like Krishna in India, is to be considered an Avatar; but one should understand well what this term means. It refers essentially to the process by means of which one of the immensely many aspects of the original divine Word in the beginning of the cycle, at least of the planetary cycle of the Earth, is precipitated into the biosphere--and later on, the "noosphere"(through a definite creative act which begins a new phase of the evolutionary cycle).

A "great Avatar" refers to the beginning of a phase of the cycle of evolution of the whole planet and of humanity. (In Hindu mythology, the first Avatars were shown with animal forms, then as half-human, half-animal entities, finally as a human, Rama, and a divine human being, Krishna; revealing thus the evolution from the biosphere to the noosphere.) But one can also speak of "lesser Avatars" referring to smaller cycles -- cycles referring to the evolution of particular races. And once a complete one-to-one relationship is definitely established between a Soul-field and an individual person, this person becomes the avatar of the Soul that is the very source of his self. Such an individual "avatarship" is fulfilled in the divine Marriage.

Jesus was an Avatar, we may well assume, not only at the level of the union of his own Soul and personality, but even more at the level of the evolution of humanity-as-a-whole. He was thus a "planetary Avatar" -- and so was Krishna, and perhaps in a slightly different sense Gautama the Buddha. The present-day Baha'is believe that Baha'u'llah, the great Persian prophet who openly declared his mission and status in 1863 in Baghdad, was a great planetary Avatar who by his presence and actions opened up a new phase of mankind's evolution -- and there are historical facts which at least tend to validate this claim.

What complicates all such matters is that there are cycles within cycles, and several levels at which one can say that a great cycle begins. When a new Archetype becomes actualized, that is to say when a new and more integral relationship is established between potentiality and actuality through the focusing of the universal power of integration, ONE, at a new level, the actualization does not occur all at once. It would not be logical if it did because the new creative action encounters ever greater resistance as it penetrates "deeper" into the materials of the past, i.e. as new "Karmic deposits" of a more primary character have to be neutralized and transmuted.

Thus I speak of an "Avataric cycle" rather than of one single Avatar-event. This has been explained in my recent book BIRTH PATTERNS FOR A NEW HUMANITY in which I speak of the eighteenth, nineteenth, twentieth and twenty-first centuries as constituting such an "Avataric cycle" which marks the transition between two Ages. Likewise what I have called "the Christ-event" should probably not be considered only in terms of the life of Jesus, for it includes a preliminary phase and perhaps a subsequent one.

Indeed one could even take a broader approach and say that the entire period from the time of the Buddha (more specifically about 600 B. C.) to the birth of Islam (the Hegira in 622 A. D.) constitutes a period of transition in the evolution of mankind. What we are facing now is I believe an attempt to implement and concretize in and through new interpersonal and social-political patterns of human relationship what was projected as an ideal Image (i. e. as merely a potentiality) during the twelve centuries from about 600 B. C. to 600 A.D. According to this view the new departure marked by the serial appearances of the Buddha, the Christ and Mohammed -- the latter, only the herald of a great Revelation, not unlikely represented by Baha'u'llah-- constituted a multilevel all-human mutation which at first produced largely negative results so far as mankind-as-a-whole was concerned. This paralleled -- we hope in a less drastic manner -- what happened in the descending evolutionary arc of the planetary cycle when "the sons of God" (Ben Elohim) came ("descended") to marry the "daughters of men" long, long ago.

Every new evolutionary departure manifests during the first period of the cycle it opens as:

(1) a few "mutants" in whom the newly emanated Archetype is successfully incarnated;

(2) a few human beings who react in a focused negative manner to the new creative release of potentiality and become definite expressions of "evil." This must be so for, as already stated, any release of potentiality implies the inevitability of a bi-polar response along the two opposing lines of acceptance and rejection, thus of what I have called "success" and "failure" in the most essential cosmic-spiritual sense of the terms;

(3) the more or less uncertain, unclearly focused and essentially mixed reactions of the mass of mankind, but with the negative response at first as a more or less dominant feature. This means in concrete social, religious and cultural terms that false starts are usually made; good

intentions and fine ideals are rapidly perverted or deviated by the pressures of unavoidable circumstances -- the Karma of the past -- and by a state of mental and emotional confusion produced by fear of letting go of familiar, even though perhaps painful, trends and allegiances -- a fear bolstered by the influence of "evil" forces acting at the level of psychic energy.

During times of collective crises the opposition between the various types of response to the new potentialities becomes acute, and much is said concerning the struggle between "forces of Light" and "forces of Darkness." At the end of every cycle the division between the symbolical realm of the immortal "seed" and that of disintegrating "leaves" (disintegrating after perhaps a glowing golden episode) becomes definite and irrevocable. The religious mind speaks here of the separation of "the sheep from the goats." It should be clear that such processes of division refer to the collectivity of men. Two statistical groups are observable. Yet each individual person should be considered free to choose. But this refers to the problem of the nature of "free will" which I shall discuss more specifically in subsequent chapters.

As already stated, according to the Hindu tradition humanity-as-a-whole is now living in the Kali Yuga. However the four great Ages (Yugas) refer to planetary evolution, not to the evolution of any particular race, whose subcycle may operate in a direction opposite to that of the planetary Age. And as Kali is also the symbol of the Mother, Kali Yuga actually represents the process of gestation of a new humanity within Mother-Earth -- an Earth which may be deeply disturbed by its pregnancy!

The process of individualization which presumably began at the time of the beginning of Kali Yuga is only a phase of human evolution. At first this phase brought the negative results of egocentricity. The ego, still bound to the compulsive drives of the biosphere ("eat or be eaten") represents in its negative aspect the shadow of the true self, the self which is an expression of the Power-aspect of the Soul-field, as we shall see presently in greater detail. However, the ego can also be the positive reflection of the self; it should eventually become the consecrated servant of the Soul.

This is the process of transmutation which goes on during the Kali Yuga. The successful individual person leaves the body of the Earth-Mother, the biosphere, and "enters" the embryonic form of the humanity-yet-to-be growing within the noosphere. As this takes place the individual Soul becomes the divine Soul. Each heartbeat of the Mother-Earth, symbolically speaking, witnesses an individual Soul reaching the condition of divine Soul on the Mount of its Transfiguration. This human person is being, in the real sense of the term, "initiated"; he enters upon the Path, and eventually joins the divine Company of perfected Beings which constitute the Soul-field of the Earth, the Pleroma-in-the-making.

Humanity-as-a-whole is thus gradually transformed; and not only humanity but the entire planet. But this does not occur in a straight line of progress, as the nineteenth century fondly and naively believed. Evolution moves in a spiral through the interplay of opposite polarities. Every light brings a shadow. He who seeks the light must accept a confrontation with his own shadow; and this is more than most people today can stand. A whole race and a whole civilization can also project a collective shadow. Indeed the scientific mind also has its shadow; and it could bring mankind to disaster--a violent condition of catharsis which either would cure its present state of generalized schizophrenia, or make a total crisis of rebirth from a relatively small group of "seed men" necessary.

In due time however the Omega state of the cycle of Man and the Earth will come. It may not be the kind of fiery conflagration which Teilhard de Chardin seems to have envisioned. It is more likely to resemble the Image of the "Gnostic" individual and the Gnostic Society which Sri Aurobindo evoked in the last chapters of his great book THE LIFE DIVINE, written long before Teilhard's works. Such a consummation will no doubt occur on an Earth no longer "physical" in the sense in which we understand this word today. As H.P.Blavatsky stated in THE SECRET DOCTRINE nearly a hundred years ago, humanity will then be "a humanity of Christs and Buddhas." What the Theosophist calls the White Lodge will have become humanity-as-a-whole on a transsubstantiated Earth. The Seed Pleroma will be ready to enter the infinite Ocean of potentiality.

It may all end in a cosmic Nova, in an immense burst of Light -- who knows? But there will also be the waste-products, the remains of all the failures, the disintegrating shells of evil which will also reach the state of pure potentiality, but in a passive and negative condition. Eventually a new cycle will begin again once the sublime Compassion of the Pleroma-Host merges in a fecundative union with the "Eternal Virgin" -- once this Pleroma-consciousness stirs "Her" infinite Potency into a new release of Power through the Ideal Form which this consciousness envisioned.

VII. SOUL-FIELD, MIND AND REINCARNATION

In outlining the most essential factors in the world-process it was necessary to omit many things so as not to make the picture too complex. The difficulty in such an attempt is that the definition of every term depends to a large extent on the meaning given to other related words. Any world-picture of existence is like a vast polyphony of concepts, each melodic line acquiring its real meaning only in the ever-changing, dynamic relationship of all other lines. It is also like a tapestry revealing abstract forms and a vibrant interplay of colors which change to a large extent according to the angle of vision of the onlooker and the quality of the light which illumines the tapestry. As we shall see in another chapter, what is to be sought is not a kind of analytical and fully objective "Truth" but the development of a capacity to "see" reality in its multifarious and interdependent aspects; to be a conscious witness to the immense, rhythmic process of unfoldment of potentiality into actuality, which is what we experience as "Existence."

Such a capacity for "vision" is a matter of no small importance. It is at the very root of our everyday approach to interpersonal relationships and to life in general. This approach depends not only on the quality of our consciousness and the power of assimilation and organization of our mind, but also, and indeed primarily, upon the data and the ideas made available to our image-making and intuitive faculties. The average person in any culture and under the influence of any particular religious organization is introduced through his education to but a relatively narrow range of concepts. These are conditioned by definite socio-psychological pressures and based on rigid methods of thinking, feeling, and observing through the senses. Even modern science, at least in its most academic and popularized aspects, operates under some very definite presuppositions and postulates. Perhaps the most basic of these undemonstrable hypotheses is that the "laws" and the "universal constants" it has discovered and successfully applied within a l i m i t e d space-time environment, are always and everywhere true and unchanging. Another limiting attitude is science's exclusive dependence upon empirical procedures which are not considered conclusive or even acceptable unless every trained researcher can repeat them and obtain the same results at any time.

In contrast to such an attitude I have stressed the concepts of an infinity of potentialities and of an ever-changing process of cyclic transformation which, during its many phases, reacts to always new needs by important changes of rhythm. The attitude taken is therefore basically o p e n to change. There is, it is true, in the world-picture I present, a basic factor which remains permanent throughout a p a r t i c u l a r cyclocosm of existence; this factor is the creative Word, which impresses itself upon the original release of potentiality at the beginning of the cycle and which controls the process of actualization of this set of potentialities from the a l p h a to the o m e g a states of the cyclic process. However this creative Word is a "constant" in a sense which differs from the one given to the constants of modern physics. It is a constant in terms of g o a l rather than in terms of m e t h o d -- a very important distinction.

What the Pleroma-Mind of the old universe had "envisioned" and impressed upon the Eternal Virgin (the Infinite Potential) w i l l be actualized at the o m e g a state of the new universe; but (1) the scope of this actualization is, I believe, not determined; that is, the group of Perfected Beings who constitute this omega-actualization may be relatively small or large depending on the success of the entire cyclo-cosmic scheme, and (2) the methods used during the cyclic process can change considerably at any time. In other words even if the basic character of the end-results is predeter-mined when the process begins at the level of actual, concrete existence, the conditions of the actualization are not neces-sarily determined.

This must be so if our idea that potentiality and actuality are two polar principles which, like the Yin and Yang of Chinese philosophy, are present in ever-varying proportions in any state either of existence or of what we call non-exist-ence. In a sense we could say that this is the basic meta-physical "Fact." These two polarities, potentiality and actu-ality, are "contained" (a very awkward term) within what I mean by ONE, the Principle of Wholeness; and this "con-tainment" is symbolized in the Chinese Tai-Chi figure by the circle within which the two forms, Yang and Yin, white and black, interact, waxing and waning in relation to each other.

Practically speaking this means that the potentiality of change is never absent at any time. We do not live in a uni-verse of only "law and order"; it is also a universe in which the dominant fact of the capacity of a divinely created Image-logos to reach perfect actualization at the end of the uni-versal cycle does NOT preclude the possibility of important variations in the methods used at any time to produce this result. These variations may be required because ex-istence is relatedness, and the possibilities of in-terrelationship between the multitude of existents is so vast, though not exactly "infinite," that the results are never "fat-ed." They are indeed at least partially unpredictable except for the fact that at the end of the cycle, the omega state, what was potentiality in the beginning will be actualized in a group of "successful" Beings. What is at stake here is a qualitative result -- i.e. there will be a Pleroma of perfect Beings in the omega state -- but not a quantita-

tive fact -- i.e. the exact number of Beings having reached
"perfection" or full actualization of the logos-potentiality.

What this implies should be clearly stated: If we consider the two factors in existence spoken of in Part One of this
book, "selfhood" and "relatedness," the fact of selfhood constitutes the permanent changeless polarity in a cyclic development, while that of relatedness refers to the nearly infinite possibilities of change. Relatedness therefore introduces
the factor of unpredictability into what, according to the
principle of selfhood, would be a totally expectable end-result. In selfhood there is "determinism"; in relatedness,
that "indeterminacy" which leads to what we usually call freedom. I am what I am as a self; the fundamental Tone of my
field-of-existence remains identical from birth to death --
and, in a sense at least, beyond the death of the physical
body. It is the unity aspect of my existence. But the
consciousness of the whole organism of personality which operates on the basis of this individual selfhood is at all times
affected by the multiplicity of relationships to which I
am at first subjected, and into which I later enter more or
less "freely."

Thus unpredictability and predictability are co-existing
facts during the whole cyclic process of existence. They can
be abstracted into the concept of the polarized co-existence
of "order" and "randomness." No process of existence is
ever totally and rigidly ordered and pre-determined; chance
is an ever-present reality. Yet chance is not the basic
fact of existence as modern scientists seem to believe.
Chance is only the result of the nearly infinite complexity of
interactions between existents. Because of this complexity
many, if not most, existential situations cannot be plotted
down exactly and quantitatively expressed. Some people
might say that the human mind cannot do it, but that God's
Mind, being omnipotent and omnipresent, can know precisely
and at any time, past, present and future, the total situation
of every atom in the universe. This, however, does not fit

into the world-picture which I am presenting, because it creates an idea of God which seems unnecessary, unwarranted
and actually unacceptable at the present stage of the evolution
of human consciousness -- unless it be today the consciousness of human beings at its least developed level. Because
such a level represents a condition of almost complete mental
passivity and of feeling-subservience to the overwhelming power of "Life," the consciousness operating in such conditions
has to deify and personalize this Life-power.

MIND AND ITS MULTI-LEVEL OPERATION

In the ever-changing polar relationship between polarity and
actuality "mind" occupies a most important role which, so
far, I have not sufficiently discussed. I have spoken of mind
as "formed consciousness," but this was only a temporary
statement which lacked precision. Let me now try to define
the different aspects of mind, and to state how mind operates
at the various levels of the process of actualization of potentialities of existence. Mind is indeed a crucial factor in this
process of actualization.

Mind is the capacity to hold images of
existence in a coherently interrelated, consistent and formal state of consciousness.
The character of a mind depends therefore on the nature of
the images which it is its function to interrelate and more or
less formally to integrate into a system. It is at some level
of existence a system of concepts; but we should be able to
think of a mind which operates at a level at which we can no
longer speak precisely of concepts, but rather of "Images."

In terms of existential facts, the word, mind, refers normally to a more or less well organized field of activities which transcends the sense-perceived activities of
what we call the human "body." The activities referred to
the field of "mind" include all types of thinking processes:
memory and anticipation, generalization and abstraction of

data of perception, the formation of concepts or mental images and the formulation of goals through the use of words or other kinds of symbols.

Also mind is able to move back and forth as it were in time-sequence; it remembers, and it projects what it knows into the future. Indeed mind and time are closely interrelated. A mind is a whole of consciousness; it is the structured field of consciousness of any existential whole--and not only of a human being. Wherever there is consciousness there is, structuring it, some kind of mind, and it is very unfortunate that most people and even many eminent philosophers speak of a type of consciousness transcending mind. The intellectual, conceptual mind is only one kind of mind. Sri Aurobindo's "supermind" is still mind though it transcends what we ordinarily call mind; it is a mind that "sees" rather than a mind that cogitates and argues pro and con in dualistic terms. But it is mind in that it integrates images of reality, even though it be a supersensorial and superconceptual reality, the experience of which can hardly be formulated in words. It is the Pleroma-mind.

Many modern psychologists of the academic type are bent upon proving that mind can be entirely reduced to the activities of the nerves and particularly of the brain of the physical body. That such activities, explainable in electrical and chemical terms, exist is evident. The question is whether they may not be the end-results of the operation of a formative principle inhering in the t o t a l field-of-existence which constitutes a human person.

Mind also operates in a whole species which manifests through a myriad of organisms of the same type, and not merely through the nervous systems of these organisms. If it could be demonstrated that a conscious individual person is still able to think and perform certain kinds of mental operations a f t e r the disintegration of his physical body, the position taken by materialistically inclined scientists would become untenable. For some individuals today it is already untenable for this very reason.

There are on the other hand philosophers and even eminent scientists who are "reductionists" in the opposite sense. For them a body is but a projection, concretization, or sensorial interpretation of a mind. All is mind, some say; God, too, is Mind -- divine or cosmic Mind.

The position I am taking resolves this dualism of mind and body by stating that the Principle of Wholeness, ONE, operates at three basic levels of existence, that is, at the levels of Materiality, of Life and of "Ideity." We saw that "consciousness" is inseparable from "wholeness," therefore consciousness must also operate at these three levels. "Mind" can likewise exist at these levels, but with a fundamentally different character at each level. And I repeat that by mind I mean the capacity inherent in any existential whole to hold images of existence in a coherent, interrelated and structured field of consciousness.

We can only speculate on what form consciousness and mind take at the level of Materiality. Yet in view of recent developments in atomic physics -- and of what scientists like the French professor at the Paris University, Robert Tournaire, and the Director of the Superior Institute of Sciences and Philosophies in Brussels, Robert Linssen, have written (cf. Linssen's book LA SPIRITUALITE DE LA MATIERE, and works by the Roumanian philosopher, Lupasco, and other European scientists) -- I do not think it at all fantastic to speak of the atom's mind. Wherever there is consciousness there is at least some rudimentary type of mind. The potentiality of mind, that is, of coherent forms of consciousness, is implied in any field-of-existence; and it is the structure of this field which determines, or at least conditions, the structural directives of the mind.

Obviously the question one should answer then is: What is it that determines the structure of fields-of-existence? The answer is: the multitudinous aspects of the creative Word, which is "imagined" by the Pleroma of the previous universe. Through this Word the release of the original creative Power pours forth, starting the World-process -- somewhat, I repeat, as the light of a motion picture projector pours through a film. This creative Word has, symbolically speaking, a multitude of "Letters." Each Letter is a "Soul Image." Because this Image is invested with power, we should rather speak of a "Soul field."

At first the Soul Image is very broad, referring to the form of vast cosmic movements, like the form of spiral nebulae; and the power integrally associated with it is only slightly differentiated, producing tremendous whorls of energy sucking in the inert dust of cosmic space barely emerging from a state of negative potentiality (i. e. of nearly total indifference to existence) and indeed resisting integration out of sheer inertia. But even then a diffuse, unitarian, cosmic kind of consciousness can be imagined, which passively reflects the most primary aspect of the consciousness of the creative Logos. This creative consciousness, in its focalized condition, can be called the "Divine Mind." It constitutes the transcendental aspect of mind -- mind "beyond" existence, yet mind as the structuring power of a new cycle of existence.

Mind always acts as a formative power; it gives form to consciousness. Any active, dynamic type of consciousness needs to be focused through a mind-structure. It is always consciousness which changes potency into power, but consciousness can only achieve this in its focused state as mind. It is mind rather than consciousness which acts. Consciousness is inherent in an existential whole just because it is whole; consciousness is wholeness reflected upon the field-of-existence. It is in this sense a feed-back process, but a process inherent in existence. What can be blocked is not consciousness itself but its operative aspect as mind. Consciousness can be unfocused; then it produces no definable mental activity. *

*Mind structures whatever is available in terms of ex-

To the question: What is it that determines the structure of a field-of-existence? we answer therefore: A mind inherent in a Soul-Image and active within the Soul-field. Here of course we should not confuse Soul-field with field-of-existence. What I mean by field-of-existence is simply the field of electro-magnetic energies, and no doubt of other as yet unknown types of energies, which both pervade and surround a material entity and a living organism. And in the case of a living organism we can speak of the "auric field" -- even though the word, aura, has received varied and confusing interpretations when used by clairvoyants or pseudo-clairvoyants.

A Soul-field, on the other hand, is the field of energies of a spiritual type which are differentiations of the unitarian release of power originating in the Creative Act that started the cycle of existence. In a basic sense all types of energies originate in this creative release of power; but when we reach the level of Life much of this initial stream of energy has become "locked," as it were, in the atoms of the realm

---

perience and more generally in terms of the contents of consciousness. But if there is nothing or very little to structure, mind turns as it were upon itself and tries to refine its methods of operation; it acts for instance as logic and epistemology. It matters little what it operates upon provided the operation is done perfectly; and we have excellent examples of this in modern art, in academic philosophy and even in surgery -- heart-transplants and the like, which are essentially an excuse for the demonstration and improvement of surgical virtuosity, an excuse camouflaged under humanitarian motives needed to rouse the emotional thirst for existence of egos of prospective patients. The ego enjoys its intellectual virtuosity which bolsters its prestige; and in a strictly egocentric society, and a consumer society, this is the stuff of which success, fame and wealth are made.

of Materiality. We might illustrate this fact by referring to the locking in of electrical power in a car battery. The kinetic energy of the current which charges the battery becomes potential energy in the battery. In this sense every atom is a charged battery which can be used by existential wholes at the levels of Life and Ideity.

Such a process of transformation of kinetic into potential energy operates in a human body in terms of the type of energy specific to the realm of Life, as we shall presently see. It operates also when the process of individualization of a human being reaches a more concrete phase; that is when a one-to-one relationship is established, even if only tentatively, between a Soul-field and the field-of-existence of a particular person.

THE SOUL-FIELD AND THE SELF

I may not have made sufficiently clear the relationship between the Soul-field and the self of a human individual, for at first I could only hint at the existence of three levels of operation of ONE, the very principle of Existence. I spoke of these three levels as Materiality, Life and Ideity without elaborating upon the meaning I gave to the last term. The realm of Materiality refers basically to atoms and molecules; the realm of Life to living cells and organisms, human bodies included; and the realm of Ideity refers to the operation of individually conscious minds and to the integration of these individual minds into groups -- groups which reach an ultimate integration in the unanimistic activities of the multi-une Pleroma, spiritual Seed of a vast existential cycle.

I used the neologism, Ideity, because minds operating at this level do so in terms of "ideas" to which the human being relates himself (theoretically at least) as an individual thinker. Even the division of the word into "I" and "deity" evokes the possibility, inherent at that level of existence, of eventually reaching a "divine" state of consciousness and being.

Such a state has its root-beginning in the establishment of a
s t e a d y and increasingly pervasive and effectual one-to-
one relationship between a Soul and the living organism of a
particular man -- a relationship which normally can only become totally encompassing through a series of ever-closer
contacts between the Soul-field and a succession of human
persons. This is of course the basis of the concept of "reincarnation." The term, reincarnation, is however a vague
term to which various meanings can be given; and I shall try
to elucidate what the process actually refers to and implies.

But in order to do so we must first of all get a clear picture of what I mean by "self." I have spoken of the self within a human being as a "fundamental Tone," a basic rhythm of
existence, which powers and sustains the entire field of existence of this human being. This "Tone" resounds throughout this auric field. It is the AUM-Tone of the existential
cycle. In this Tone the presence or catalytic action of ONE
is operative. It is basically unchanging throughout the existential cycle.

What complicates the human situation and the character
of the self in man is the fact that man, who f i r s t is a mere
unit in the vast entity we call mankind or h o m o s a p i e n s
which belongs to the realm of Life, can become and is des-
tined to become "individualized," and through the process of
individualization to become operative at the level of Ideity.
This means, as we have already seen, that the individual
person actually operates at two levels: the level of Life and
the level of Ideity. Moreover, the operations of Life are dependent to a large extent, but n o t e x c l u s i v e l y -- a fact
which science has still to discover -- upon the energy locked
in material atoms. Thus briefly stated a fully individualized
human person operates as matter, as life and as an individualized mind.

As a living body, man is a field-of-existence in which
inhere a "vital" type of consciousness and mind. For the
sake of clarity we should call this vital mind a proto-mind

or organic mind; and the "vital" consciousness it structures is to modern man sub-consciousness, or instinctual consciousness. Through this human field-of-existence a self vibrates. This self is the fundamental Tone of the human organism as a whole; and this organism-as-a-whole includes many overtones constituted by the feelings, emotions and various psychic activities. It includes even the proto-mind which man shares with animals and even plants, according to recent experiments already mentioned.

Life is not Ideity; the two levels are distinct and become increasingly so as evolution progresses toward the Pleroma-state at which Life presumably ceases to operate, except perhaps in a transformed and reflective sense. Nevertheless Life is the "root"-foundation of the human "plant"; and it is only when the "seed" is completely mature and leaves the old slowly disintegrating plant that this root-foundation is no longer operative, its potential energy having been locked within the seed. This means that the self which is the Root-tone of the living organism of human beings only is the foundation of developments which will pertain to the process of individualization. Without deep foundations a soaring tower cannot exist. Neither can there be in man individualization and individual mental development at the level of Ideity without the steady vibration of the Root-tone in man's auric field. When this vibration ceases death immediately ensues.

However, this fundamental Tone of selfhood has overtones. The power inherent in this Tone spreads through these overtones; and the main focus of this power can be transferred to one of these overtones, particularly to the second overtone the frequency of which is, in relation to the fundamental Tone, in the proportion of 3 to 1. This refers in acoustics and music to the interval of the twelfth -- an octave plus a fifth. If the fundamental Tone has a frequency of 100 vibrations per second, the first overtone has a frequency of 200 (it is the octave above) and the second overtone a frequency of 300 (the fifth above this octave-sound).

This musical illustration is most valuable because it explains, accurately I believe, the process that takes place when a man who is truly individualized and "autonomous" sees the Root-power of his existence re-focused at the level of the "individual soul" -- which means, at least symbolically, in the region of the heart. Such a re-focusing does NOT mean that the fundamental Tone, the self, no longer operates. What it means is that the power of self is now focused at the level of the second overtone, the heart center to which we already referred (page 102, chapter IV).

The self was originally focused in what the Hindu yogi calls the Muladhara chakra at the base of the spine, that is, in the pelvic region. There too (more forward in the body and a little below the navel) is what is known in Japan as the Hara region. "Mula" means root. In that pelvic region the Root-power of Life is focused; within it the seed of man develops. The vital-physical seed moves downward through the sexual organs; on the other hand the full process of individualization in its more occult sense represents a moving upward of the seed-power toward the heart, then toward the cranial region in which, according to Hindu yoga, the descending light of the divine consciousness, Shiva, becomes united with the ascending energy of the vital organism totally concentrating in the Ajna center -- the center between and back of the two eyebrows.

In the Hindu Kundalini Yoga, Kundalini which is to be raised from the pelvic root-level to that of the frontal region (Ajna chakra) is the fundamental power of Life. The Hatha Yogi deals with Life-energies. He gathers into a thin stream of light the energies of all the cells of the body and focuses them in Ajna. This utter integration of Life-energies normally dispersed through the physical organism calls for a response from the Soul; but this is Soul at the level of Life, non-individualized Soul. What occurs is not super-individual, but "pre-individual." The type of consciousness and power which is released is consciousness and power at the level of Life --Life being experienced then in a cosmic sense. The Tantrik officiants who perform the sexual rites experience the sexual power, basic in the realm of Life, also in a cosmic sense. We may call these experiences "spiritual" for they deal with "pure" potentiality and immediacy of response to ONE, the Principle of Wholeness; but they are not spiritual at the level of Ideity. At that level the experience of pure potentiality and unity is only reached in the Pleroma, that is in the unanimous consecration of perfected Beings to ONE, a consecration which manifests actively as pure Compassion. *

As the Root-Tone of the human organism, the self contains only the potentiality of full, conscious individualization; it is an expression of Life. A man is at first only a "human" being, a member of the human species -- a species which fulfills only one particular function in the planetary organism of the Earth. And when I speak thus of the Earth I am not thinking only of a mass of matter but of a field of activities extending far beyond the physical level. It extends beyond the physical because Man, and undoubtedly Beings above the level of present-day mankind, are active

---

*Actually the pelvic region should be symbolized by the interval of octave separating or, one could also say, linking the fundamental tone and the first overtone -- thus the relation 1 to 2. The region between the solar plexus and the heart center is symbolized by the interval of fifth (the relation 2 to 3); that between the heart region and the throat center, the "creative" center from which words are uttered, by the fourth above (relation 3 to 4). Above the throat center we find the Ajna center which represents No. 5, producing the musical interval of the natural third; and above Ajna the Sahasrara center, the multi-petalled Lotus which corresponds to No. 6, an octave above the No. 3 of the heart center.

within this Earth-field -- and are indeed integral parts of it.

The development of a fully conscious and autonomous individual is potential in the self; it becomes actualized only when a one-to-one relationship between a human organism and a particular, differentiated Soul-Image is established. As this occurs ONE operates in a new way, bringing together Soul and human organism. It operates at the level of Ideity -- at the level of what in India is called karana sharira, usually translated as "Causal Body," though the term, body, is quite confusing. It should more correctly be called the "Causal Field."

It is this operation of ONE at a new level which sooner or later causes the re-focusing of the power of self from the pelvic to the Heart region. As this refocusing process (or "modulation" musically speaking) occurs the energy of the differentiated Soul-field can also flow into the field of existence of the individualized human being, and this can produce almost "miraculous" effects. Unfortunately, however, and as we have seen in previous chapters, the individualization process in most cases at first passes through a negative phase. The individualization of consciousness has to move through the phase of ego-formation, and the ego gets hold of the new power which it at first uses to its own purposes. This ego-centric and ego-glorification phase cuts off the human organism from the power of the Soul-field. The Soul can only "watch and wait" until through crises and catharsis the ego collapses and finally realizes that its only function was to provide some sort of "scaffolding" for the development of a truly autonomous consciousness, structured by a mind that is widely "open" to the possibility of unceasing renewal and thus able to respond to the vibrations of the Soul-field.

The consciousness of a human being cannot at first respond effectively to such Soul-vibrations, or at least it cannot reach a state in which focused activity is possible unless a "mind" is developed to allow such a focused activity. The building of the mind necessitates at first subservience to the collective patterns of a particular family, culture, and society. As we have previously seen these constitute "matrices" for the development of a conscious mind. As long as such matrices feature egocentricity as a constant fact of existence and are based on acquisitiveness, aggressiveness and competitive drives toward financial or political power, the child and adolescent can only develop minds that are also ego-controlled--or that react violently and confusedly against this ego-control and the hypocritical procedures of their society.

As long as this is the existential situation the one-to-one relationship of the Soul to the personality can only remain mostly ineffective. A "link" is formed between the Soul-field and the field-of-existence of the human being, and the Soul tries to reach, at least on critical occasions, the consciousness of the person. But as long as the ego is dominant such inner promptings -- the "voice of the conscience" and various "hunches" -- can easily be blocked or misinterpreted.

During such an egocentric phase, which covers probably many millennia of human evolution, man operates in a state of inner conflicts as well as in a society rent by the struggles between classes, groups and ambitious individuals. The inner conflicts are essentially the results of the fact that the human field of existence is oscillating between two foci of power -- the pelvic and the heart centers. The circle with one center has become an ellipse with two foci. Men speak of lower and higher selves. Yet self is always one power; what fluctuates is the place and character of the focusing of this power -- a fluctuation which reflects itself in the state of the consciousness and the concentration of the mind. *

---

*For the Christian mystics, particularly those related to the tradition of Mount Athos monasteries, the focus of the unitive life and of meditation is the Heart, or the Rose-Cross center already mentioned. The focus of selfhood is already

The "blame" for such a difficult situation in terms of the relationship between Soul and physical organism is however not to be laid upon the human individual alone. The situation, tragic as one might think it, is a seemingly inevitable result of the evolutionary process which, as we have already seen, operates in two directions. There is the involutionary movement of the Soul towards the kind of precise qualitative differentiation which will make it possible for the one-to-one relationship with a particular human organism to work out; and there is the opposite evolutionary movement within the Earth's biosphere which manifests as gradually more complex, refined and clearly conscious biological species, and eventually as ever more intelligent and sensitive human races and social groupings. Both of these movements can probably be partially frustrated for a time; and the frustrating factor is what we call "evil."

In many mythological traditions "Wars in Heaven" are spoken of. These Wars refer to a struggle between opposing factors in the realm of Soul-involution. One may well assume that an antagonism of cosmic forces can operate at the

---

established there potentially; it is the meditator's purpose to center it vividly and effectively in that region. Thus the mystic may concentrate on visualizing Christ in the Heart and repeating the great Christian mantram, the Kyrie Eleison, imprinting it as it were upon this Heart center. However there is another Christian way of the spirit: the exercise of compassion or real "charity" -- living a life which no longer concentrates on the raising of the Life-force, kundalini, but rather on raising the consciousness of other human beings. This way is the Western equivalent, at a new level, of the Indian Karma Yoga, the yoga of works accomplished for the sake of "the One" without any thought of ego-satisfying results, or even of ego-destroying results; for thinking of any result or goal, or of success or failure, would be a deterent to dedication to the One Actor, God-Ishvara.

level of the solar system and especially of the galaxy; this
simply because, as already stated, every release of potentiality can and indeed m u s t, lead to both positive and negative results. This is a fundamental principle in our cyclocosmic approach to existence. Besides, in some cosmog-
onies, as is stated in H. P. Blavatsky's SECRET DOCTRINE
with reference to various traditions, it is clearly implied
that the origin of evil on this Earth was due to the failure of
many Souls to incarnate in the primitive human forms at the
time when such a process was needed according to the pattern of development of the planetary cycle. This is no doubt
a mythical way of saying that a certain kind of inertia can
develop concerning the process of gradual differentiation of
the Soul.

What such a differentiation means is that the "Oversoul"
of the human species, which operates strictly at the level of
Life and o v e r s h a d o w s and controls the whole of mankind, may resist being differentiated into Souls able to establish a one-to-one relationship with only one human being.
There is a relationship of course between this Oversoul,
Man, and the human species -- and we might say, in Biblical
terms, between Yahveh as Ruler of the Life-forces of the
Earth's biosphere, and the collectivity of mankind. If one
thinks of this Yahveh as a "tribal god," then this god, whose
Being is actually the Soul-field of the tribe, rules over the
tribe -- if it is truly an archaic tribe -- with compulsive power. But when the process of individualization actually begins, this compulsive power is challenged by the development
of more and more differentiated and, from the Soul point of
view, individualized Soul-images and Soul-fields.

The basic "Image of Man" (which is what the concept of a
M a n u essentially means in Hindu mythology) differentiates
into a multitude of Variations on this one Theme, Man. Each
Soul is such a particular unique Variation. The basic Theme,
Man, remains; but much of its power is transferred to the
many individual Soul-Variations -- a process which parallels

that of the "modulation" of the fundamental Tone of the self in a human organism to its overtone related to the Heart center.

The Theme that was being reiterated unceasingly in every specimen of the human species can "resist" its being transformed into individual Soul-Variations. It is such a resistance which we find mythified in the story of the conflict between the god Jupiter and Prometheus. Prometheus by giving to all human beings the fire of individualized selfhood was actually differentiating the one Power of the god into a multitude of at least potential power-centers, one for every individual. The fact that it was at that remote time in history only a potential gift is shown by the tragic fate of Prometheus chained to a rock by Jupiter. Prometheus' liver moreover was devoured by a vulture; but was immediately reconstituted and re-devoured -- the liver here symbolizing man's capacity for assimilating and metabolizing as an individual the results of his relationship with other individuals.

In other words Jupiter managed to defeat the process initiated by Prometheus -- or in India by the kumara Host said to have come from "Venus" -- but not forever. Prometheus was to be delivered from his chains and his torments by a hero. This hero was the Christ. In Wagner's Tetrology it is symbolized by Siegfried who frees the Walkure condemned to lie asleep, imprisoned within a ring of fire by her divine father, Wotan, because she showed compassion for human beings; thus thwarting Wotan's "law."

As Prometheus is freed, the long frustrated process of individualization starts again on a larger scale. An increasing number of Souls achieve a more differentiated state through their successive relationships with a series of human individuals born in societies which embody in their increasingly more "open" institutions the ideal of individualism.

KARMIC PATTERNS OR MONADS

At this point it is necessary to bring into our study of the process of individualization a factor which I did not want to introduce earlier so as not to make the evolutionary picture too complicated. I hinted at it however in a previous footnote. In a sense, and in terms of the present-day mentality of human beings, it is a most important factor. Yet its existence does not actually alter anything that has been said thus far.

What this factor refers to is the apparent and logical, or perhaps I should say "cyclo-logical," problem posed by the concept that a vast cosmic cycle of existence should end in only two extreme conditions: that of total "success" -- the Seed Pleroma of Beings having actualized perfectly the potentialities released at the beginning of the cycle by the divine, creative Word -- and that of total "failure" (the disintegrating remains of all that dropped by the wayside during the evolutionary process furnishing "manure" for a new universe). It seems necessary to believe that there are also intermediate states of actualization of potentiality between these two extremes of success and failure.

This does not alter the idea that all releases of cosmic potentiality imply the inevitability of a negative as well as a positive outcome, and that therefore a cosmic cycle of existence ends in a dualistic success-failure situation. What it refers to is the realization that, when a one-to-one relationship between a Soul and a living human organism has been reached in the process of evolution, something has happened which must have special consequences. The action or presence of ONE at the very core of that relationship constitutes a new type of integration. A field of relationship is established which encompasses and gradually integrates the Soulfield and the field-of-existence of the human being becoming linked with the individualizing Soul. This field of relationship is presumably what some Hindu philosophical systems spoke of as Hiranyagarbha, and which has been referred to in Western occultism as "the Auric Egg." It could be called the "Ideity field" because it represents the manifestation of ONE at a new level, the level of what I have called Ideity.

In a merely living organism, a plant or an animal, ONE is also present but in a lesser form of integration and at a less explicit stage of the universal Principle of individual existence. Life is compulsive and ruthless in its operation for it must deal with multitudes of specimen of the same basic archetypal structure. Thus there can be no individual freedom of choice in its realm. By contrast, at the level of Ideity, individuality is a basic fact. The presence of ONE operates in its most precisely focused condition. It not only brings Soul and human organism together as interrelated factors within the field of their one-to-one relationship -- even though for a long time the human consciousness has a very vague and distorted picture of such a relationship -- but it is "present" as the definite potentiality of a fully individualized selfhood. It is present and focused in the Heart of man.

As the level of this manifestation of ONE is reached, it is what takes place within and through this "Ideity field," and thus between the Soul-field and the human field-of-existence, which is the deciding factor. Not the Soul alone, not individual man alone, but their relationship.

This relationship however is not something entirely "new"; it has back of it a karmic inheritance. It is conditioned from the very moment it was established by the karma of a relationship which, in its place and function in the past universe, corresponded to it. This must be so because this entire present universe is karmically related to the past universe. The present universe exists in order to take care of the "unfinished business" of the past one. As individual persons related to a particular Soul, you and I exist in order to take care of a tiny part of the vast unfinished business of the past universe.

Let us put it very crudely to stress the point: If at the hour of 11:00 in the "Day" of a past planetary or cosmic evolutionary process a failure in relationship occurred involving a Soul and a "human" being, at the same hour in the "Day" of this present universe, that failure can be neutralized and transmuted into success. What failed during the past universe has now a "second chance" to achieve success.

This can be interpreted by saying that "I" lived at that time in the past universe and now "I" have to deal with this karma; and if successful I shall then contribute to the "success" aspect of this present universe in however microscopic a manner it may be. This would be the popular attitude generally accepted in India and among our present-day "esotericists." But one could also take the "I"-concept out of the karmic picture and simply say that a small pattern of karma -- a failure in relationship in certain existential conditions -- led automatically to the present emergence of a particular human being having reached the stage of individualization, such an emergence being necessary in order to re-establish the Harmony of the universal whole. This would be more like the official Buddhist view of the matter.

In terms of the first-mentioned approach, we can speak of "monads" that partially failed in past cycles and that now once more have incarnated in order to better "learn their lesson." This term, monad, was popularized by the German philosopher Leibnitz in the seventeenth century and adopted by the Theosophists two centuries later. A monad is simply a "one." It is one number in the infinite series of whole numbers. If we consider such a series, then the first monad, from which all others have derived, as overtones derive from a fundamental tone, is No. 1. This No. 1 monad is of course "the One," the One God, the Logos, Ishvara, the Supreme Identity of the cosmos; and to that No. 1 all "universal religions" pray. The No. 1 of our universe is "karmically related" to the No. 1 of the past universe, in that the original Creative Word of this universe was conditioned by the overall type of failure of the past universe.

However when I speak of ONE I have in mind a Principle not a Being. I speak of That which manifests in and through every number, whether it be No. 1 or No. 365,432. ONE is the Principle of Existence -- existence as a whole of activity in an unceasing state of relationship to other wholes. Any whole that has reached the human state of conscious individualization and has failed to meet fully the challenge of relationship with other human wholes can be said to "generate karma"; that is to say, he has acted "against" ONE. He has repudiated the presence of ONE in his field-of-existence and his mentally focused consciousness. To that extent he is at least a partial "failure" however much he may be successful in other modes of activities. He is thus given another chance of neutralizing this failure in a future cycle.

The question is whether one has to say that the "he" who failed actually reappears in the future cycle as the same "he"! When the phase No. 365,432 appears in the new cycle, its appearance carries the karmic imprint (in Buddhism, the skandhas) of the failure that occurred at this very point in the development of the past cycle. It is this failure which in a sense "reappears" and has to be met and dealt with. It is dealt with in the Ideity-field linking a new Soul-Image and a new human organism. As both are "new" so is therefore the Ideity-field new. Yet while the Ideity-field is new, it is also conditioned in its structure by the karma produced by the failure that occurred in the past cycle. It is existentially new but structurally conditioned by an event in a past cycle.

It is to such a "structural conditioning" that the believer in the popular process of reincarnation refers when he says that a monad that partially failed in the past is now -- the same monad -- reincarnating in the present cycle. Should we speak of "the same monad"? This is the question. If we do we personalize, or at least "entitize" what can as well be considered an impersonal conditioning factor in a vast process. This personalizing produces a simpler picture of what is happening; and at a time when man tends to personalize or individualize everything it is easier to think of the reincarnation of "the same monad." Modern science nevertheless has been trying to "dis-entitize" what we normally consider objects with fixed characteristics; the concept of process is superseding that of set entities. Instead of speaking of an entity having a particular form, the progressive physicist speaks simply of "form," that is of the successive aspects or phases of a structured process. What structures the process, in occult terms, is the karmic imprint of a previous cycle during which, as it reached a parallel or "synchronistic" phase, some basic event occurred affecting the success-failure balance of the process. There is "good" as well as "bad" karma. Success leaves its structural mark as well as failure.

In other words, in thinking of such matters one can focus the attention on the cyclic process as a whole and its many phases, or else one can "entitize" the balance of success and failure at any stage of the process and speak of it as a "monad" -- an entity which is partially successful and partially a failure. I repeat that "success" (or "good") means allowing ONE to operate as the Principle of integration without fearing or obstructing this operation; whereas "failure" (or "evil") means hindering or perverting the integrative process within which ONE is a constant presence. At the human level ONE, as the Principle of Integration, can be called "Love" -- but Love in a universal sense rather than the emotional and inherently possessive love found in the relationship between two or more mainly egocentric individuals.

In the cyclo-cosmic World-picture which I am presenting, I emphasize processes and cycles rather than entities with fixed characteristics. I stress the flow of existence rather than any particular snapshot taken of it and given a definite particular name. I am speaking of "fields" in order to present a more "modern" picture of reality -- a picture in which

the most basic factor is r e l a t i o n s h i p rather than entities related to each other yet never quite losing their essential character as "entities" -- which means, at the individualized human level, single persons and, beyond the personal realm, single monads. Nineteenth century occultism and
Theosophy emphasized most strongly the individualistic approach, indeed very often the "rugged individual" at even
supposedly "spiritual" levels. The original concept of "the
Brothers" in early theosophical books later gave way to one
of "Masters" -- of the powerful Adept, either "white" or
"black." The "White Lodge" ideal was largely replaced by
that of a "Hierarchy" of Super-Individuals having personal
names and performing very definite personalized functions.

The two types of pictures are in a sense complementary.
ONE focuses itself at the level of Ideity in individual persons
-- persons who, when completely attuned to and integrated
with a particular Soul-Image, fulfill indeed particular functions within the planetary field of Man. But these particular
Soul-Images and functions are actually parts of a vast process of existence. They are all derived from the One Word
in the beginning, the One Logos, Ishvara. In terms of activities they have their individual fields of operation; but in
terms of consciousness and of purpose, they all commune in
an integral Whole of which I speak as the Pleroma -- the fullness of perfected "being-ness". We might say that at close
range they appear as "individuals"; but in their wholeness
they constitute a sphere of White Light -- which is what one
should understand when thinking of the "White Lodge." In this
White Light all colors are interrelated. Indeed this Light is
the relatedness of all the component illumined Souls.

At a much "lower" level -- if we are individuals qualify-
ing for the New Age -- we should concentrate in our thinking
upon the Ideity-field within which the Soul-field and the human field-of-existence gradually interact more consciously
rather than upon an individualistic monad that keeps reincarnating from time to time. T h e m o n a d i s t h e I d e-

ity-field conceived as an entity. It is a "snap-shot" of one brief phase (a human life) in the development of the Ideity-field.

In atomic physics light is described at times as a "wave"; at other times as a stream of "particles" called photons; and many scientists still think of an atom as a kind of sub-microscopic solar system with electrons revolving around the proton as planets do revolve around the sun. But this model of the atom, described by the physicist Bohr, is no longer valid in terms of the most recent concepts of physics.* It may be that the picture we make of the solar system is also not a truly correct one in an absolute sense; it is "true" only because our sense-perceptions operate the way they do and our intellect organizes them in a manner adapted to our state of consciousness.

In ancient astrology the "real" planet was not the mass of physical matter on which man may land someday, but the orbital space defined by the revolution of that physical mass around the sun; in other words the "field" of the relationship of that planet to the sun. Likewise most people think of the zodiac as a circular sequence of actual groups of stars called constellations, whereas it is rather the field of the yearly relationship of the earth to the sun. Constellations are only symbols -- symbols of the cyclic relation of the earth's biosphere to the solar source of the energies which in their totality we call Life. In the same way the monad,

---

*"By atomic particle we mean a manifestation of energy or of an amount of motion localized in a very small volume and susceptible of displacing itself with a finite speed. The electron... is a particle only to the extent to which it can manifest its presence in a locality with its total energy. The wave associated with the electron is not the physical vibration of something; it is only a field of probabilities." (Louis de Broglie, CONTINU ET DISCONTINU, page 56).

considered as a fixed single entity, is a "myth" which expresses by means of a convenient Image the operation of a universal Principle of integration, ONE, at the level of the one-to-one relationship of Soul to the individual human person.

It is a very valuable "myth," a powerful Image-symbol, which at the particular level of evolution of most human beings in this individualistic Age is most effective as an incentive for individual integration. But a New Age will soon open -- it has presumably been opened potentially since the days of Gautama, the Buddha. This New Age will demand new Images and symbols, as we shall presently see. A snapshot of a person in the midst of a series of operations can indeed be most valuable if we only want to study analytically that person's features and movements. But we are now in an Age of motion pictures. The whole life of a person from birth to death is to be seen if we want to know the real "eonic" meaning of any single event or any single action of this person. We are at the dawn of the development of eonic consciousness.

This eonic consciousness can be applied not only to the total process of actualization of the set of birth-potentialities in the life of an individual person, but to a far more extensive process which, starting at the very beginning of the evolutionary process of individualization of "Man," will lead to a generalized state of Divine Marriage -- the omega state of Man's evolution on this planet, Earth. If we consider only one Soul-Image and its relationship to human organisms, the process of individualization begins when the Ideity-field is first actualized. Yet it was a potentiality the moment the process of individualization began for Man as a whole, i.e. the moment symbolized by the "gift of fire" made to mankind by Prometheus.

This actualization of the Ideity-field begins when the human being reaches a point in his development at which he is able to give at least a faint, intuitive but conscious response to the near-presence of the Soul-field. We may also say that then the monad, which is the developing energy of the Ideity-field, is able to focus this energy upon the Heart center of the human being. Then the "modulation" of which we spoke early in this chapter also begins to take place, transferring the focus of the self from the pelvic center to the Heart center. Only then can we speak of the beginning of a reincarnation process, a process which is but one phase of the larger planetary or cosmic process of actualization of the potentialities released into existence by the creative Word.

THE PROCESS OF "REINCARNATION"

The Purpose of this process, as a phase of the larger process of Man's evolution, is the full actualization and concretization of a Soul-Image in and through a fully responsive individual person, so that this whole person -- by which I mean a total field-of-existence with its activities at several levels -- becomes transfigured and transsubstantiated. The "transfiguration" refers to the consciousness and the mind within and through which the Light of the Ideity-field pours; and the "transsubstantiation," to the very substance of the material organism, cells and atoms.

This is the essential Purpose; and we should not limit it to any one aspect of the human person. The culmination of the process must change every factor within the Ideity-field. It changes the existential person. It changes the Soul-field which has as it were assimilated the existential person making it relatively "immortal." It changes the Ideity-field inasmuch as it brings "success" to the monad that had failed in the distant past, and thus it removes one small, very small block from the path of the total evolution of Man toward the omega state of fulfillment. It affects not only an individual person, but Man as well because the individual is only one small aspect of Man -- one Variation on the planetary or cosmic Theme of Man.

The process of individualization operating within one Ideity-field cannot be isolated from what is happening to mankind-as-a-whole. The geographical location, the period, the culture and the society within which the process unfolds, are important factors which our individualistic Western mentality, alas, is only too prone to ignore or dismiss as unimportant. Races and societies have cycles of reappearance which indeed can greatly condition the individual cycle of "reincarnation" of a monad. And as I said before, rather than speak of the reappearance of a monad one should study the periodical rhythm of activation and inactivation of the Ideity-field.

This Ideity-field, or "Auric Egg," is the limited and apparently ovoidal "space" within which the Soul-to-person relationship has to work out. The relationship operates on an active basis as long as the human person lives, exceptions notwithstanding. When the man or woman dies the Ideity-field becomes inactive. It enters into a condition of "obscuration" or latency. When a new human being is conceived or born with whom the Soul enters into relationship, the field is reactivated. But the person who had previously died and the new one are not the same person. The Ideity-field and thus the monad are the same; the Soul-field is also the same --but a new human organism is drawn into the Ideity-field, and the social-cultural environment of the new birth differs in most cases from the one in which the first person was born.

What we have to consider thus is a succession of human persons, each completely new, who constitute the "negative" ever-renewed pole of the Ideity-field, of which the Soul-field is the permanent "positive" pole. Individual persons born at more or less lengthy intervals succeed one another in assuming the negative pole of the Soul-to-person relationship. During the period between the death of one of these persons and the birth of his "successor" the Ideity-field is, as stated above, inactive.

When this field is inactive the monad, which simply represented the focusing of the universal Principle ONE upon that field, is also in a state of relative latency -- a state confusingly and variously described according to the metaphysical School describing it. It is nevertheless evidently a "subjective" state. It is presumable that in that state, or more likely series of states, the monad gravitates toward the positive pole of the Ideity-field, i. e. to the Soul-field; for in this Soul-field is gathered the "spiritual harvest" of the experiences of the individual person who is now disintegrated. What remains of this individual person is an "ideistic" factor, that is, the seed product of the activities of the individualized mind during the person's recently terminated lifespan.

The Ideity-field is indeed of the nature of mind; but mind as used here does not mean what is usually meant by the term, that is the cogitating, arguing, dichotomizing and classifying intellect. It is mind as a creative power of consciousness, mind, as the "stuff" out of which the Ideity-field is composed-- mind as the result of the interplay of the Soul-field and the bio-psychic human organism while the latter was alive.

Many students of modern "metaphysics" as well as Theosophists, Kabbalists and the like teach that in the individual person mind exists at two levels; thus they speak of a "higher mind" and a "lower mind." The latter is still closely affected by the compulsive energies and drives of the level of Life; it refers also to the type of mental activities over which the ego rules. The "higher mind" on the other hand is the mind that is open to whatever comes to it from the Soul-field. It is the truly "intuitive" mind that is able to resonate to the large rhythms of the all-human and planetary evolution. It also can become infused with "eonic consciousness" as well as with promptings and Images emanating from the Soul-field with which it is definitely connected within the Ideity-field.

And when the "Divine Marriage" occurs which is the spiritual culmination of the Soul-to-person relationship, this higher mind reaches the state of the Pleroma-mind, focusing a fully developed eonic type of consciousness.

As this Divine Marriage occurs, the Soul-field and the human field-of-existence become one -- and one with the Ideity-field. The human individual reaches a state of "personal immortality," which is "personal" only in the sense that the personality has become absorbed in the Soul-field while at the same time retaining its structural identity, its Form, which has indeed become the likeness of the Soul-Image. What was once a bio-psychic organism of Life-power has become an "organism of mind-power" -- the Diamond Body of Asiatic lore, the "Resurrected Body of Christ." In it the Presence of ONE glows in a condition of perfect Pleromic consciousness. This is the goal of human evolution; and, if the term "Man" is used in its most general, cosmic sense, the goal of all evolutionary processes.

The belief in reincarnation usually does not consider the complex process discussed in the preceding pages. It is based on the desire innate in most human beings to escape what seems to be an inevitable process of disintegration in and after death. It may be bolstered also by what are usually called "memories of past lives"; and of late various procedures more or less involving hypnotic suggestion have been widely used, claiming to lead to "regression to past lives."

In most discussions concerning reincarnation and past lives the question of what is meant by the "I" that has lived before and that is supposed to remember is almost never asked. It is taken for granted that there is an "I" -- a spiritual superphysical entity -- that incarnates in various "bodies." This "entity," as Edgar Cayce called it, is even said to "select its parents" as well as the life-circumstances into which it will be born. If there is such an entity it would be, in the world-picture I have outlined, the "monad"; but when most persons say "I" they actually refer only to the ego which was gradually formed out of the contacts between a human organism, operating at the level of Life, and its family and social-cultural environment. They know nothing but this ego and the name given them by their parents. Ego and name define what so many modern psychologists unfortunately call "the self," meaning really the person-as-a-whole. It is this "self" and all its idiosyncrasies which most men today want to see perpetuated. They try to accomplish this physically in the organisms of their children, or in some work that will bring a "social" kind of immortality; but this does not work too well in most cases, so they yearn for a more "personal" kind of permanence. And the modern movement of Spiritualism which began in the Forties of last century provides them with rather vague but at times seemingly comforting "proofs" of such a permanence of the personality-self after death. But are such "proofs" valid and convincing? And if "memories of past lives" register in the consciousness of the now living person, are these truly "memories" -- except in rather special and unduly publicized cases, especially those of children who "recall" events in the life of another child who died at a very early age?

I do not mean to say that events of past human lives may not somehow register in the consciousness of now living persons under certain critical circumstances and perhaps under quasi-hypnotic states which do away temporarily with the ego-mind and its more or less rigid structures of consciousness. The real problem is whether or not the "registering" of such past events, scenes and surroundings is to be considered as the r e m e m b e r i n g by a now living entity of what took place in a p r e v i o u s e x i s t e n c e of this s a m e e n t i t y. Is it really the same entity or do we assume it to be "the same" because our life-philosophy, or our deep unconscious desire, w a n t s it to be the same?

As I see it the Ideity-field, or Auric Egg, does record events and responses which affect the relationship between the Soul-field and the living human person; and it is these records in the Ideity-field which can be activated to impress the consciousness of the new human being. But the fact that this new human being is able in some circumstances or in special states of consciousness to be impressed by these records does NOT mean that the recorded events happened to "him." They may have happened to a person who was his predecessor, i. e. who, centuries or years before, occupied the place which he now occupies in this Ideity-field.

If we speak of a monad that is the integrating power of the Ideity-field, the life-events recorded did not happen to this monad; they happened to the living person who constituted only one pole of the field. One might say of course that the monad was in some way "involved" in these events; yet they really happened to the living person, not to the monad as such. I would rather think of these events as being recorded in the Ideity-field because of their importance to the relationship between the Soul and the human being, and that later they are reanimated at significant times in the life of the new individual so as to warn him or to enlarge his consciousness of the process of existence. Through such experiences with the reanimated past a person may be led to develop at least the first stage of "eonic consciousness" -- a type of consciousness not limited by the ego-boundaries of its present field-of-existence but able to "feel," or sense intuitively, the cyclic tides of the process of individualization.

The process is tidal, because it includes periods of activation and periods of inactivation or latency of the Ideity-field. Each on-surging tide takes for a time the form of an individual monad--an "I am" which transcends the ego-sense and becomes focused in the Heart center of the existent. Each receding tide dissipates this feeling of individuality-in-existence; but the seed harvest of the existential cycle is nevertheless gathered within the Soul-field (the Buddhi of early Theosophical writings -- a kind of Soul granary). It is not only gathered, it is assimilated. It assists the Soul in its final stages of individualization and sharp focusing. Faculties are built into the Soul-field which call for a new and higher type of human organism to be drawn into the Ideity-field when the time for re-activation comes.

Humanity as a whole and indeed the entire Life-field of the Earth strive to be able to answer such a "call" of the Soul-field, so that the very living substance of the planet may evolve and sensitize itself further in a symmetrical effort. This effort is symmetrical to the involutionary "descent" of the Soul-Image, which, as it comes "closer" to the human Earth-level, becomes more differentiated and sharper in its outlines. A two-fold movement -- descent and ascent -- yet but one process of existence. To feel this process slowly, rhythmically unfolding in essential harmony in spite of all temporary set-backs is to develop eonic consciousness. And such a consciousness has no need to entitize or personalize every phase of the process. It is gradually becoming o n e w i t h the process, one with the Eon. It exists in the constant presence of ONE.

The Ideity-field (the monad, in a sense) draws to itself a human organism about to be born which will be able to resonate to the vibrations of the Soul-field in such a way that the next stage in the differentiation and focalization-process of the Soul Image can best be fulfilled. It is not really a matter of "selecting" parents and a particular environment, except perhaps at the most advanced stages of the process of individualization. It is much more a matter of "karma," that is, a question of dealing at a certain time with the evolution of humanity and of a particular racial group and culture, of dealing with a particular phase of the process of individualization referring to a particular Soul-Image -- a "Letter" of the Creative Word. That phase is conditioning the state of the Ideity-field to which a new human organism will be drawn.

As it is drawn into such a field, the human organism finds

itself, unknowingly in nearly all cases, the "successor" of the person who previously occupied the negative pole of the relationship operating within that field. That is to say, the development of the new human being is structured as much by the fact that it occurs within a particular dynamic Ideity-field as by its occurring within a certain family and social environment. Nevertheless the new human organism is first of all "human." It is an expression of trends in the Life-field of mankind. Only later on in its development will the human being become individualized. Of course, it is already potentially individualized by virtue of its presence within an Ideity-field; and the more nearly the Soul-field is ready for the Divine Marriage, the closer this potentiality of individualization is to actual individualization.

The very young child may already seem to be an individual; but this appearance merely reveals the influence of the Ideity-field which he then passively reflects in pure "innocence." The reflection may, and usually does, fade out when, toward puberty, the specific energies of Life forcibly assert their power, or even before puberty under the psychological pressures of school and comrades. Likewise, even at the very beginning of its existence, a discordant family-situation may incite the nascent ego to become a positive, aggressive or neurotic force in order to hide the shock of disparateness between the inner situation (the condition of the Ideity-field) and the outer family environment.

The development of a human person is indeed a complex matter. It is already complex at the level at which the ordinary psychologist operates when he deals with the transition from a state of instinctive subservience to life-energies in the child to a state of more or less effective individualization in terms (at first, at least) of ego-development. But many things cannot be accounted for or understood in their true basic meaning if another dimension of existence is not considered.

One might say that the realm of Life is three-dimensional; and that any organized state of Society is four-dimensional because it includes the sharing of experiences and of concerns and ideals with many other human beings. It includes also the capacity of "time binding" -- to use the well-known phrase of Korzybski in his early book THE MANHOOD OF HUMANITY. The vegetable kingdom displays a "chemistry binding" capacity in transmuting solar energy into potential food for other lives; and the animal kingdom displays a "space binding" capacity as it brings out in the evolutionary picture the factor of displacement in space, of migration, of roaming in search of its food and water, of adventuring. Man "binds time" because he is able to transfer the harvest of his experiences to future generations by means of symbols, words and in terms of "values." And this is a "fourth dimension" of existence.

There is, as already suggested, still another kind of "binding" -- and we could speak of it as a fifth dimension of activity and consciousness. It refers to the "personality binding" power of the Soul-field. The permanent Soul is, as we saw, the positive pole of the Ideity-field, while a succession of many human persons occupies the negative pole. The Soul "binds" the spiritual harvest of all these personalities somewhat as a human civilization or culture gathers the knowledge of past generations of men in vast Libraries and Encyclopedias. As a result the Soul-field gradually becomes filled with the quintessence of an immense variety of human experiences; and it is by integrating and "assimilating" these harvested products of individual lives in the Earth's biosphere that the Soul-field gradually becomes more differentiated and individualized; that is to say, the Soul-Image which was at first essentially but a general "quality" -- let us say, a broadly defined aspect of LOVE or INTELLIGENCE or CREATIVITY -- differentiates this "quality" until it becomes precisely defined in such a way that one single human being can respond to it totally. And this fact makes the Divine Marriage possible. This Divine Marriage is, philosophically speaking, simply the total and perfect actualization of this precisely defined Soul-quality in the very substance of the living materials of the Earth integrated in a human field-of-existence.

I repeat that this Soul-quality or Soul-Image in the beginning of the evolution of the universe, was inherent in the Creative Word or Logos. It was, symbolically, one Letter of this cosmos-engendering Word. But it was only a most broadly and universally defined quality of existence that had been "envisioned" by the Pleroma of the past universe. It had to pass through a long series of cosmic and planetary stages in order to acquire definiteness and the capacity to focus its precise character upon one single human organism who had become sensitive enough to act and think as an "individual."

Even at this stage of its one-to-one relationship with an individual man, the Soul should not be considered as "a being." It is rather a quality of being-ness. It is an "ideal" to which the "reality" of the human individual is called upon to attune itself. Unfortunately most religious have given to the realm of Soul-Images attributes which make it appear to be a separate world of "being" essentially distinct from the realm of "becoming" -- that is, of actual existence. It is we, human beings, who give to the Soul -- and to what we personalize as "gods" -- this character of "being." We personalize Soul-qualities, giving them almost human features. We ought to recognize that an ideal is not a "real" fact of existence; it is the potentiality of a multitude of real existential developments.

This potentiality is nevertheless affected by human efforts to actualize it existentially. The reality does react upon the ideal, or at least upon the possibility of the future substantiation of this ideal as a perfect manifestation of the creative intent of the ancient Pleroma. For this reason, the relationship between the Soul-field and the individualized person is to some extent a two-way relationship. The two poles

interact; and their interaction determines what happens to
the Ideity-field. In extreme cases this field can be completely sundered, and as a result the individual is truly "soul-
less." Eventually he totally disintegrates. But the karma of
that failure, which can be interpreted as the failure of a particular "monad," remains. It will have to be faced in a new
universe; but it is not necessary to believe that it will be the
s a m e monad, reawakened from a latent state within the Infinite Potential, which will have to do the "facing." Such a
belief is no doubt of value at a certain stage of human evolution. However, an increasing number of human beings
should now be reaching a state of consciousness beyond that
stage.

It may be worth while, in concluding this discussion of
the character of the relationship between Soul and human
person, to picture a Soul-Image as a kind of "Office" -- an
Office which is assumed successively by a series of individual persons. He who occupies the Office can add luster and
prestige to the Office, or he can discredit and disgrace it.
The Office does not "exist" without an officiant who gives it
existential reality; yet in a sense "it is there" as an ideal or
mind-structure, and it remains regardless of the person
who occupies it and who defines its meaning by his behavior.
Let us consider the Office of the President of the United
States -- that is, the Presidency. One individual person after another seeks, is elected to and assumes this Office.
He becomes President; which means that a one-to-one relationship is established between the Presidency and a human
being, the President. The Presidency is an "ideal." Ideally, i. e. legally and constitutionally, it has certain functions
to be performed by a particular man to whom is given the
power to discharge them. He may do well, indifferently
or badly. This will affect to some extent the power and prestige of the Presidency as an Office, perhaps not crucially

however, and after the President's term is over another man will assume the Office. As a successor to the first-mentioned President the new man may inherit a heavy load of unsolved problems, of unfinished business, thus of karma. But he may act brilliantly and perhaps restore the temporarily tarnished prestige of the Presidency.

Now if we say that a Soul "incarnates" in a human body, can we also say, in terms of our illustration, that the Presidency incarnates into Mr. Hoover, later Mr. Roosevelt, then Truman, Eisenhower, etc. ? This would not give a revealing picture of the situation. It would be even less significant to say that Hoover reincarnated into Roosevelt, Roosevelt into Truman, etc.; this kind of reincarnation applies only to the Tibetan belief that a Dalai Lama actually reincarnates into the next child to which the Office will be given after years of preparation. Each President of the U.S. is the "successor" of the previous one, and the "predecessor" of the one who will follow him into the White House.

The White House in a sense symbolizes in this illustration the "Auric Egg" -- the Ideity-field within which the Office and the man who holds the Office operates. The President "chooses" his Administration; according to this choice and to his actions when confronted with crises, the particular relationship between Office and the holder of the Office will be a success or a failure -- or half-way between success and failure, as is usually the case under present-day circumstances. Each President's Administration will have to bear the karma of the preceding one.

Can one say, then, that the Presidency "chooses" a President? It sounds rather absurd to say so, and yet in a subtle sense this is true. The Office, at a particular time in history, tends to require a certain type of "Officiant." The requirements for the Presidency of the U.S. today are not the same as they were in the days of President Jackson. The Office of executive Head of a large business firm, like General Motors, demands intellectual, social and personal qualities very different from those needed for the Presidency of a small and local firm. In this sense, the Office chooses at least the type of person who will succeed in getting the job and satisfactorily performing his work either directly or through his Administration and the bureaucracy. It has often been remarked how an individual man changes once he assumes the responsibility of the Presidency --and often any office which brings to him social power.

Such a type of illustration is obviously not to be taken literally, but it may show more clearly what I have meant all the while by Soul-Image and Soul-field. In an often strange way the organization of society and the social factors which derive from it can illustrate rather effectively the type of relationships operating at a cosmic level. One may think of course that if this is so, it is because we give a "socio-morphic" character to the cosmic patterns of organization, just as most people today give an "anthropomorphic" character to their conception of God and Soul. If so, then this means that man has reached a stage of consciousness at which social and cultural problems are in need of broader and more cosmic principles of organization.

Indeed the very concept of the coming of a New Age implies such a need, especially as it seems quite obvious that the main outer fact which will characterize the New Age is the planetarization of human society, which inevitably implies the planetarization of human consciousness and the rise of a new type of human being. Global man -- man in the fullness of actualization of the potential inherent in the archetypal Image of Man -- this is the "Man of Plenitude" of whom I have spoken for many years and to whom a number of progressive thinkers have referred in different terms, each term stressing a particular ideal aspect of the future reality.

As we face the possibility of emergence of such a new type of human being we should realize how valuable the concept of "fields" which has been developed here indeed is. It is a deeply needed concept because the more one thinks of individual entities, of monads and the like, the more difficult it is to integrate these individual entities in some all-encompassing Whole -- Man, or the Earth-as-a-whole. We have been living through a period of intense and acute individualism; and a change must come about if the process of planetarization is to take place in a harmonious manner, and not in a totalitarian and anarchistic way, totalitarianism and anarchy being two sides of the same coin.

The change from the concept of rigidly defined and more or less static "entities" to that of "fields of energies" would make the integration of mankind, and of all knowledge as well, far easier. A field can more readily be seen as a limited zone of operation within a larger field, than an individual person can be understood to constitute but one unit within a larger social and planetary Entity. The consciousness of Man is entering the realm of forces and force-fields. This realm used to be known and feared as the "occult realm." We have now reached a point in evolution at which a "dis-occulting" of the occult is possible, nay inevitable, at least in a relative sense.

That this step can be a very dangerous one is quite evident. We have its symbolic evidence in the possibilities inherent in the processes of nuclear fission and fusion -- and in the atom bomb. But the real danger does not reside in taking the new step but rather in taking it in terms of man's old concepts of the meaning of existence -- existence as an insulated and competitive individual still motivated by the compulsive drives of the Life-field, to which must be added a generalized kind of fear and a sense of alienation inherent in egocentricity. What is crucially needed today is a new concept of what individualism, and at the social level, democracy, should mean in the global world of tomorrow -- a new approach to knowledge -- a new sense of value -- a new ethics to supersede the still persistent puritanism of the past, and as well the anti-puritan reaction which is merely its negative aspect.   Humanity needs new symbols, new ideals, a new vision, and a new type of man to substantiate and make real this new vision.

This new type of man is coming. It is beginning to appear here and there, everywhere, in strange forms and in unlikely places perhaps. But the unfamiliar always seems strange and even repugnant to the sclerotic minds of defeatists and fear-riddled men. We must have faith in tomorrow -- even more in the day after tomorrow. We must have faith in Man, and act out this faith.

Part Three

IN THE SOCIO-CULTURAL MODE

Chapter VIII: KNOWLEDGE THROUGH COSMIC ATTUNEMENT

The problem of knowledge (218); Sruti knowledge based on revelation
- Smittri knowledge derived from the senses and the intellect (219-220);
Existential knowledge and structural knowledge - their different forms
(221-222); Need to include both in human experience (223); An original
Divine Revelation and its imprint in the collective memory of mankind
(224); Carl Jung's interpretation (225); The power of Archetypes challenged by the ego (226); Centripetal integration and the true meaning of
synthesis (227); The structuring Power of the Eon, and how it operates
through individuals (228); Horizontal and vertical relationships as they
appear in the cyclocosmic world-view (228-229); What is primary: the
individual or society? (230-231); Man's twofold character and the process of education (232); Man's objective experience of the Earth from
"space" changes his relationship to the planetary whole (233); The three
evolutionary stages of human knowledge - thesis, antithesis (ego stage)
and synthesis (234); Eonic consciousness based on the resonance of
smaller wholes to the greater whole which contains them (235); Holistic consciousness, clairvoyance, and the problem of communication
(236-237); Man in relation to the Earth considered as an organized
whole of existence (238); Structural knowledge and prophecies (239);
Statistics in the Bible (240); Statistical determinism and existential
freedom (241); Difficulty of passing from one time-scale to another
(242-243); The cyclocosmic picture as a framework for synthesis -
Unity in diversity (244); Validity vs. truth: the danger of premature
knowledge (245); Immediacy of feeling in experience vs. the knowledge
of structured process - Seeing events as phases of cyclic processes
transform their impacts and meaning (247-248); The conscious assimilation of mystical experiences (249); Attunement as the key to basic
knowledge (250).

Chapter IX: VALUES AND SYMBOLS

The structuring of individual consciousness by collective images - Symbols as answers to existential needs (252-253); The Buddha symbol and
the Crucifix (254); Symbols as abstractions of human experiences (255);
Symbols vs. facts (256); Symbols as structural factors, and their existential aspect (257-258); The power of symbols at critical moments
of history (259-260); Einstein's equation as a symbol of transformation
(261); The relativity of truth (262); Subjective experiences which release new human potential (263-264); The "true-false" dichotomy (265);
The cycle as frame of reference for all values (266); Truth, as relative to each evolutionary phase of man's development (267); The prob-

lem of free will vs. determinism (268); The symbolic projection of the man-to-God relationship (269-270); The function of a "dialogue" with a personal God (270); The symbols of the individual and the "free and equal" citizen (271); And the need for these to operate within a more inclusive symbol such as Man, Humanity, the Globe (272); Transfiguration of the tribal ideal and the personal God-image in Free Masonry (272-273); Culture and Art (274-275); The basic function of Art in different epochs (276-278); Art in a cultural-existential and in a planetary sense (279-280); Art for the sake of Man (281); Deculturalization and the war of symbols (282-283); The planetary function of mankind (284-285).

Chapter X: THE ETHICS OF WHOLENESS AND THE PLENARY SOCIETY

The new basis for ethical judgments in the synthesis phase of our evolution (286-287); Definition of ritual (288); Comparison of instinct and intelligence (289); Rituals as social instincts, and moral "right" (292); Training and correct performance, in magic and in science (294); Morality in terms of human relationship (295-296); Religion as a unitive force (297); The enforcement of morality in a society of egos (298); The Golden Rule - Our Society as a transition stage of human development (299); The ambiguity in the concept of freedom of choice and moral responsibility (300-301); The individual-collective dichotomy (302); The evolution of morality (303); The Mosaic experience and its shadow (304); The present crisis of morality - The dharma ideal (305-306); The need for a new quality of relatedness (307); Man in the "Age of Plenitude" open to the Presence of a "greater Whole" (308); The revolt of youth (309); The new communes and the conditions for their survival (310); The new morality (311-312); The acceptance of catabolic forces and evil (313); To be open, but not afraid (314); The New Age commune and the "Love" ideal (315-316); The future multi-leveled society (317); Beyond quantitative democracy (321); The Auroville experiment (322).

VIII. KNOWLEDGE THROUGH
COSMIC ATTUNEMENT

The problem of knowledge has occupied the attention of the most questioning and critical minds in all highly developed cultures. How is man conscious of existence -- conscious that he exists and conscious of what occurs in his environment? On what foundations is knowledge based? Are there several essentially different modes of cognition and as a result several basically different types of knowledge? And if this last question is answered in the affirmative, could it be that mankind is in the process of developing collectively a new way of knowing what it now needs in order to insure survival and above mere survival a full development of man's potentialities, which certainly are as yet but partially actualized? This "new way" of knowing may indeed not be new at all, for a relatively few individuals here and there may already have experienced it. But when they tried to interpret and explain the actual mental process which produced this special type of knowledge it may well be that these individuals (who might be considered "mutants") had to use concepts and words heavily laden with emotional glamor and egocentric or geocentric biases -- concepts and words rendered inadequate by the fact that they emanated from a type of culture and mental imagery formed by local geographical and racial conditions.

It is not my intention to build here a new theory of knowledge and to present subtle or rigorous epistemological arguments for its validity. All that is intended is to state the problem of knowledge in terms of a holistic approach to existence and to man's relationship to the universe, and to suggest how, if one follows this approach, some of the old concepts can be reformulated and integrated with the cyclocosmic world-picture which seems best to satisfy the needs of humanity at the threshold of a new planetary Age.

REVELATORY VS. SENSATION-BASED KNOWLEDGE

The idea that there exist two essentially different modes of knowing and types of knowledge was fundamental in the philosophies of old India -- and I use the term philosophy in the plural, as did Heinrich Zimmer, to stress the fact that there were and still are completely different "Schools of Philosophy" in India, and not only one type as many people seem to believe. According to the Vedas and the systems of thought derived from these ancient texts, a type of knowledge is available to man which is characterized by the term s h r u t i, that is, knowledge based on "revelation." The other type, s m r i t i, refers to the knowledge resulting from the progressive accumulation of information gathered by succeeding generations of men -- information derived from sense-observation and their generalization through intellectual assumptions and the building of abstract theories.

The s m r i t i-type of knowledge is therefore not only based on the testimony of man's senses and on data furnished by instruments extending the range of our sense-perceptions, but it is conditioned by a cultural tradition, a collective mentality and a particular language. It represents what most people today understand as knowledge. It is the knowledge which modern science seems to make available. Yet the majority of people do not quite realize what is actually implied in our sense-knowledge and especially in modern science; thus we shall have to try to elucidate what is inferred in this mode of knowing.

As to the shruti-type of knowledge, it has been presented in most cases as a revelation bestowed upon man by God, or by divine and semi-divine agencies mediating between God and man. The problem however in such cases of "revelation" is to ascertain what is meant by God and quasi-divine intermediaries, and whether the human being apparently "chosen" as a recipient for a revelation is an effectual and reliable transmitting agent; and moreover whether what he receives from a divine Source can be formulated in words and images or concepts understandable to the men of the particular culture and society for whose benefit the revelation is apparently bestowed.

We shall deal separately with these two forms of knowledge. But first of all let us stress the fact that the men who believe exclusively in the validity of sensation-based and intellectually or rationally devised systems of concepts in most instances refuse to call any type of supposedly divine revelation a valid form of knowledge. On the other hand, to the religious devotee or the spiritual seer of old, sense-based knowledge is actually a form of "ignorance" (as Hindu philosophers like Sri Aurobindo use the term). It may have value in everyday life, but from the "spiritual" point of view this everyday life is itself an "illusion," and the testimonies of the senses are ultimately unreliable and deceiving for they refer to a world of "unreality" (Hindu concept) or a world of darkness and sin (the Christian approach) from which the Soul in man should divorce itself as soon as it can -- a divorcing process made possible by the super-sensual knowledge obtained through divine revelation.

This being so, do we have to infer that these two opposing attitudes toward knowledge refer to irreconcilable levels of human consciousness or evolutionary status, or is it possible to see that they can be reconciled and that they are indeed complementary?

The answer to these questions can be found in the fact,

stated at the beginning of this book, that man becomes aware of existence in two different ways. On the one hand he experiences the continuous flow of existential activity as if it were a tumultuous and haphazard sequence of unrelated events which pass through and around him, leaving a confusing or bewildering series of impressions or shocks on his whole organism and his senses; he is buffeted by the waves and whirlpools of life whose essential character is that it implies a multitude of ever-changing relationships between existing entities. On the other hand man becomes aware, either through or beyond this existential tumult, of patterns of order and periodicity, of rhythmic processes and cyclic recurrences, and thus of essential order.

This two-fold character of man's basic awareness of existence is at the very root of the two approaches to knowledge, even at the more cultured and sophisticated levels. Basically one can therefore speak of existential knowledge and of a structural kind of knowledge. Existential knowledge refers to the direct and immediate perception of the passing of events -- internal and organismic, as well as external and environmental events. Structural knowledge derives from man's ever growing consciousness of the order inherent in all processes of existence, and from his attempt to learn the mode of operation of this principle of order. What complicates the situation is that both the "existential" approach and the "structural" approach can be, and have been, interpreted in different ways, according to man's basic temperament and the character of his particular culture.

Existential knowledge, in its more developed form, deals with the ever-changing relationships between existents and with the activities of these existents within a particular environment and a particular social setup. If these relationships are felt to be negative, frustrating and oppressive, and particularly if their sequence or their implications appear to be meaningless, utterly chaotic and indeed absurd, existential knowledge may become pervaded with a sense of anxiety, fear and defeat. It may indeed take on a very pessimistic character, the more so the more emphasized the belief in universal order and divine purposefulness had been in the past of the culture and of the individual person. On the other hand, existential knowledge, even without any postulated reference to a divine or cosmic order, can be colored and glorified by a total acceptance of existence per se and a conscious and serene identification with the continuous flow of events. Man then is contented to keep his mind open to the rhythm of life and the universe, to gather whatever information chance relationships bring to him and perhaps to transfigure his sense-perceptions and internal feelings by the use of his poetic sense and his capacity to discover symbolic meaning in whatever comes to his attention.

Structural knowledge can also take different forms and embody seemingly divergent temperamental approaches to life and consciousness. In its most traditional aspect it is interpreted as "divine Revelation"; it is then knowledge endowed with absolute certainty and given to consecrated human beings, either by God or by more or less divine or superhuman Teachers. For some cultures, the revelation occurred as a unique event which took place either at the beginning of human evolution on this Earth or with the appearance and the teachings of a "one and only" Son of God, the Christ. In the latter case, the revelation is seen to have taken an essentially spiritual and moral character oriented towards the individual person.

Modern science is also a type of structural knowledge but in a totally different sense, especially in its dependence upon mathematics and logic; yet what has limited thus far our Western science is its insistence on relying exclusively on empirical observations and strictly intellectual procedures along the lines of the old Aristotelian logic. The reason for this exclusiveness is quite obvious, historically speaking, because our modern science developed in the sixteenth and seventeenth centuries as a strong protest against the dogmatism of the Church. As the Church was able to enforce its claim that only religion had the key to the knowledge of the soul and of all spiritual or ethical values, the only field left open to the emerging group of scientific researchers was the realm of material objects and of all that belongs to the realm of sense-obtained data.

Thus the new structural knowledge of science established as a new dogma the idea that all reliable knowledge could only come through empirical data organized by the rational intellect into "laws of nature." The result of this forced concentration of the enquiring minds of men of the Classical European Era upon matter and the intellect proved to be spectacular. Modern technology developed rapidly, and it has transformed the ways of life of mankind. Whether such a transformation will turn out to be an unmitigated success is highly doubtful. It may lead to a nuclear catastrophy and to the mechanization of most human beings. There are, however, many indications that new trends are developing among the most progressive scientists and "generalists" of our day, and that instead of reducing man to a physical mechanism, future science may be repolarized through a psychological and indeed spiritual interpretation of matter (cf. Robert Linssen, LA SPIRITUALITÉ DE LA MATIÉRE, Paris, 1967).

The main points which I wish to make here are:
(1) That the two basic factors in human experience should be included in our approach to knowledge: the structural and the existential, and
(2) That both of these factors should be given their fullest and most positive implications; that is to say they should not be restricted to some special aspect of the total nature of man, for man should be considered as a vast and multi-leveled field-of-existence rather than as the creature of either a personal God or of local geographical, cultural and historical circumstances.

The concept of divine revelation as the foundation of valid

knowledge is as limiting as the idea that knowledge is only reliable if acquired through sense-data and laboratory experiments which imply certain more or less unacknowledged postulates. The ancient opposition between revealed knowledge and experimental knowledge must be reinterpreted and given a new meaning; and this I believe can only be done in a way acceptable to the modern mind of man, when freed from traditional biases, through a cyclocosmic type of approach to existence.

Before we discuss this approach in its application to the problem of knowledge, it would seem worthwhile to mention briefly recent attempts to give validity to the concept of revelatory knowledge in the broadest sense of the term.

REVELATION AND THE COLLECTIVE UNCONSCIOUS

If there was some kind of divine Revelation at the origin of the development of man's consciousness -- a Revelation bringing to mankind the basis of a knowledge originating in a "source" outside of man's everyday awareness of the flow of existential data -- it would seem probable that one should still find ideas, images, or modes of thinking today at least relatively identical in most cultures and religions. Indeed the comparative study of old and new cultures and religions has shown conclusively that a number of similar ideas, symbols and even ritual forms of behavior have existed in one form or another almost everywhere on the face of the globe. They can be found in the Bible and the Sacred Books of the main religions, in the great myths, the fairy tales and the popular legends of cultures separated by time and space.

However, such a fact can be interpreted in several ways. One of the first interpretations, emphasized during the last century, was that all races originated from one geographical region constituting the cradle of mankind; that there, a more or less coherent whole of ideas, symbols and magic or religious formulas were developed. Later on human races became progressively differentiated as they evolved in different localities, each race or tribe isolated from the other and creating particular traditions and systems of beliefs influenced by its environment, as well as demonstrating specific bio-psychic traits.

This type of interpretation evidently was in accord with Biblical doctrines; it also fitted in with the idea, found in many places, that an "Original Revelation" had been bestowed upon primitive man by great Beings who had come either from another planet or from a superior sphere of existence. This idea is found expressed in a variety of forms among men of all races, so that it is possible to state that there actually is a "collective memory" -- imprecise as it undoubtedly is -- of a remote condition of human existence in which divine Instructors taught men the foundations of agriculture and primitive industry, of language and moral behavior, of medicine and all the arts.

The term "collective memory" may however be inappropriate. It may hide more than explain the basic nature of revelatory knowledge. Rather than say that there has been at some special time in the remote past a revelation, brought by superhuman Instructors, which left its mark upon all succeeding cultures, is it not more logical, and especially more fruitful and stimulating, to speak of an always possible contact between a form of superior consciousness and the minds of particularly sensitive human beings acting under special circumstances? That such a contact is perhaps more likely to occur at some periods of human development than at others may also be true.

The psychologist, Carl Jung, gave this problem a seemingly valid solution, yet one which he has not been able or perhaps willing to carry far enough because of his point of departure and of his eagerness to remain at the level of an empirical psychology. He refers the ideas and symbols at the core of most religions and cultures to what he calls the collective unconscious, and gives them the names of archetypes. According to him, these archetypes are "psychic structures" which are inherent in the collective consciousness or archaic humanity, i.e. of humanity still in a non-individualized state of openness to direct contacts with nature. He believes that these psychic structures are direct expressions of primordial instincts in human nature and that these instincts themselves are moulded by the structures and functions of the total human organism.

These Jungian archetypes in many cases refer to the relationship of man with the planet and with its daily and seasonal rhythms. They are, according to Jung, the psychic end-products of a multitude of human experiences repeated through many millennia and, one might say, incorporated in the deeper level of the psyche. These psychic depths, especially today, are outside the usual field of consciousness, because most of the time man's consciousness is hypnotized by preoccupation with everyday social life and enclosed within the more or less rigid framework of a dominant ego. This ego wants to remain precisely itself. It clings to what makes it different from others and rejects or pushes back into the unconscious that which all men have in common, because to this proud ego whatever is common appears more or less valueless in the intensely competitive and "success"-oriented society in which men operate today.

Such a state of affairs is productive not only of often dynamically stimulating tensions but, in its exaggerated form, of acute neuroses and psychosomatic illnesses. It also affects the very nature of the knowledge sought after by the men of such a society. It transforms "universities" into highly competitive "multiversities" operating as factories of knowledge under perhaps unofficial, but powerful and ever-present pressures from Government and big business. Nevertheless, a most significant and growing reaction against this atomization of knowledge and the competitively technological goals of official education is developing. Integration of knowledge (cf. Oliver Reiser's book bearing this title), integration of educational departments and fields of research, interdisciplinary conferences, etc. have become ideals toward which to strive. But of course what is sought is a type of integration which proceeds mostly from separate fields of technical knowledge -- thus from an existential type of knowledge based on sense-data and empirical procedures. It is a c e n t r i p e t a l type of integration which dreams of establishing, through the convergence of diverse intellectual theories which at first appear unrelatable if not opposite, an all-embracing concept or system of knowledge.

The keyword is thus: synthesis -- the last stage of a dialectical process of knowledge. Jung's "collective unconscious" is, in one sense at least, a kind of synthetic formation, the condensed and unified harvest of all human past experiences. The attempt to show that all great religions teach fundamentally the same body of spiritual-ethical truths (Aldous Huxley's perennial philosophy) takes the form today of an ecumenism which seeks to reduce the diversity of doctrines to a unity of beliefs acceptable to all men, even in spite of the cultural and traditional differences feeding their emotional and harassed egos. What is sought is a consciously accepted all-human c o n s e n s u s, a passage from the stage of "antithesis" to that of "synthesis." But can such a passage be accomplished without regard to the "thesis"? Is it not illogical to hope to reach a synthesis of antithetic viewpoints without incorporating in that synthesis the very essence of the thesis which is the root of the dialectical process of evolution of human consciousness and knowledge?

It is because a more or less clear realization of this need to rely upon an original human thesis, a root reality, is felt by many seekers that we often find mentioned the idea, and what is more the practice, of a "return-to." But a return to what? This evidently is the basic question; and any answer is likely to be unacceptable to a great many minds, because they are still strongly committed to their own or their culture's position at the antithesis level. The "return to source" which inspired certain European thinkers always means the return to some particular source -- to the alpha state of the cycle of a particular culture, but not to the original state of mankind as a whole.

On the other hand, Jung's concept of the collective unconscious fails to be entirely satisfying, not only because of its imprecision which makes it appear as a convenient screen behind which to hide anything one does not know, but because it offers no answer to the problem of what is at the root of human consciousness. The concept of a "primordial Revelation" as the root-foundation of human knowledge, and indeed of the human ability to be conscious of being conscious, is a more logical belief; but it is a metaphysical or religious belief which cannot be proved valid except, one might assume, if we undertake to follow certain disciplines for occult-spiritual development which claim to provide the consciousness of the "disciple" with indisputable and certain knowledge. Unfortunately such claims are many and varied, and rarely if ever open to objective checks and counterchecks.

What makes the idea of such a "primordial Revelation" difficult to accept is the personalized manner in which it is so often presented, whether it be in Asiatic or Western traditions. Great events, it is true, do occur through persons; but "through" rather than "by." The person focuses a critical situation in a process of unfoldment of potentiality into actuality--an existential process; but this does not really "cause" the transformation. The person is an important fact at the existential level; but he is an "agent," an instrumentality, at the structural level of understanding. A structuring Power acts through this agent. The agent is, existentially speaking, a Source; but a source is merely a place on the surface of the Earth at which -- through which -- water flows as a result of certain geological structures. What is this structuring Power? We have spoken of it as the Eon. It is the "greater Whole" in relation to us, men, who represent "lesser wholes."

THE CYCLOCOSMIC BASIS OF HOLISTIC KNOWLEDGE

The fundamental proposition in the cyclocosmic world-view is that existence is a process of transformation of wholes which are organized systems of activities and are composed of a more or less vast number of components or parts, each of which is in turn a whole composed of many parts, etc. The terms, whole and parts, are interdependent -- just as, let us say, mother and child are. One cannot speak of a whole without implying its parts; and to speak of a part indicates the existence of a whole within which it is contained. Likewise no woman can be called a mother unless she has a child; and the existence of a child presupposes a mother -- at least in our natural Earth-environment!

I have spoken in a preceding chapter of two basic types of relationship: matricial and associative. I am now considering an even more general and fundamental dualism. There are relationships which link wholes operating at the same level of existence in time and space, that is, whose life-span and size belong to the same scale of magnitude; and there are relationships in which the two terms of the relationship are constituted by a relatively small whole and the much vaster whole of which it is a part. Thus there are two kinds of relationship: of whole with whole belonging to the same level of existence -- and of whole to part, and part to whole. These might be called "horizontal" and "vertical" relationships, if one wishes to adopt a recently publicized concept; but these terms do not accurately define the character of the relationships. The qualificative "vertical" indeed misses the basic point, i. e. the fact that in such a so-called vertical relationship the supposedly "higher" factor in the relationship actually contains the "lower." The same confusion exists if one speaks of higher self and lower self --a very unfortunate way of expressing a most important fact of human existence by the use of an archaic type of symbolism. The consciousness of a human organism is not "higher" than that of the cells of this organism; it is first of all more inclusive; it is also as far as we can imagine more complex. It refers to a longer span and a larger field of existence.

The consciousness of a living cell in a human body has its own "cellular" character -- whatever that exactly is. The consciousness of a primitive man or a newborn child has its own "organismic" character which belongs to a different order, an order of great complexity and scope of operation. This primitive man or infant develops beyond the organismic state when he reaches a state of evolution or of growth in which he experiences even more complex "associative" or "horizontal" relationships, that is when he is able to participate in a larger whole which we call society -- and ultimately on this Earth, humanity. He then relates himself "associatively" with other human beings who are at least potentially his "equals." But at the same time he also finds himself related to the greater whole constituted by his community, his nation and its cultural traditions, and eventually humanity as a whole.

Present-day thinkers, hypnotized as they are by the physical sense-obtained character of what they conceive as "reality," will object to the preceding statement on the basis that a nation or humanity is not a "real" existential whole; and people love to repeat, without giving too much thought to the matter, that a society, or humanity, is made up of individuals. They assert that the primary fact, the only real concrete fact, is the individual; the individual alone can be thought of as an "entity," while mankind is simply a concept or a category. But is this really so? Is not this attitude of mind a prolongation of the Romantic approach glorifying the individual and of Rousseau's rather absurd idea of a "Social Contract" at the root of primitive societies?

As a strictly physical organism, a human being is more or less evidently the primary fact of human existence; yet would he survive if alone on this Earth? Is he not an integral part of the human kingdom which occupies a certain place and function in the planetary biosphere, which is itself but one layer in the Earth's total field of infinitely complex, yet closely interrelated and interdependent activities? The human organism's existence depends on the maintenance of a narrow range of temperatures, on the availability of food, on the behavior of animals, indeed on a great many factors which are all related to the extremely precariou⸱ balance of terrestrial and climatic variables refe⸱ ing t⸱ ⸱e Earth-as-a-whole. These are the facts to consider, and the modern mind should forget Adam and his being born alone on a planet made strictly for him and his descendants -- except as a myth expressing a very significant view of the evolution of consciousness.

When, moreover, the baby grows into a man, his growth is not only conditioned by the associative relationships he enters into with youngsters of his age or even with older persons; it is moulded most effectively, and most often irrevocably, by factors and influences which do not refer to individuals. They refer to the collective power of the culture, religion and social-economic conditions in his environment -- to the language his mind has to learn if he is to think in communicable terms (or perhaps even to think at all!) -- to whatever mode of behavior and feeling-response surrounds him and which he readily imitates. Family, school, military service, university training, business apprenticeship -- all these force upon the growing child various kinds of relationships which have not the character of equal-to-equal, but of container to content.

The child grows as a social being contained within his society and whatever national-cultural whole he was born into. He is no doubt potentially an individual; but only potentially so. He is first of all an exemplar of the type of human being his family and his culture imagine as a model of human existence. Society existed before the individual. He is born into it, just as helpless at the psycho-mental level as a baby born in a jungle would be biologically helpless. Only the over-emphasized individualism of our period blinds us to this fact. And as the child grows up into adult manhood, in spite of whatever possibility of asserting his true individuality may exist, the grownup man in the vast majority of cases finds it very uncomfortable not to conform to what society expects of him. As a result he remains controlled by the ubiquitous power of this society and its traditions.

The situation one faces, therefore, as one studies man in his relationship to what contains his physical and psychological-mental existence, has a twofold character. Man, as a biological organism, is contained within the vast planetary field of existence of the Earth; while as a psychological-mental being, as a person, he is contained within a social-cultural field of activities (of thinking-feeling and behavior) with more or less extended boundaries: i.e. a small community, a nation, or at the limit, humanity-as-a-whole.

What we call "education" -- in the widest sense of the term -- in a process according to which a particular man and his mental-emotional-physical activities are being attuned to the needs and the aspirations for progressive changes of his society.

This, I believe, is a very basic definition which clarifies much of the turmoil going on at present in the educational field. This turmoil is occurring because we are in a period of human evolution in which an ever increasing number of men and women -- many young, and not a few older ones -- have come to feel inwardly or to realize mentally that the traditional needs and aspirations of their society, Eastern as well as Western, are obsolescent, if not obsolete and often ludicrous -- perhaps even suicidal.

How did this happen? Simply because human society is today passing from a local to a global state of organization. All cultures up to now have been based exclusively on the characteristics of a "local" environment -- small or extensive as the locality may have been. Even the Mediterranean world of the Roman Empire was a local region with reference to the entire globe. Besides, all societies have operated under a regime of "scarcity." Now for the first time abundance is possible for every human being, but possible ONLY if mankind is organized on a global scale even though local ethnic and regional groups retain their root-individuality, becoming as it were the extended "family-groups" of cultural communities of the future -- an important point I believe. However, the moment we extend the concept of "society" to include all human beings, thus mankind as a whole, something is bound to happen. The container of man at the b i o l o g i c a l level (i. c. thc planct, Earth) becomes identical in scope with the container of human persons at the p s y c h o - m e n t a l level (i. e. a worldwide global society). The relationship between a man and the Earth as a planetary whole therefore becomes all-embracing. Humanity begins to see itself as one complex system of activities within the total field of existence of the Earth -- perhaps, we might say, as the voluntary-nervous system (brain and spinal nerves) of the planetary "organism," the Earth. This is made more evident as it becomes more possible for individual men to look at our planet f r o m t h e o u t s i d e, thus objectively -- just as a doctor looks at a human body, analyzing its complex structures.

What has this to do with the nature of knowledge? A great deal indeed; for the man who can think of himself and feel himself as a functioning existential unit in the vast body of the Earth in which all men "live, move and have their being," this man can come to experience vividly his relationship with this planetary Whole in a super-social, indeed a "spiritual" sense.

At the tribal level of social organization man was bound by local life-circumstances and local needs. His aspirations were moulded by a religon stressing local symbols and the power of gods identified exclusively with the tribal community and its ancestral past, and also with the land cultivated by this community. The spiritual was a transcendent expression of the biological, based on a "psychic" attunement with these gods which were identified with race, land and tradition. Knowledge was acquired through such a psychic attunement. What spoke to the medicine man of the tribe was the "divine" Power that structured the very way of life of the tribe through almost unceasing rituals. It was structural knowledge as a psychic attunement to the will of the tribal gods. And this is the level of knowledge which represents the THESIS of which we spoke earlier.

The ANTITHESIS developed with the sense of individuality and the preoccupations and claims of the human ego. Tribal gods, expressions of local needs and aspirations, vanished --yet often to reappear in the Christian world in the form of "saints" and "archangels"! The "one God" answered the needs and aspirations of isolated individual egos no longer able to enter into and still less to maintain total psychic relationships with other egos, and therefore longing for a "dialogue" with a divine Comforter and Redeemer. In such a state of consciousness, unidentified with anything at the deeper psychic level except in terms of the peculiar and subordinate relationships of creature to Creator, the mind of man was compelled to seek evidence of a structural order in the world of his sense-perceptions. He was compelled to break up the immediate intuition of order -- so vivid in the primitive because so necessary to his inner security -- into knowledge of a multiplicity of laws of nature. While he sought to experience love and emotional-spiritual comfort inwardly through his faith in, and his moments of communion with, the "divine Other," he strove at the same time -- and the more intensely he did so the less did he come to believe in the Presence of God -- to find security of mind and the satisfaction of his ego-will in a knowledge of physical laws. The use of that knowledge in terms of technological skill, moreover, enabled him to satisfy his ambition -- a tragic ambition because alienated from everything beside its own ego-limitations.

Now however the hour of the SYNTHESIS is coming: Man and the Earth -- Man as component part of this vast field of activities, the planet, within which the Principle of Wholeness, ONE, operates, as it does as well in every human being and every existential whole -- Man and the Eon -- Man "resonating" to the vast cyclic rhythms of the Eon, Man with an eonic consciousness. A new type of structural knowledge is now possible. In a new sense, a concrete and far less mysterious sense, we are able to speak of "revelation"; indeed, of the possibility of a constant state of revelation, i. e. of "eonic" consciousness.

Such an eonic consciousness should undoubtedly not be considered an entirely new development. Great creative and inspired minds as well as true seers and prophets have experienced moments of eonic consciousness in which their individual minds, being brought to a condition of "resonance" to the planetary Mind of the greater whole, the Eon, were able to partake of a knowledge which was "transcendent" only in the sense that it belongs to a far more inclusive existential whole -- the Earth, as a multi-leveled field of activities.

The reader may react to such statements by thinking that I am merely substituting the word, Eon, for the word, God. But so to think is to miss the most fundamental point in the cyclocosmic picture of reality. Here the term, Eon, does not apply to our planet only or to any particular macrocosmic whole. An individual human being is an Eon to the consciousness of the cells of his body. The solar system and the galaxy can be seen as each having its Eon. As there is a "hierarchy" of existential wholes, so there is a hierarchy of wholes of consciousness. All that is stated here is that the consciousness of any "lesser whole" can, under certain conditions and in certain phases of its evolution, resonate to the consciousness of the "greater whole" within which it has its being and, as a result, in the vast activities of which it to some extent participates. In such moments of "resonance" man reaches a state of eonic consciousness which to him seems transcendent and supernormal, yet which is transcendent only in the sense that it partakes reflectively of the consciousness which is normal for the Eon. A communication is then established between the consciousness of the greater whole and that of the lesser whole. The sensitive, open and attuned individual is inspired; he "sees"; he may receive a "revelation."

Such a state of communication may arise spontaneously and unexpectedly in the lesser whole, caused by the focusing of the greater whole's attention upon a lesser whole occupying a position which is particularly important -- and perhaps vulnerable -- for the welfare of the greater whole. Then the lesser whole becomes, as it were, the "agent" of the greater whole, and thus in some degree (and there are evidently many such possible degrees) an "avatar" of the Eon.

The lesser whole (man-the-individual-person) can also reach a stage in his development at which his consciousness even in its everyday functioning becomes holistic. That is to say, man may reach, naturally and through his own efforts, a state of consciousness which refers to the "synthesis" phase of the evolution of human consciousness. He may be able, when faced by any life-situation, to perceive it in its wholeness -- thus holistically rather than analytically (in terms of intellectual concepts) or emotionally (in terms of uncontrolled organic reactions or of precedent feeling-responses).

THE PROBLEM OF CLAIRVOYANCE

Such a holistic perception can manifest as what is usually called "clairvoyance." The truly clairvoyant person when faced with a stressful situation -- either one in his own life or one brought to him for elucidation by friends or clients --

"sees" some kind of symbolic image or scene which somehow reveals (it is thus a form of revelatory knowledge) the character, meaning and perhaps the outcome of this situation. The problem however which the clairvoyant faces is how to interpret the symbolic picture or scene or (if a certain type of "clairaudience" is involved) the often ambiguous statements which register in his brain-centers as words seemingly heard by the ears. This is the problem which often makes the "messages" of clairvoyants, and of the "oracles" of ancient times, so confusing, if not misleading.

This problem arises, at the level of the usual type of modern clairvoyance as well as at that of ancient oracles, because of the fact that what is involved in the process does not as yet actually refer to the level of "synthesis," but is still at the level of the "thesis"; that is to say, the faculty which operates in these cases is essentially "archaic," and a symptom of psychic passivity to "the passing" aspect of time. It is not founded upon a consciousness able to apprehend the wholeness of a cycle from beginning to end -- which is what an eonic consciousness should do. Only in an Eon does this kind of consciousness fully and actively operate; but a human mind can either reflect it or resonate to it. Any lesser whole -- when sufficiently evolved, open and responsive -- should be able to reflect or resonate to at least partial or fragmentary aspects of the consciousness of the greater whole in the cyclic activities in which it participates.

What is involved is a problem of communication -- or to use a fashionable term, of "information." Channels of communication have to be evolved if there is to be a truly reliable transfer of knowledge. A mere capacity to "reflect" more or less imprecisely some fleeting aspect of the consciousness of the greater whole is usually uncontrolled and easily unfocused by the ego-reactions ("statics" of consciousness!) of the receiving mind of the "sensitive."

An essential factor in such a matter of communication between greater and lesser wholes is whether or not the communicated knowledge is needed. The attention of the greater whole is drawn to the lesser whole, in most cases, only when the latter has a real need for it; just as a person's attention is drawn to a small section of his body (say, an ingrown toenail or a cut) when this part of his total organism requires help as a result of some crisis-producing event. The idea that the Earth as a total field of activities operating at several levels, i.e. as an Eon, is able under certain circumstances to affect the life of one of the organisms which are active within this field should be no more strange or startling than the fact that a human body immediately sends antibodies to one of its fingers when it has received a deep cut through which infection-causing microbes could enter and infect the whole body.

Such an idea is startling only to minds that have never thought or that refuse to think, of the possibility that the Earth is an organized whole of existence every part of which is related to, and thus able to injure, every other part. Such a thought runs counter to the concept, deeply ingrained in our Western mentality, that man is a totally special creature -- the only creature made in the likeness of God, Creator of all that is. But what pride such a concept reveals! We can assume that only man has what Teilhard de Chardin calls "reflective consciousness," and thus that perhaps only he among all living organisms on this Earth can develop an eonic consciousness. In this sense man is potentially "God-like" in his consciousness; but this does not mean that the Earth-as-a-whole, of which mankind is only a constituent part, does not have consciousness of a planetary type, provided we do not think of the Earth as only a mass of material substances. This planetary type of consciousness includes the normal consciousness of humanity; but there is no reason to believe that it does not include as well other types of consciousness, and perhaps the consciousness of forms of existence of which man is not normally aware today.

Indeed the only obstacle to such a type of concept is Western man's exclusive dependence upon sense-based knowledge and upon a set of dogmatic assumptions which characterize his official culture -- not to mention his neurotic desire to isolate himself from a universe felt to be alien, just to satisfy his remarkable pride which is primarily a disguised sense of anxiety and guilt. The realization that such dependence is not exclusively valid is beginning to percolate into the minds of some scientists and "free" thinkers, and the interest in parapsychology is a symptom of an impending "change of "mind -- a m e t a n o i a, to use the Gospel's term so badly translated as "repentance."

The concept of statistical knowledge which is now so basic in modern physics may also have much bearing on an appreciation of what I call "structural" knowledge in contrast to "existential" knowledge, as this structural knowledge deals with cyclic processes which affect the behavior of wholes rather than that of individual parts.

THE STRUCTURAL CHARACTER OF PROPHECIES AND MAN'S FREE WILL

The basic point here is that while a greater whole experiences its own existence in relation to other existents at the same level of wholeness in e x i s t e n t i a l terms, its approach to the lesser wholes which participate in its "inner" life is, in most though not all cases s t r u c t u r a l.

For instance a human being is conscious of the organs and cells within his body mainly in terms of the over-all rhythm of their functions, except in unusual instances. A man pays attention to his digestion, his blood-pressure and heartbeats, his sexual responses and potency, but not to how a particular cell of his liver, of his heart or of his testicle behaves. Even an entire organ, like the pancreas or the thyroid, draws the man's attention only when the o v e r - a l l f u n c t i o n i n g of all his organs in their interdependence and "polyphonic" interplay has become disharmonic. This knowl-

edge which man has of the rhythmic and polyphonic interplay
of the basic functional systems of his body is a "structural"
type of knowledge. It deals with the balance of anabolic and
catabolic activities in the body; and if the catabolic functions
prevail -- which, let us not forget, in themselves contribute
to the health or wholeness of the body -- then a danger sig-
nal begins to operate which draws the attention of the man
and should impel him to "take a cure" of some kind.

Any knowledge of the balance of two operative tendencies
is, in a more or less instinctive or sophisticated sense,
"statistical." So many "units of action" operate in one way,
so many in another, more or less opposite and complementary. The knowledge acquired can be formulated in terms of
percentages; it is the type of knowledge obtained from computers operating in a binary manner, and as well from popular political or economic "polls." Such knowledge is valid
only in an investigation of large numbers of units or at least,
as in the Gallup polls, in relation to units which can be considered representative of a large class or segment of the
population. Medical blood-tests and the like also provide
this kind of statistical knowledge; they deal with large numbers of cells, bacteria, viruses, etc. They become significant in relation to averages carefully determined through
many observations and samplings.

Now let us consider this Biblical statement (Zechariah
13: verses 8 and 9): "... in all the land, saith the Lord, two
parts therein shall be cut off and die; but the third shall be
left therein. And I will bring the third part through the fire,
and will refine them as silver is refined, and will try them
as gold is tried..."

What such a statement should indicate to anyone considering it as a true and reliable "revelation" made by God to
his prophet is that God is not concerned with individual
persons but only with statistical averages, i.e. with initiat-
ing and/or maintaining a certain structural process-- a third

will be saved, two-thirds destroyed. It is like saying: When autumn begins, so many seeds will have been produced which have in them the potentiality of surviving the winter and of giving birth to a subsequent cycle of vegetation -- and so many leaves, which will fall and decay in order to become manure for the new vegetation. Whether an individual person will join the third which will be saved and tested (successfully or not -- let us not forget!), or the two-thirds which will be lost, appears to be of no concern to "the Lord."

What this "Lord" -- who can here be considered as the Eon, the personalized aspect of some planetary or cosmic greater whole -- is interested in is the over-all structure of a process involving large numbers. The atomic physicist uses a similar type of structural knowledge when he ascertains that so many electrons will go one way, and so many the other. He is not really interested in finding out -- nor could he apparently do so-- what course one particular electron will choose to adopt. Modern physics has given up the idea of tracking down what "substance" really is; it is satisfied to study the structure of large groups of events.

These are very important facts wherever one can be sure of their validity, for when generalized they give us a fundamental picture not only of the universal process of existence, but of what we may have to understand by the confusing terms "freedom" and "determinism." If the Biblical statement truly refers to a basic fact of existence in terms of the over-all destiny of such groups of human beings as tribal communities or modern nations, then we can logically conclude that man operates not only in terms of statistical determinism, but also in terms of existential freedom. Considered in the collective sense as mankind, Man's behavior and choices are determined, in broad structural outlines, by the very rhythm of the process of evolution of the entire planet, Earth. But a particular man is existentially free to choose what he will belong to, i.e. to determine freely and selectively the type of allegiance he will accept or seek.

A planetary "Lord," ruler of the Earth's system of organized activities -- of men, beasts and plants; of seasons, winds and earthquakes, etc. -- may enter into existential relationships with other planetary Lords, as the Ancients indeed believed, because They operate at the same level in the vast scale of cosmic magnitudes. But in His relationship to these "lesser wholes" which men represent to Him -- as cells in His total field of existence -- this Lord would normally think in terms of structural knowledge. An exception might be in rare cases where perhaps one particular man occupies a position of control over far-reaching possibilities of development; for instance, perhaps if this individual man were the President of the U.S. and able to press a button which would initiate a nuclear holocaust and thus possibly a "fatal" crisis for mankind and the entire biosphere.

The consequence of all this presents much interest and a real challenge to individuals; for it if is possible for an individual human consciousness to "reflect" some aspect of the consciousness of the greater planetary whole, the Eon, it is most likely that what would be reflected is the structural aspect of that Eonic consciousness. The existential aspect, involving the relationship of this Eon to other Eons, would almost necessarily be totally beyond man's possibility of understanding. If therefore there are elements of existential knowledge in the "revelations" bestowed by the Eon (the greater whole) upon a sensitive and well-attuned man (the lesser whole), it is indeed most probable that these would be added to the true and pure "communication" by the consciousness and the feeling-nature of the human recipient. This would account for the unreliability of so many of such communications.

As to the difficulty of accurately dating the ambiguous prophecies of seers and oracles, it is evidently caused by two different factors:

(1) If a "day of the Lord" equals a thousand years defined

for man by the rhythm of the seasons -- and in ancient symbolism the term "thousand" should rather be translated as a "myriad," or a near-infinity -- then it may be difficult for the inspired seer or prophet to pass accurately from one time-scale to another.

(2) Moreover, and this is probably the most basic point, if the "communication" refers to existential facts in the life of an individual person or of a relatively small group, whatever is imparted to the seer or sensitive is always subject to the unpredictability associated with the factor of existential relatedness. In other words, the clairvoyant may symbolically perceive a structural trend or a statistical possibility; and this is what he would directly receive from the eonic level of consciousness -- a structural factor. But this kind of perception would not actually refer to an existential event or series of events. The existential data would be provided by the human consciousness of the recipient of the communication, and might be colored by personal biases, expectations or wishes.

Nevertheless if a genuine state of resonance is induced between the eonic and the normally human levels of consciousness, because a certain event which could occur within one human year may actually occur in a few minutes according to the eonic time-scale, this event may be entirely expectable in terms of eonic consciousness; yet it is presumably not determined. We can be fairly certain in most cases of what will happen to us within a few minutes; but these few minutes could constitute a large part of the life-span of some microscopic particle. A prophet may predict that a cataclysmic earthquake can be expected in fifty years or it could be one hundred years -- a greatly annoying uncertainty! But the Earth-as-a-whole, whose life-span is of billions of years in contrast to our 70 or 80 years of human life, may already register in its body at the human time of the prediction the very first tremor of the quake.

The relativity of the experience of time in terms of the

time-scale of wholes whose spatial dimensions and spans of existence vary from the microcosmic to the macrocosmic should be an absolutely basic factor in discussions concerning the nature of knowledge the moment we accept the possibility of communication, in one form or another, between greater and lesser wholes. But if we do not accept such a possibility we are confronted with even more baffling problems which can only be given transcendental or miraculous interpretations and solutions. Religious beliefs and dogmas, and as well basic scientific assumptions usually left unquestioned, have tried to solve these problems in a great variety of ways. But all these complexities can be resolved into a fundamental simplicity if one accepts the holistic cyclocosmic picture presented here. Of course this picture represents a bold generalization of the facts of human experience, but so are theism and Einstein's Theory of Relativity bold generalizations. The essential point, as we shall see later on, is not whether such world-pictures are "true" in an absolute sense, but whether they are v a l u a b l e -- and valuable for a particular phase of the evolutionary process of man's consciousness.

Because mankind has quite evidently reached a point in its evolution at which a trend toward synthesis of knowledge is inevitable in view of the rapid development of a world-wide mentality and globally interrelated social-cultural activities, some kind of framework for these efforts toward synthesis has to be formulated. It could be, of course, a totalitarian type of synthesis which would increasingly exclude what does not fit a glorified "Science" and an all-powerful scientific and technocratic Establishment. But this certainly does not appear to be a desirable prospect, camouflaged as its motives may be by such imposing words as "democracy," "free enquiry," etc.

To speak of "unity in diversity" is to utter beautifully sounding words; but the question is: How? There has to be some kind of integrative principle to reveal the manner in which diverse attitudes to life and approaches to knowledge c a n be seen to constitute a "unity" -- which actually means a whole. The cyclocosmic concepts constitute such a framework, because to the mind that accepts such a framework, every diverse manifestation of human consciousness, every form of mind, every social, cultural and religious system can be seen to FIT in its proper place and accomplishes its valid function during one particular phase or at a specific level of the entire cycle of human evolution. Moreover as the cycles of human civilization do not all run at the same time and with the same speed or rhythm, and as there are sub-cycles and sub-sub-cycles within the larger cycles, it follows that what is eminently valuable in a certain culture may also awaken significant and valid resonances in other cultures having related problems, perhaps at other levels and in terms of different environments.

I said "valuable," but this also means "true"; knowledge is true, in the deepest sense of the term, o n l y when it is valuable. Knowledge has value in terms of the relation between the knower and the known. Prematurely disclosed knowledge can be deadly to the knower, or at least a source of great confusion. Our wild proliferation of intellectual and technological knowledge may well bring about man's ruin for a time. Yet the rationalistic and scientific approach to knowledge, whether in the Greece of the sixth century B. C. or at the time of the early Renaissance in Europe, was a valuable approach because it was n e e d e d at the time. But the satisfaction of an evolutionary need quite often becomes a form of self-indulgence; the originally constructive trend can become uncontrollable and gain a dangerous momentum as it becomes "institutionalized" -- and all institutions and bureaucracies develop an unwholesome inertia. They have to become neutralized by complementary new trends against which they of course often fight bitterly.

Still, because the more inert mass of human beings is slow in reaching new levels of consciousness, the old "truths" and the institutions which crystallized them into dogmas may still be valuable for the mass-mind. Einstein's Theory and his fateful formula $E=MC^2$ which inspired the atom bomb project came at its "time of destiny" in the cycle of our Western civilization which still dominates human evolution as a whole. But the New Physics with its almost mystical world-view in which material objects are dissolved into waves of energy and light in multi-dimensional space-time, has not yet thoroughly changed the mentality of low-level materialistic science, nor been re-interpreted at the psychological and metaphysical levels; and the masses of humanity, even though worshipping science and technological achievements (such as the landing on the moon), are still powerfully involved in nearly medievalistic fights between political and religious ideologies.

NOW-FEELING AND CYCLIC KNOWLEDGE

I want to make it clear, however, that by applying a formula of cyclic unfoldment one cannot expect to experience directly, as an inevitable result, the unique quality of a particular process of existence itself; any more than Einstein could have been expected to have an actual "feeling" of atomic power when he conceived his formula. To bring experiences into a meaningful order does not mean to have these experiences actually and personally. Two factors in man's consciousness are here implied: the experience, in its immediacy of feeling or realization; and the ability to make sense of the experience by relating it to other experiences and to the needs of the whole person and, perhaps, of other persons with whom one is associated. The experience as such is simply what it is; it is subjective, private and in itself essentially uncommunicable though, if it is a great experience, one may communicate something of its energy-release, its dynamism or tragic intensity, by means of a person-to-person transfer.

However, the experience does not just happen and then is no more. It is remembered; it is formulated, to oneself if not to others. Thus words and concepts must be used; and these imply relationship to a culture, a tradition, etc. -- and perhaps a resulting sense of conflict or irreconcilability with the past, and all kinds of secondary psychological by-products. It is then that the concept of cycle reveals its value; for the mind of the individual and its complex mechanisms, always subject to pressures from the ego and the emotions, have to come into the picture. They tend to remove the experience from the natural process of existence and thus to isolate it, to make of it a "thing in itself."

At first, in the case of an inner experience which reveals a previously unknown reality, doubts may well arise -- a feeling of "What was it, after all?" In many cases a typical reaction follows: an upwelling self-assertive sense of "It was true" (i.e. a fact and not an illusion). If then the experiencer finds himself confronted with the disbelief of others or their seemingly emotional and egocentric opposition, the assertion that it was "true" acquires in him a fighting strength -- unless he allows himself to be "brain-washed" by his entourage! But this very strength changes the memory of the experience. The experience and what it brought to the consciousness may well cease to be regarded as only one phase of the existential process of actualization of the innate potential of the individual; it acquires a separated, exclusivistic and psychically "inflated" status -- or, if the post-reaction has been negative, a process of subtle self-destruction often begins at the subconscious level.

The value of applying the principle of cyclic unfoldment to psychology and to an interpretation of individual experience is that it is an effort to integrate (or re-integrate) the many components of personality and the elements of the experience in the whole process of individual existence. When we speak ordinarily of self, or soul, or ego, or of any "complex," we tend unfortunately to separate and to isolate these, and very often we personify them; we say "my soul," "my ego," as if these were the very distinct possessions of a mysterious "I" which, nevertheless, can in no way be pinned down, and which only a very transcendental explanation may imprecisely define. Also when we think of some memorable event, happy or distressing, in our life, it seems quite "normally" to stand all by itself as an event which has "happened" to "me," yet which is somehow unconnected with and independent of the process of existence which reaches consciousness as this "me."

The cyclic or "eonistic" approach seeks to discover the place which the event occupies in the overall pattern assumed by the rhythmic flow of existence with reference to that particular person who says "I." It studies the event as a phase of a sub-cycle of the large cycle of personality -- as a phase of personality growth rather than as an isolated event. Moreover this approach seeks to define and understand the function of the various components of personality in the individualized whole of existence which, for instance, carries the name, Peter. By so doing it removes some of the psychological terms, which still carry a certain halo of religious-occult meaning, from the realm of more or less transcendent mystery. It makes them more existentially real, even though their reality can only be e x p e r i e n c e d in many cases through the play of faculties or powers of consciousness which are still mostly latent or barely developing in most contemporary individuals.

The eonistic approach is not necessarily a help in experiencing with an immediacy of feeling these still mysterious components of man's total being; but, when properly used, it should be of immense value in indicating where the experience fits and what its meaning is a f t e r one has this experience. For it is after the experience that the mind and the ego get hold of its imprints in the consciousness and begin to i n t e r p r e t or formulate, according to cultural and traditional Images, whatever change or new realization has taken place. The subtle (or not so subtle) desire of the ego for increased self-assurance and prestige can indeed be another factor in the interpretation.

In other words, the eonistic approach deals with the structure of the process of personality-unfoldment -- the form which the experiences assume when they are seen as integral factors in this process. The contents of the experiences, the "feel" of personality or of cosmic impersonality, the elation of the "I am" proclamation or the sense of being one with the universe -- these remain untouched, directly and in themselves, by such an approach. Yet the eonistic approach can also most definitely induce many experiences of extreme validity, for it predisposes the mind to respond to unusual impacts and distant influences which otherwise it would not have been able to accept. The experiences it induces tend to be very quiet and very simple, for they are unemotional and by nature inclusive and essentially compassionate. They emerge from the fulfillment of relationships serenely met as encounters induced by cyclic necessity.

The so-called "mystical" approaches may well lead to effulgent experiences of great intensity and power -- experiences which may mean a sudden reshaping of the consciousness, a brilliant illumination of the mind. But the problem they always pose is: "Yes, wonderful -- but what now?" Human confusion and psychological tragedy all too often come as the aftermath of the exalted and transforming experience; for once the light has vanished, darkness seems more intense.

Granted the experience has done something to you, what will you do with the results of the experience, the memory of it? Unless you see it as an integral and recognizable phase of the cycle of your individual unfoldment, unless you can meaningfully situate the elements of the experience and the factors in you which it has affected, the danger that it may greatly unbalance you will always be there, and especially the danger that it may subtly feed or inflate the ego or else dissolve it into a formless kind of psychological "ectoplasm" susceptible of being pressured into elusive and fundamentally meaningless shapes.

This danger is particularly real today, as the normal collective restraints of old traditions are being shattered by the pressures of a massive expansion of man's field of activity which has rendered obsolete so much that constituted the foundation of our sense of order. Modern man eagerly wants to experience directly, existentially, all that now confronts him; he wants to play with the tremendous new energies his intellect and his collectivized scientific mentality have released. The great problem is, thus, for him to discover what it is in him that provides a secure foundation for his existence, for his individual experiencing of a more than ever bewildering reality -- bewildering because the old patterns of steady relatedness have broken down. The problem is to understand what in him can safely and constructively use this new power. It is to realize that his ego is neither a secure foundation nor a reliable user of power of planetary or cosmic magnitude; and to discover, then to attune his consciousness and his capacity for response to the challenges of his actual personal existence, to his "fundamental nature," his self -- and beyond this self to the Soul-field, and still beyond that to the vast Mind of humanity and the total field of existence of Man and of the Earth.

"Attunement" is always the key to the most basic type of knowledge. In the ancient past man attuned his consciousness to the great rhythms of universal Life through the intermediary of a mind, either passively and naively reflecting the cyclic play of the seasonal life as it was revealed in his local environment, or totally conditioned by a rigid psychic-occult tradition. Later on man tried to grasp by intellectual-rational means the "laws" of the universe in an objective and formalized scientific manner. But beyond such an intellectual and quantitative-statistical approach, and by reawakening some of the lost capacities of his earlier evolution, man may now begin to attain a new, more truly conscious state of resonance to "That," in the field of existence of which he participates.

Man may "know" beyond mere cogitating and rationalizing; he may "see," feel, respond to the great planetary and cosmic Play of forces and powers, and vibrate to the everlasting, though ever-transformed Harmony of existence. That Harmony he had lost -- but only to regain it in a truly conscious and participatory sense; not merely in terms of the world of Nature, of materiality and life, but as a direct experience of his divine Source and of the Principle of Wholeness whose presence illumines his total being as well as the universal Whole.

IX. SYMBOLS AND VALUES

In the preceding chapters I have stressed the fundamental importance of the concept of the cycle, a concept which gives universal scope and meaning to the order and periodicity which we find inherent in existence the moment we consider it objectively. I have defined time as a function of cyclic evolution through which what is potential in the release of an original creative impulse gradually becomes more differentiated and complex through a twofold process of actualization of latent relationships. In the beginning of the cycle the release of energy and structural potentialities, of power and basic forms of existence, operates compulsively; but throughout the long process of differentiation, specialization and refinement, and under the influence of unceasing interexistential relationships, consciousness takes ever more definite forms in progressively more complex and more individually structured minds.

The individualization of consciousness occurs under the direction of individual egos which in turn are moulded by the intellectual and cultural structures of the society in which they take particular forms. As much of the time the ego does not succeed in emerging from these collective matricial structures it is impossible for it to evaluate them objectively. The ego remains mostly their creature, passively taking them for granted. As long as this is the case and as long as the ego controls the totality, or near-totality, of the conscious reactions of a human being -- his modes of thinking, his everyday feeling-responses and his customary behavior -- this human being can hardly be considered an autonomous individual. He is merely one of the many elements which together constitute a particular community; and this community, small and local or national in scope, is structured by a definite culture, an organized religion, a special type of morality, a certain way of life. These collective structures are essentially related to the special geographical and bio-psychic conditions surrounding their slow growth; and men are not only related to their birth-environment and specific bio-psychical inheritances but they are usually deeply and passionately attached to them. They are proud of these collective roots and fiercely defensive when their validity is questioned.

All forms of established collective behavior and cultural-religious beliefs are structured by groups of symbols; but there are also symbols which refer only to the individual person. Symbols are indeed found in every area of human existence. But what precisely do we mean by this term, symbol, which today is being used perhaps more extensively and ambiguously than at any other time in human history? Directly defining its meaning is not a simple task, because this meaning is so pervasive and the word is used in such varied frames of reference that one can hardly define it without implying by the definition one's basic philosophy.

In terms of the approach to existence which I am presenting in this book, a symbol is the answer given by a person of a community of persons, and in some instances by humanity-as-a-whole, to a group of experiences or situations which, diverse as they may appear when considered individually, yet when seen as a whole reveal an existential need which the evolution of the consciousness of this person or this community demands to be met and satisfied. The need may only be "personal"; the most significant dreams of an individual are symbols answering to his psychological

needs, and in most cases only to the needs of this individual. Most characteristically, however, a symbol is an answer to a collective need; it provides, at least potentially, the
solution to a problem affecting at least a section of humanity
or a certain type of human being. This solution is more or
less essential to the well-being of this group; it is communicable and it elicits a reaction from the community, whether
it be in the area of religion, of culture, or of socio-political
and economic behavior.

Let us take the image of the Buddha in his characteristic
posture of meditation, an image reproduced in Asia many
millions of times throughout the last twenty centuries. This
image is based upon the actions and the weltanschauung
or attitude to life of a particular person, Gautama; but the
immense and lasting influence of such a personage can only
be explained, from an existential point of view, by the fact
that Gautama focused and embodied in his personality and in
his radiance of spirit an essential answer to the collective
need of the Asiatic people. The image of the meditating Buddha came to represent at a certain time in the evolution of
these people the ultimate solution to the problem of human
existence.

The Christian crucifix is likewise the symbol of an existential attitude which the people of the Western world
believed, and many still believe, to be a fundamental answer
to the "human condition" as they understood and deeply felt
its nature at the time -- that is, as a temporal and im-
permanent state of crisis which could only be successfully
and significantly met by means of a total sacrifice, thanks to
which, and to it alone, man could experience a transcendent
resurrection in the "other world," the realm of pure spirit.
The Mediterranean people at the beginning of the Christian
era evidently needed such a solution; and Jesus' life became transformed into a symbol pointing to the possibility of
satisfying this need. This life was made into a mythos. It
was "imitated" and reproduced an infinite number of times

by and for the members of the Catholic and Orthodox Churches
under the abstract form of the ritual of the Mass, and also
in various rites and festivals of the liturgical year.

A symbol is an abstraction in the sense that it is an image, or a sequence of images and actions, drawn out, i. e.
ab-stracted, from a certain number of actual facts which are
or have been essential parts of the lives of human beings.
Here however we have to use the word "image" in its broadest sense. Some symbols appear to be entirely intellectual
images or concepts; nevertheless they are made up of elements which once were abstractions of human experiences
and feeling-responses. In the origin of words, and even in
the letters of our alphabet and the shapes of our numbers,
we can find forms which, long ago, referred to existential
activities and images. We have forgotten these archaic connections, just as we have forgotten the onomatopoeic origin
of the basic words used in ancient tongues, or even the relationship existing between the sounds of vowels and consonants
and certain bio-psychic structures of the human organism;
nevertheless these connections between what now appear to
be purely conventional "signs" and original human experiences are often not only real but most revealing.

A language should be considered as a complex group of
symbols inasmuch as, with its special words and forms of
syntax, it answers to a basic need of humanity: the need for
communication. The algebraic formulas used in modern
chemistry, mathematics and physics are likewise definite
answers to the need, not only to communicate precise forms
of knowledge from generation to generation, but more generally still, to establish on solid and secure foundations a
sense of the order inherent in all existence; and man must
have such a sense of order if he is to retain his sanity. All
human cultures are means of conveying to particular types
of human beings a specific feeling and intellectual realization
that they live in a world of order.

I stated that the symbol is an abstraction in the sense

that it is an image, or a sequence of images and actions, "drawn out" from a certain number of actual facts which are or have been essential components of human experience. As the term, abstraction, is susceptible of various interpretations, let us try to see clearly in what way symbols differ from facts.

A fact is what it is particularly and exclusively as a fact; it can be described and recorded in such a manner that, at least theoretically speaking, its precise character is not open to doubt. That is to say, everyone fulfilling the specific conditions required for the perception of this particular fact can identify it from its description.

When the geometrician draws a circle on paper he sees in it the exteriorization of the relationship between a central point and the mathematical locus constituted by an infinity of other points which together make up the circumference of the circle. When one reads the exact technical description of a series of operations needed for the construction of a machine, these operations have a strictly objective character and may be repeated identically forever. In a sense we might also say that "facts" belong to the category of rational entities: these entities can be precisely defined inasmuch as the definition implies all that they are not -- that is, the definition essentially excludes other conceptual entities.

On the other hand when one deals with a symbol one is in the presence of something that goes beyond the rational and the factual, something that is more than it is, because the symbol describes not only what it appears to be rationally and objectively, but also the relationship between a specific human need and the possibility of satisfying this need.

When in an ancient magical ritual the performer of the rite traced a circle around himself with a spear or a sword, this action had a symbolical character. The magician did not think of the geometrical and rationalistic formula defining the relationship between the radius and the circumference; instead he focused the energy of his life-force and his will upon a psychological and "magical" process of isolation, of psychic protection and integration. Also if a Catholic or a Buddhist believer contemplates the golden halos around the heads of saints or buddhas, he is not impressed by the geometrical character of these circular forms, but he is deeply and emotionally moved by the greatness and radiant purity of the state of sanctity symbolized by such a halo. Likewise when a priest celebrates mass, his gestures have a quality and a carrying power essentially different from those of a workingman putting together the parts of an automobile's engine. The priest's gestures are symbolic because they evoke a r e s o n a n c e in the innermost being of those who believe in their ritualistic efficacy and in the value to humanity of the ancient facts evoked and perpetuated by these gestures. His actions are symbolic because they are an answer to the psychological need which is one of the dominant features of the particular phase of human evolution which is represented by the Christian era.

The same thing could be said of any truly religious symbol, be it archaic or modern. An image or gesture, a consecrated object or sacred ritual, are symbols for men who feel themselves fundamentally related to the culture which produced these symbols, and who resonate to the basic rhythm of the evolution of humanity as a whole; the symbol relates a vast number of living human beings to a particular phase of the cyclic process of unfoldment of both mankind and the planet, Earth. Thus the symbol has b o t h an existential aspect -- because it moves human minds and souls; and a structural aspect -- because it identifies the need arising from a particular phase of the evolutionary cycle.

As a s t r u c t u r a l f a c t o r, the symbol has an objective and predictable character; it concretizes a value characterizing a particular and inevitable phase of the cycle. It represents a particular way in which the human species becomes conscious of activities and events which it must experience during a specific era. The meditating Buddha and the crucified Christ symbols not only express but may also initiate or intensify two different modes of feeling and of becoming aware of the basic meaning of the relationship between man and his earthly life. Each corresponds to a specific historical period and to a specific state of development of the collective evolution of man's consciousness. This evolution proceeds according to a cyclic and dialectical rhythm; it proceeds in different ways, in different earth-localities which give rise to different cultures.

Yet symbols have a strictly existential aspect for they can be referred to an immense variety of personal experiences and situations vivid with an immediacy of feeling. The symbol evokes a response yet does not limit or actually predetermine it. It cannot be considered an element in rationalistic thinking because it goes beyond such a type of thinking. It cannot impose upon the persons emotionally moved by its contemplation strictly defined forms of behavior or feeling-response. The symbol refers rather to the potentiality of collective or personal reactions to a category of situations which have some essential features in common, yet which can lead to existential results at one of several levels of consciousness and variously affect diverse types of human beings.

A symbol gives us no strictly particular information concerning the events to which it may give a decisive initial push. It can refer to a cosmic process, to a social or religious activity or a drama of consciousness and a personal crisis, or to an organic function of the human body. Moreover it may either operate or not, for its transforming influence depends not only on the fact that it answers to an essential need in the development of human consciousness, but just as much on the capacity of human beings to react and respond to what it brings to their attention, whether this reaction is conscious or not. The symbol releases a potential of evolutionary transformation, of emotional and intellectual dynamism; but nothing warrants that this potential will be factually, existentially actualized. Likewise the character and quality of this actualization is not defined by the symbol, it is conditioned by the nature of the individual and collective response of human beings. The royal crown and scepter are symbols of authority and of social power, but they do not define the character of this or that king who uses them, or the loyalty and respect of his subjects. These symbolic and "sacred" objects express the structure of the activities derived from the relationship.

When one says that a symbol has to be "interpreted" it means that one has to ascertain the existential contents which fill the structural container, the symbol. The symbol relates him who contemplates it, physically or intellectually, to a vast possibility of activities or events which are evidently of concern to this person so long as he is moved, physically or emotionally, by what emanates from the symbol. To discover the meaning of the symbol is to discover what in the nature of the onlooker has need of the potentiality of action or understanding implied in the symbol. For instance, to discover the meaning of a dream which has made a deep impression is to come into existential contact with the structure of events which will help the actualization of that which in the psyche was thus far only unconscious potentiality, but a potentiality dynamized by the deep movement for personal fulfillment inherent in the self of the person.

Likewise after his experience on the road to Damascus, for Paul to interpret such a subjective experience meant for him to understand the profound meaning of the Christ symbol, and to see in it an answer to the fundamental need not only of this Saul shaken as a person by this "revelation," but of a vast category of human beings then in an ambiguous psychological state resulting from the conflict between the values of the old Mediterranean world and those of a universal civilization which the Roman empire was making possible. This Hebrew who was also a Roman citizen might theoretically have considered his experience from a purely existential level and attributed to it very natural or strictly psychological causes; but he referred it to a social and religious situation which reached beyond his own personality while integrating it into a vast historical process. Paul felt himself to be the agent for a potential transformation of humanity at that time. He gave to the Christ of whom he had become intensely conscious -- a Christ who differed greatly indeed from the existential Jesus whose words and very simple actions are recorded in the Gospels -- a structural and historical meaning. He dramatized the life of Jesus and made of it the symbol of a radical crisis indicating the transformation of human consciousness from one state to another. Thanks to him and to the apostles who accepted his vision, this life became a turning point in human evolution. In them the symbol became action and power to act.

Is it "true" that the life of Jesus was the essential turning point in the evolution of human consciousness? From an existential point of view there can be no question of absolute truth. One can nevertheless realize that a turning point in history occurred at the time Jesus lived and one can say that the power to act inherent in this life, when transformed into the symbol and manifestation of new values, gave a basically new character to the collective mentality of large segments of humanity and, at least indirectly, to the entire Mind of Man. In this sense the Christ symbol -- and before it, the Buddha symbol -- should be considered as manifestations of critical phases in the cycle of mankind and of the planet, Earth.

The power of symbols is often immense. It is the very power of the process of human evolution. This power acts through men who condense it and who at the same time extract from the evolutionary crises confronting them new values and symbols which, externalizing these values in striking and moving forms, initiate a process of transformation. Such men constitute the creative elite of mankind; they are the seed-men, the great mutants of humanity.

The concept of the cycle which is at the root of our holistic world-outlook is a symbol; and so is the famous equation discovered by Einstein, $E=MC^2$, and his Theory of Relativity. If I consider this symbol, the cycle, as being eminently valid and indeed essential today, it is because I deeply feel that the idea of the cyclicity of existence and of time constitutes the basic answer to the philosophical, psychological, religious, ethical and social need of our times. This need has reached a point of great intensity because of the conditions in which our present-day humanity lives, and because of the conflicts which it inevitably faces in the process of synthesizing, assimilating and organizing a multitude of traditions within the structures of an all-encompassing global civilization.

Einstein's formula also answered a historical need, even though the use which modern nations are making of this great symbol of the fundamental relation between energy and mass may lead to catastrophy. But, who knows, a civilization may need to destroy itself so that a new quantum of potentiality of human existence may be released. Radioactivity could be tamed by a radically new society, and who can say that the emergence of a new type of human organism may not depend upon a much greater quantity of radioactive elements in the biosphere. Why do we always tend to expect our knowledge to be more or less final, our so-called "laws" to remain forever valid and our little truths to be absolutely true?

TRUTH, VALUE AND SYMBOL

For most people living today, the formulas of modern physics and higher mathematics express structural relations that are unquestionably "true" and reliable representations of existential realities. Yet this "truth" is more apparent and temporary than absolute. Newton's formulas are also true, but we know now that they are true only up to a certain point and under certain conditions. We hardly know what gravitation or even electricity "really" is; our definitions of light are quite ambiguous. Even the most exact sciences imply postulates, of which one cannot say that they are absolutely true.

We can construct non-Euclidian geometries based on the postulate that two parallel lines meet. It is not necessary for us to say that a proposition and its opposite cannot both be true. There may be universes, or even long periods in our universe structured by "laws of nature" different from those we observe today. We claim that the speed of light is a universal constant, that the laws of thermodynamics and the principle of conservation of energy are true. Should we not rather consider them more fundamentally, as did Henri Poincarre, to be "convenient"? They fulfill a function which is to enable us to define our feeling and experience of existential order and periodicity, then to act with confidence so as to achieve relatively certain results in a relatively near future. These laws and principles of structural order have validity. We do not know whether they express "Truth."

This word, truth, has a character of ambiguity to which we should not be blind. According to its current everyday use we may indeed rightly say that it is true that the state of Ghana is in West-Africa; that the sun, late in March, sets exactly in the West, and that the earth is a spheroid. These statements refer to facts which are part of our common human experience; they are "facts" simply because it is possible for any man who fulfills the required conditions of observation and possesses the necessary faculties of perception to experience their factual character. On the other hand, if we deal with our own feelings or inner experiences which other persons are not able to feel or experience -- or at least not as directly and precisely as we experience them because an essential individual factor enters into such interior events -- then the qualificative "true" can only have a relative significance. The same can be said of most metaphysical concepts and of the meaning a person attributes to such ambiguous terms as God, time, soul, mind, etc., for these terms are loaded with emotional and personal overtones.

If I suddenly hear a voice, seemingly originating from a place at the end of my studio, yet I know for a certainty that no one and no instrument is there to produce the sound, and the voice gives me an important message, I cannot honestly say that this experience is true or real in the ordinary sense of the word, for no one is there to share the experience, and no one perhaps would have been able to share it. Nevertheless it is my experience, and no one has any right to contest this fact. The experience may well have an immense value for me; it may answer to a deep need within my personality.

Yet if, having had this experience, I say to a friend that the message constitutes a "revealed truth," this would only cause a semantic confusion in his mind. If he is not, at least theoretically, able to share my experience, it is not true for him; yet it might be very valuable to him. It would be valuable as a symbol, that is as an answer to a need which my friend and I have in common. We have the same need, but the event which contains an answer to this need is an experience only for me; for my friend it is a symbol. I cannot actually communicate the experience; as soon as I formulate or in any way exteriorize it, it becomes for those who learn about it either merely an interesting event or a deeply moving symbol.

What Paul related that he experienced on the road to Damascus cannot be said to be "true" as a fact; yet all men feeling psychologically and morally related to Paul and to his state of consciousness at the moment of his cathartic experience may rightly consider Paul's vision and its consequences as a symbol deeply affecting their innermost being. The same thing could be said of Moses' experience on Mount Sinai, or of the Buddha's attainment of Nirvana under the bodhi tree, or of the revelation received by the great Persian prophet Baha'u'llah while chained to criminals at the bottom of a horrible airless cistern -- the revelation of his mission as a "divine Manifestation." The radiance released by such transfiguring experiences has changed the lives and minds of millions of human beings; yet, existentially speaking, one cannot assert that they were "true."

Nevertheless, such types of experiences occurring at the beginning of important historical periods actually represent essential phases in the cyclic process of the evolution of human consciousness. From the point of view of the s t r u c - t u r e of this process, and when considered by a mind able to perceive this eonic process as a whole, the experiences of great historical personages have a profound meaning and value; they, and the modes of cognition they exemplify, have a structural value. They exist -- which is the existential way of saying s u b   s p e c i e s   e t e r n i t a t i s ! -- as a function of the cyclic order of the evolution of Man's consciousness. These experiences represent successively actualized aspects of Man's original potential. To the individual person having these experiences they have an irrefutable existential character; but, I repeat, to the disciples and the millions of believers who follow after them, they are symbols. They have a deep, radical, structural and eonic value; but they are not true according to the existential meaning of the word, truth.

The importance of this distinction is fundamental. First of all when someone affirms that his experience is "true," such an assertion, at least to the rationalistic and logical mentality of the West, inevitably evokes the opposite statement; it may be false. A basic dualism at once appears and we find ourselves on the plane of the moralist who establishes opposite categories of judgment -- the good versus the evil. Just the same, dualistic modes of consciousness and ethical judgments are basic factors in human evolution, for men are constantly confronted with the necessity of choosing between seemingly contradictory possibilities of action or of intellectual interpretation. Some persons or groups of persons follow a certain path; others take an opposite road. As a result in a majority of cases an acute conflict is unavoidable, whether it be a physical or an ideological conflict.

Conflict is inevitable the moment human beings who face opposite paths of action or belief give to their choice an absolute sense, i.e. if they affirm that what they see as the "truth" or the "right" is absolutely and forever true and right. No individual need take such an attitude; or at least men need not take it throughout the entire evolution of humanity. The dualistic attitude is necessary during long periods of evolution; but a time comes when it must be left behind if there is to be growth. The dualistic mode of consciousness can be overcome when one begins to introduce into true-or-false and good-or-bad judgments the factor of time; that is to say, when one takes into consideration the character of the phase of the cyclic process of evolution at which the judgment takes place. A certain phase of the evolution of consciousness emphasizes the need for a certain type of decision, for a particular kind of desire and attraction, or for specific categories of intellectual concepts; another phase will present other needs, which may well be opposed to the first. The solutions of these needs are each "true" in relation to the human beings experiencing the contrasting needs. The different solutions represent different human values.

The concept of a multi-level cyclic process of existence itself constitutes a fundamental value. Thanks to this concept we can understand and appreciate all the moral, intellectual and emotional solutions to the ever-changing needs of evolving man which successive and even simultaneous societies have sought to embody in collectively glorified ways of life and cultural institutes. We can recognize that all these values were adequate and legitimate at the time and at the place where they met the structural needs of human beings -- individuals as well as groups -- inasmuch as they were geared to particular phases of the cyclic process of human evolution.

Values must change the moment a new phase of evolution -- whether it be of mankind as a whole or of a single individual -- begins. The forces which oppose the change -- social groups and privileged classes in society, or habit-patterns, obsolete allegiances and complexes in the individual person -- are obstacles to the process of growth; yet in some cases they may be useful as brakes to slow down a chaotic rush toward new but hazy and as yet dangerous goals. In any case (and there can be such a variety of circumstances!) we should not speak of an absolute opposition between truth and error, or good and evil, but only of a state of transition from one set of values to another. The new values are the answer to new human needs, and we always find these values condensed, exteriorized and formulated in terms of existential facts as new, or at least radically renovated and reactivated, symbols able to enkindle as well as focus the imagination of men.

The concept of the cycle is at least potentially the most inclusive of all symbols, because it constitutes a frame of reference for all symbols; it enables us to situate and to give a structural meaning to any and all symbols. It answers perhaps to the most profound need of the human mind, the need to harmonize, within an intelligible pattern of order and significance, ideas and beliefs, modes of feeling and behavior which though radically different must all be granted an objective and historical-geographical value.

This can be done convincingly only if each point of view or way of life is seen on the background of a whole cycle of existence, and each one is understood as a function of the particular phase of the cycle which it characterizes. As cycles with different starting points and of different lengths interact constantly and overlap, it follows that a great variety of values can be embodied and proclaimed in contrasting societies and cultures during the same period of time -- as is particularly the case today. The values differ simply because each of these societies is at a different phase of its evolutionary cycle, and therefore has different needs. If we are able to understand what these different phases are, we can accept the conflicting values as eminently worthwhile, at least for the people whose existence they guide or rule; and we can do this not merely in a spirit of perhaps hypocritical "tolerance," but with deep and respectful understanding.

From such a spirit of understanding new techniques of inter-group and inter-cultural harmonization can emerge which would be more sound and stable than are our modern procedures of communication, discussion and conciliation, usually based merely on some half-hearted compromise. Humanity crucially needs such new techniques as it heads, willingly or not, toward a state of highly complex planetary integration. All people need the capacity to grasp structurally the place of their own cultures and value-systems within the cyclic framework of the planet-wide process of evolution of the all-encompassing mind of Man; and they can do so only if they cease thinking of the symbols, born out of the particular need of a particular phase of the cycle, as absolute truths. I repeat that absolute truths inevitably imply absolute errors, and that belief in some timeless Absolute beyond existence tends to lead to a devastating form of evasion from reality and human sanity. If the factor of time is not integrated into any judgment of value, such a judgment will nearly always be based on a deviated sense of value; then also problems cannot be well formulated nor can there be found a valid solution, and the inevitable result is either a state of deep confusion or constant warfare between irreconcilable values.

A banal example may show how, if one does not introduce the factor of time into the formulation of a problem, one can often not find an acceptable answer. A young student is given a written test phrased as follows: "Does the sun set in the west? Answer: true or false." What should his answer be? Actually there is no possible yes-or-no solution to this problem, for the sun sets exactly in the west only at the time of the two equinoxes; at any other time the setting is more or less northwest or southwest. Therefore without bringing in the factor of time and without referring actually or implicitly to the yearly process the student cannot give to the test the type of answer which has been asked.

A very similar kind of ambiguity is inherent in most of the metaphysical problems which have haunted Western thinkers. Consider for instance the famous problem of free will vs. determinism. The question of whether a man is free or controlled by fundamentally preordained patterns, or by the power of God, makes no real sense if one does not introduce into it the queries: w h e n,   h o w and w h a t f o r. The meaning of "freedom" changes at every basic step in the evolution of human consciousness, be it the consciousness of the entire human race or of a person evolving from birth to death. Likewise the meaning of a term like "God" is understood differently by a child during the first stages of his mental development and by a 60-year old wise philosopher.

One may retort that there is a "Reality," God, to which different persons relate themselves in different ways; that while the approaches of the child and of the wise man differ, God is always what H e r e a l l y i s. But from the point of view presented in this book, what is "real" is in every case the approach, that is, the existential need which human beings apparently have to imagine and evoke the presence of something or someone called, in one language or another, "God." It is an existential and therefore an always changing need; it changes according to the phase in the process of evolution of the consciousness of the race, the group, or the individual person.

Actually the term, God, represents a c y c l i c   a n d s t r u c t u r a l   r e l a t i o n s h i p between one of the myriad of human existents appearing throughout the vast planetary cycle of mankind and the state of unity of the cycle-as-a-whole, the Eon. This relationship is a cyclic reality; and it is expressed by a multitude of symbols to which different meanings and values are given, all of them being equally valid and indispensable at that particular moment of the cyclic process of the society and the culture which gave them form and power.

Today as we approach the birth of a civilization planet-wide in scope, the imperious need has arisen within human consciousness to integrate these many symbols of the past. We are impelled, and indeed spiritually compelled, to discover where each of them belongs historically and intellectually and to attempt to give to the relationship, man-to-God, an all-inclusive cyclic meaning. Thus we will find ourselves obliged to use the basic symbol which expresses as broadly as possible this total relationship, because it includes and situates all other symbols, i. e. the symbol of the cycle.

THE INDIVIDUAL AND THE COLLECTIVE

We actually face the same situation when we consider the meaning of the relationship of the individual person to his community or to humanity as a whole. This inevitably leads to different conclusions according to the "when" and "where" of such a study. At an early stage of human evolution, when man is an almost completely undifferentiated part of the tribal unit, the condition of self-sufficient and self-determined individual selfhood, is for some few tribesmen, a dream, an ideal perhaps; for the ordinary religious leaders and the myth-makers of that period, this condition represents something evil, and they symbolize it in the figures of "rebel angels" or (in India) asuras (no-gods) against whom the gods wage a relentless "war in heaven."

The Prometheus myth in Greece has the same meaning but it already includes some new elements; Prometheus gives to as yet unindividualized, tribe-bound men the "fire" of individual selfhood which makes them self-conscious and potentially free individuals, and for this he incurs the hatred of the great god, Jupiter. Why does Prometheus steal the fire and give it to men? Out of compassion. This is the new element, compassion; and because of it Prometheus is in the end freed by a human hero who has become the symbol of the victorious and free individual. A new phase of human evolution has begun; it brings to the fore new symbols which glorify the new possibility -- indeed the new need -- of spiritual unfoldment for man.

The process of individualization very soon reveals itself fraught with great danger unless it is referred to a more encompassing reality. A solution must be found and at first it is sought at the psychological or psychic level. Man, the individual, oppressed by his loneliness and his struggle, in order to counteract an inevitable trend toward total isolation and a self-destructive glorification of the ego, i m a g e s forth a personal God with Whom he can hold an intellect-transcending "dialogue." This gives man the possibility of fully developing his potential of individual selfhood in relative psychological security. Everything that seems ideal then becomes oriented toward the attainment of "pure individual selfhood," an attainment which is given a transcendental sanction by the "higher religions" and leads to the realization, by the single and essentially isolated individual person, of a mystical union with an absolute Reality beyond time and space.

At a more concrete and social level, the glorification of the individual person has its n e g a t i v e aspect in the "rugged individualism" of the American Frontiersmen, or of any frontier type of life. Its p o s i t i v e aspect is the ideal of the "free man" who, secure and strong in the realization of his individual self and his own truth-of-being, is able fully to cooperate with his companions in the building of the ideal democratic society of free men everywhere. Actually however the concept of the individual person as a "citizen" endowed with uneradicable social rights represents a highly abstract ideal and evolutionary goal. What human consciousness faces and meets everywhere are collectively ordered factors even though theoretically individualized persons are so often blind to this evident fact.

Individual differences between men are very small compared to all the life-factors these men have in common. Moreover most members of a particular society are ninety per cent controlled by collective cultural patterns of behavior and thinking; they speak the same language and use the same symbols in terms of basically the same needs. Even the feelings of these culture-bound men and women very often coalesce into mass reactions. When slightly deeper differences arise -- of color, of race and climatic environment, of culture and religion -- they tend to take disproportionate and danger-provoking forms, and the supposedly individual person hastily withdraws into the safe enclosure of identification with his group, his people, his culture. The evident facts point to collective factors in human life; truly individual characteristics are magnified out of all proportion in most cases. Likewise a creative artist tends to overstress his originality, his uniqueness, but to the art-critic of a couple of centuries later, his works and those of his colleagues, often regarded in his day as motivated by a sharp conflict of ideals, are seen as manifestations of the single collective style of the epoch.

The purely individual person, just as the "free and equal" citizen, are mostly "myths"; they are symbols answering to the evolutionary need of this historical "Age of Conflicts." However these symbols inevitably call for another great symbol: a personal God with Whom an individual can hold an inner dialogue whenever he needs reassurance, guidance and a sense of total communion. When the belief in this God and in the possibility of dialogue with Him fades from man's mentality, then a psychological crisis -- which can most easily develop into a social crisis -- is inevitable. We are today in the midst of such a crisis. It compels "Godless" human beings to seek in some other way a real dialogue and total communion. For the vast majority of restless modern individuals sex seems to be the only other way; but except in rare cases, it leads to disappointment, perhaps to bitterness or perversion, and even to individual or collective crime.

These facts, under the pressure of which our society is today reeling, point to the need for new symbols. We have just begun to understand, and what is more to experience, the necessity to refer the symbols of the individual person and of the free man in a democratic society to a larger process of human evolution. We dimly realize that of themselves alone these symbols have but a transitory and illusory meaning; they acquire a "real" and a safe meaning only when they operate within a larger frame of reference and in terms of a new and all-inclusive symbol. The terms Man, Humanity, the Globe, the Planet-as-a-whole, constitute conceptual attempts at giving a definite form to this need for such symbols. But the attempt must fail if it does not include the older symbol, God, and even that of a closer human community, re-evoking but with a new meaning the sense of "belonging" found in tribal units. We are reaching a state of evolutionary synthesis; and both the thesis and the antithesis have somehow to participate in that synthesis, even though it be in a "transfigured" sense.

The transfiguration of the tribe ideal has been demonstrated in Free Masonry -- or at least in the original form of this movement some 250 years ago. The Masonic Lodge represents a new and modern version of the ancient concept of "occult Brotherhood" which today is usually so little understood. Its most significant corollary is an ordered process of transformation of the human person through a series of initiations which measure and identify his progressive steps toward the mastery of super-personal power and faculties. These are acquired when a man becomes an "agent" for the over-all purpose of the "Great Architect of the Universe" -- unless he came to follow the way of self-destruction and total isolation. This symbol of the G. A. O. T. U. is a repolarization of the personal God-image stressed in Near-Eastern religions. Whereas a personal God enters into a dialogue with individual persons (God and the individual constituting actually two aspects, infinite and finite, of the same concept) the Great Architect is seen rather as the creative Source of a vast universal process in which men who have reached the third degree of Mastery are able consciously to participate as His agents, as Builders of the Temple of Man.

This Great Architect of the Universe is the hidden Father Who "structured" in Mind the process of evolution of the universe before it began to operate. For us men this process has concrete meaning basically in terms of our planet, Earth, seen as a vast field of interdependent activities operating at several levels. Indeed this planet is, for humanity as a whole, the Lodge. Within this one Field of activity all men are potentially co-builders of tomorrow. Out of the co-ordinated and companionate efforts of those individuals who have agreed to live in terms of a symbol -- the Globe, the Lodge -- that includes their inter-related basic selves and their differentiated and self-controlled capacities for the building work, the omega state of the planetary cycle will gradually take a concrete form.

In this symbolic image of a united mankind the principles of individual selfhood and personal freedom are certainly not absent; they are transfigured. They have to prove their validity by the only proof that matters -- the proof of works. If a man claims to be an individual person he should prove it by demonstrating his freedom from the matricial power of family, culture and traditional beliefs. If he demands "equality" he should be able to meet his equals at the level of their activity and their quality of response to life's challenges. Nothing should be assumed that cannot be shown to be real, here and now, either directly or through its immediate and actual consequences; and the ultimate proof is the one made tangible by a man's total consecration to whatever his participation in the process of human evolution demands. Everything else is a means to an end, including mystical experiences or mysterious revelations.

What is always essential for human beings is that they should at any time be able to answer the need confronting them. New symbols arise when new human needs call for them. We should recognize these needs objectively and dispassionately and seek to open our consciousness to those events or especially significant actions which seem to be pregnant with symbolic meaning. Some symbols may evidently have only a personal meaning, answering only a temporary need -- a need conditioned by the tensions and conflicts which in most cases are inevitably associated with what I have called the ego-consciousness. Other symbols emerge out of collective situations and experiences in which a vast number of people share for a relatively long period. Some symbols may be so fundamental that they no doubt have a sort of "archetypal" character inasmuch as they are integral parts of "man's common humanity" -- which can be interpreted to mean the Image of Man within the creative Mind of God-ELOHIM; an Image which is but a theme susceptible of an almost infinite number of variations.

In any case however the symbol has no real meaning unless it is deeply felt by a human person; unless it releases existential power, that is, the power to transform some concrete and perceptible aspect of his existence. To legislate the character of symbols or to make dogmas out of their validity is essentially futile. The only proof of the validity of a symbol is the fact that it acts upon human beings -- and it seems probable (though we certainly cannot be sure) that only human beings can be vitally affected by symbols. Animals respond to signs which lead them to expect certain actions or coveted gifts of food or delicacies; but human beings can be moved and transformed by symbols, for in these they find clues to the solution of basic problems which can only be solved when referred to a larger Whole in which these men participate more or less consciously -- and at the limit, to entire cycles of human evolution.

As Count Korzybski wrote in his early book THE MANHOOD OF HUMANITY, man has the "time-binding capacity." He can transfer the knowledge born of experience to future generations. This he does through the use of symbols. With his symbols he reaches beyond the end of his own personality cycle, i. e. his death, and immortalizes himself as a contributor to the One Mind of humanity. Throughout his lifespan a man shares in the treasures of the human past and, if he is at all creative, adds to these treasures the symbols -- words, recorded or remembered deeds, works of art, images and now photographs -- which together constitute not only the imprint but also the "seed" of his personality.

A culture, seen from the perspective of several centuries or millennia after its gradual disintegration, is perhaps best understood through the complex groups of symbols embodied in its literature and its art. Art -- in the most general sense of the word which includes music, literature, dance, etc. -- constitutes the most vivid and meaningful "seed manifestation" of an ancient culture, or even of one particular century-long phase in the development of a culture which may still be in the process of completing its cycle of creative existence.

Because of this it is necessary to conclude this chapter on symbols with a brief discussion of what Art is capable of conveying to present-day humanity at a time when men of all cultures all over the globe can, for the first time in history, communicate through the experience of Art, not only with all the creative manifestations of living artists everywhere, but even more significantly with the seed-products of all past cultures which have left Art-symbols as witnesses to their innermost concern with the great problem of existence, and as collective answers to the human need of their time.

THE PLANETARY APPROACH TO ART

A symbol without an existential function -- i. e. a symbol which does not answer to a need characteristic of a particular phase of the evolution of the consciousness of a person or a community -- is not really a symbol. In this sense we

may say that a symbol is essentially useful inasmuch as it
serves a vital purpose in man's evolution; and the same applies to Art in general. Yet it would probably confuse people's minds if one were to state that Art has a function of "utility"; for the word utility usually refers only to physical
everyday needs. Art serves a purpose, but this purpose
takes on very different aspects according to whether it operates at one or another of the several levels of human existence. Man has essentially a need for a deep-seated experience of order and structure. He wants to be reassured in
every conceivable way that ours is a universe of order in
which certain vitally important events -- like the sunrise,
the coming of spring, or the inundations of the Nile -- occur
periodically. He expects the recurring of such events just
as he expects the recurrence of a theme in a musical fugue
or symphony, or of a geometrical motive in architecture; and
when his expectation is justified he feels more at peace with
himself and the universe.

Art fills this human need for an ever more subtle experience of structural order; and if a work of Art presents a
person with a kind of repetitive order or structural development which disappoints his normal anticipation, he experiences a sense of frustration or even resentment and indig-
nation. An Art-work for this reason is expected to have
"form" which, however, actually means the particular type
of structural order which previous Art-works in this particular culture have displayed until then. The innovator in Art
is always accused, by critics who take it upon their stooped
shoulders to be the guardians of the tradition, of producing
Art-works "without form." The first music, in the Debussy
period, which failed to end without a definite stressing of the
tonality of the piece gave most hearers a frustrating sense
of incompleteness; it left them "hanging up in the air," they
said. Their expectation of a satisfying ending was disap-
pointed; and this fact reveals how deeply rooted is the instinctive awareness that life is cyclic and that every great

cycle normally ends with a statement of perfect fulfillment in consonance -- thus in some kind of presentiment of the omega state, or seed-state.

It does not make much sense however to expect that every work of Art should at all times present such a picture of cyclic fulfillment or formal equilibrium. While it is true that man needs to feel order and structure around him, he has just as basic and essential a need for dynamic transformation. In so-called "classical" eras the sense of structural order normally prevails; and such eras usually follow periods highly disturbed at the political-social or spiritual level. But there are times when change becomes imperative, when ego-structures and traditional moulds which have become prisons for the free creative spirit must be shattered; there are times when a narrow cultural provincialism has to be expanded or dissolved in order to allow experiences of wider horizons to occur. Then the exclusivism of a classical era must give way to the inclusiveness of a romantic and post-romantic period, and the demand for an ever greater inclusion of values which at first appear alien to the spirit of that culture is not only justified, aesthetically as well as ethically or intellectually and scientifically, it is necessary and inevitable.

We are now in a period in which our constant contacts with what are to us alien cultures that have developed on all continents make it necessary and inevitable that we include in our Art, symbols and types of structures which at first disturb our sense of order and our expectations. As most people at first resent being disturbed, and cultural institutions fight overtly or insidiously against innovations and the inclusion of the products of alien cultures, it becomes necessary for iconoclasts deliberately to aim at shocking the public into a realization that the old traditional patterns are obsolete and empty of really creative meaning. Yet these old patterns may still be valid answers to the needs of large sections of the masses which lag behind the creative elite;

and the reactions of these masses may also be valid counter-weights to balance the too-centrifugal tendencies of artists, musicians, writers, theatrical producers, etc. who may be avid for novelty at any cost.

The craving for originality, today exacerbated by commercial interests profiting from swift changes of fashions in the Art world, belongs to the realm of the ego. It is the realm where the fleeting superficialities of existence give rise to equally superficial symbols. Changes in fashion -- in Art as well as in clothes, in commercial designs and in external group behavior -- reflect the surface agitation of egos moved by the winds of everyday occurrences and temporary social readjustments. But underneath the excitement of these small waves of change, which bring to the status of fleeting symbols movie stars or new "schools" of Art, fancy automobiles or highly publicized slogans, one can feel the deep currents of human evolution introducing sometimes slow, but now very rapid changes in man's basic sense of values. It is with such changes in depths that the emergence of lasting and humanly significant symbols correlates.

A new evolutionary tide is compelling every awake and responsive man to become aware of the existence, the everyday mode of behavior, and the basic culture and symbols of many past and present human societies. A global culture is almost inevitably arising with the spread of the radio and television, and the translation of ancient and modern books into all languages. For the first time Art can be seen from an all-human point of view. It can be related not merely to a particular type of men living in a particular geographical environment, but to the evolution of Man -- to the slow development of the mind of Humanity-as-a-whole. A totally new perspective is possible; a new all-human meaning can be given to Art. Art can be watched from a panoramic point of view encompassing simultaneously in space the cultural products of men on all continents, and relating in time the cultural seed-harvests of all types of societies which have left any records, from the time when men drew amazingly beautiful pictures in the caves of Central France and Spain some 25,000 years ago to this present twentieth century.

For the first time in human history these ancient records of prehistoric man, the statues of ancient Egypt and China, the Mayan and Hindu temples, the Gothic cathedrals and Arabic mosques, the Ajanta frescoes and Cezanne's paintings, the music heard on all continents and many other expressions of Art, can be seen to constitute in their togetherness the multifarious manifestations of one immense effort in which men always and everywhere participate. In such a participation human beings of all races and cultures should feel themselves united and victorious, in spite of the existential peculiarities of exclusivistic doctrines and regardless of ever-repeated social-political tragedies -- victorious not only over such tragedies, but even over the sense of futility or absurdity which at times seizes groups of over-sensitive or morally weak men, particularly today among our confused intellectual classes.

In Art, from this global and perennial point of view, we can now see at work the tireless and forever creative mind of Man. What we can witness in the great museums of our day and in the collections of music records registered in all countries of the globe are no longer only the many answers which this, that or the other culture has given to its basic psycho-social needs, but even more the proof of the continuity and indomitable strength of the human spirit operating under all conceivable existential conditions. We can rise above all the particular collective situations and the differentiated answers concretized into great Art-symbols; we can see through these specific answers to most varied human needs the one all-encompassing answer of Man to existence on this planet, and become attuned to the one multifarious passion for expression of human multitudes spurred on by the vision of creative minds that become the "seed-men" of their epochs.

It is important for us to realize that the statues, the hieroglyphs and the mythical figures, often half-animal, half-divine, of ancient Egypt or India which were answers to the psychological, social and religious needs of the people of those cultures can no longer have for us moderns the existential meaning that they had when produced. We cannot experience today the actual feelings which the men of ancient Egypt had while moving through the corridors of their temples, peopled by the strange figures of some of their gods, and preparing for initiation into the Mysteries. Our own feelings today when retracing their steps lack existential "authenticity" because our contemporary needs require new values and new symbols. Yet while the direct and immediate feeling-responses which the figures of the gods elicited from the men of that time are no longer possible for us, we can give to all these ancient records of Art, or to the present-day ritual sculptures from Central Africa, another meaning which reaches beyond the original, strictly cultural and religious meaning or purpose of these Art-forms. In and through all of these forms, we can vividly experience the indefatigable pulsing of the creative spirit in Humanity-as-a-whole; we can experience Man at work and become aware of the essential unity of the mind of Man.

Art, seen in its all-human and "planetary" reality, thus answers a deep and new need of our time. It becomes a potent and vivid symbol of what modern man should value most in this period of history. Indeed it is perhaps man's most authentic existential response to the challenge of preparing for a coming "New Age." Such a response negates the old concept of "Art for Art's sake." It gives a new dimension to Art reaching far beyond mere formalism and technical skill. It speaks of Art for the sake of Man. It realizes that, in this most basic of Art-experiences, the individual person should become conscious of the immense effort of human collectivities, everywhere and at all times, toward contributing to the one mind of Humanity the harvest of symbols which their specific cultures produced.

Mankind has reached an evolutionary level from which it should be increasingly clear that Man's essential function on this planet, Earth, is to extract consciousness from an immense variety of existential situations and personal and collective activities. However, the consciousness which until now human societies have extracted from their basic experiences has been conditioned by local factors and limited geographical environments. This stage can and should now be transcended. Its particularism and exclusivism should be absorbed in and transfigured by the unifying experience of Man at work everywhere and throughout all ages -- Man, the consciousness of the Earth, forever creating symbols to focus and dynamize the many values which, phase after phase of human evolution, contribute answers to the "needs of the times."

The lesser is always more or less an obstacle to the realization of the greater. In this sense we are today inevitably witnessing a process of de-culturalization of Art and of all modes of human activity. Global consciousness, in seeking to assert itself, necessarily tends to disintegrate and destroy the consciousness and the dependence of men upon local culture and religious forms, however broad the latter may seem. The new values emerging from this century are expressions of the planetarization of human consciousness; and Art, when understood and experienced beyond its strictly cultural meaning and importance, and when reaching beyond the mere recording of the superficialities of the contemporary scene, can and should become a potent influence in the stimulation of this process of planetarization.

However it is not only Art that is to be re-evaluated. All symbols require a fundamental reappraisal of their value as a function of the newly emerging planetary consciousness of humanity. The traditional meaning of the famous trinity, the Good, the True and the Beautiful, is at stake; for these criteria of validity must also be transfigured by the birth of a world-viewpoint transcending the exclusivism and separativeness of societies and cultures always at war with the foreign and the alien, always haunted by a yearning for absolutes and clinging fanatically to their own "revelations" as supreme and changeless.

Such a transfiguration of values can hardly assume an existential and totally convincing character unless the potent symbol of the cycle is wholeheartedly accepted as the measure of all things. Only such a concept of cyclic process enables us to s i t u a t e every truth, every moral code, every theological dogma, every aesthetical mode of expression, every social form of behavior, every institution, and essentially to accept them all as relatively valid -- valid, that is, in relation to the type of collectivities which believed (or now believes) in their value and to the historical time and geographical environment which witnessed and is still witnessing their development.

Since the Industrial Revolution and above all since the discovery of nuclear power, the concept of a tribal or nationalistic and geographically defined culture can no longer have the same kind of exclusivistic meaning. This does not necessarily mean that local cultures and ethnical values have become entirely obsolete. It means however that they should now be seen evolving as specialized expressions of humanity-as-a-whole. It means particularly that the values and symbols which are directly founded upon man's common humanity should be emphasized, rather than those which tend to divide groups and races. There are symbols and values which are essentially related to the very structure of Man in this planetary cycle of existence: but even these should be freed from limiting traditional and racial biases and prejudices. They should be thoroughly re-assessed, reformulated and revaluated, so that they can once more creatively vibrate with an intense and now a c o n s c i o u s l y all-human meaning.

Such a process of rejuvenation of symbols demands of us all that we summon from within us the courage to meet, with open eyes and minds free of archaic allegiances, the present-day release of unparalleled and utterly transforming potentialities for planet-wide rebirth out of the nightmare of centuries of exclusivism, fanaticism, cruelty and wars. We are challenged to face with emotional detachment and with intellectual lucidity and honesty all that has bound us to past cultural traditions and to the habits and fears of our ego-consciousness. We are challenged to rethink all values and all symbols, and to take nothing for granted; for whatever we take for granted is, from this very fact, for us spiritually dead.

Humanity is today actually facing a war of symbols, and every man is its battlefield. Under the pressures of catastrophies and total wars, and even more perhaps of economic conditions and of compulsory readjustments of human relationships at home and at work, many human beings, feeling their everyday lives empty of meaning, happiness and inspiration, tend to find solace, support and security in the old symbols of the social, religious and cultural past of their society, or of other seemingly more attractive cultures. At the same time the extraordinary strides of our modern technology has aroused in us all new material needs and desires for comfort; and this arousal is methodically intensified by industry and science which always need greater expansion and new horizons to conquer, unable as they are to stop the ever-accelerating momentum.

Materialistic or even artificial as these new human needs may appear, they nevertheless inevitably operate in the direction of the planetarization of human existence inasmuch as they serve the process of deculturalization. It may seem unfortunate that they most often destroy or subtly disintegrate man's allegiance to the old concepts of the Good, the True and the Beautiful; but out of the chaos and spiritual emptiness of the greater part of modern living, new values and more inclusive, less provincialistic forms of interpersonal relationships are gradually taking shape. These values and these new modes of relationship must become focalized, vivified, dramatized by new symbols if they are to have the power to move the minds and stir the emotions of the leaders as well as of the human masses everywhere.

Such symbols take form in the minds of individuals who are "open" to the surge of potentialities which is now making inevitable the planetarization of humanity--individuals whose personal experiences have produced in them the tensions necessary to such a process of spiritual pregnancy, and as well the enthusiasm, the fervor, the inescapable and perhaps torturing feeling that the traditional symbols of the past can no longer provide them with the psychic, emotional and intellectual sustenance they need to lead a totally acceptable and meaningful life. These individuals, men and women, boys and girls, seek passionately, and often feverishly and most awkwardly, to reach a new state of human existence, a state which, many years ago, I symbolized by the term "the man of plenitude."

The new values to which such a state of individual as well as all-human plenitude refers have doubtlessly not yet found their most characteristic and stimulating symbols, yet some basic ones have appeared, as we shall presently see. Whatever these may be and however fecundant their meaning, the field of the new mentality is wide open -- a virgin field for "seed-men" who have the courage and the creative imagination fully to envision what is even now beginning to emerge out of the womb of the potential inherent in Man.

Whether on this Earth or on other planets, "Man" is the form of existence in which the creative potential of evolution is essentially uncommitted to any limiting and restricted mode of response to the infinitely varied challenges of environment. Man is the conscious agent through whom the creative and forever transforming power undertoning the process of existence can become focused and released and, as it is released, acquire the character of consciousness. Conscious Man is the creator of values; and values in order to become effectual and stirring must become concretized and dramatized as symbols through the power of man's imagination.

We do indeed live in a world of symbols; and as human existence changes, at each new phase of the process of evolution of the biosphere in which human beings live, move and have their being, the need for new symbols ineluctably arises. These symbols, emerging from experiences in the depths of "seed men," become the foundations upon which new societies are built; and today we are witnessing the painful birth process of a global society.

X. THE ETHICS OF WHOLENESS
AND THE PLENARY SOCIETY

In its primary sense the term, ethics, refers to judgments of value concerning human behavior. A man acts, and by acting he inevitably relates himself to his environment which is filled with other existents -- whether these be human beings, animals, plants or elements of the earth, i. e. the atmosphere, rivers, the soil, the seas, etc. His actions are said to be "right" or "wrong," and there may be intermediate shades of right and wrong, especially when a certain level of behavior is reached.

On what basis are the ethical or moral judgments of what is right or wrong to be passed? On the basis of what the action does or means to the person who acts, of how it affects the existents concerned by it -- and also of how the action affects the whole environment (natural or social) in which the action takes place. Thus we can deal with ethical issues and judgments in two ways. Our judgments of value may be "individual-oriented" or "environment-oriented." We can think primarily of what the action does to the individual who acts and also to individual persons acted upon; or we can think of the result the action may have upon the social community and upon the general environment in which this community lives.

In view of these undeniable basic facts we find ourselves led to consider once more the "dialectic" process of human evolution; that is, the process which has at its original phase (thesis) the tribal community operating as a bio-psychic "organism" controlled by quasi-instinctual and compulsive imperatives toward which no disobedience is possible except on pain of some kind of death, psychic if not biological.

After a very long process of evolution a second phase (the antithesis) gradually takes form in which the individual person becomes the focus of attention. As this person does not exist alone but enters into relationship with other individuals, the actions and reactions, then the character of the relationship between them, constitute the substance of ethical judgments. Our present-day humanity operates mainly at this level; at least it does so theoretically, while in fact tribal-collective values are still effective in a more or less disguised form, supposedly "for the good of the individual" or "to save his soul."

A third phase (synthesis) is slowly emerging beyond the individualism of our theoretically "democratic" society. As the true character of this phase becomes clearer and more widely accepted -- first within small groups, then more generally--a new basis for ethical valuation will be formulated; and it is even now gradually and tentatively taking form. I speak here of the ethics of wholeness; but the character of this future "wholeness" will be very different from that of the primitive wholes, i. e. the tribal communities. It will be essentially different because these new social wholes will be constituted by groups of individuals who, theoretically at least, will be conscious and self-determined individual persons operating at the level of Ideity (that is, of the conscious and creative individualized mind). These persons will have chosen as individuals to come together and to become integrated into a super-personal whole. We see today very interesting and promising attempts by young people gathering into "communes" in more or less remote places away from the anarchistic jungles of our cities; and this may be a small and uncertain beginning.

We shall presently discuss what is implied in this kind of group integration and show that it can only operate successfully if the Presence of the Principle of Wholeness, ONE, is not only recognized but made an essential, determining factor in the "commune" -- and eventually in the entire planetary human society. Let me say at once that what this means is that the most central factor in the situation is the m o t i v a t i o n of the individual to consciously and deliberately join such a communal whole. It is this motivation which must always make the essential difference between what we today call "democracy" and what I envision as the "h o l a r c h i c" approach to the new type of social organization -- the p l e - n a r y   s o c i e t y.

RITES AND RIGHT

The words, rite, ritual, right, correct and the Latin r e c - t u s -- from which also come the words, erect, rectitude, rector, etc. -- are derived from the Sanskrit term, r i t a. This is not the place to dwell at length either on word-derivations or on the various meanings of r i t a in the Hindu society of Vedic and post-Vedic times. Suffice it to say that essentially this word, r i t a, refers to the precise way in which actions should be performed so that the exact result needed or expected will occur. "Per-forming" means acting through a form, or according to a formula -- which for instance in music would be a musical score, in the dramatic arts a scenario or script of some sort. A rite, or ritual, is a sequence of actions done in a precise, well-defined manner, according to a strict schedule and usually in some well-established and consecrated location.

The question inevitably arises: Who determines h o w the act or the series of actions are to be precisely done, and w h e r e and w h e n? We find an answer to this question when we consider what we call "animal instinct." An animal acting according to his instincts acts compulsively right; the instinctual act is a perfectly adequate answer to the need of the species-as-a-whole. It correctly achieves what needs to be done at the precise time and place in which it is needed in order to take care of a specific life-function -- for instance, in order to insure the survival and propagation of the species. A generic need automatically evokes a correct answer; but the answer is usually valid only in a more or less limited environment and it may be effective only under relatively stable conditions. If these conditions suddenly change or are modified progressively beyond a point representing a maximum degree of possible adaptation to geographical, climateric and biological transformations, the instincts of the animal in a natural state begin to be inadequate. They still compel, but the results are no longer "right" for survival; and sooner or later the species disappears.

The human species displays an extraordinary capacity for adaptation to even radically changed conditions of existence. Man has, like any animal, basic instincts operating at the generic, biological and unconscious level of his existence; but with the development of a highly complex nervous system and a large forebrain -- a development presumably related to his "erect" spine and his special kind of hands -- generic man, homo sapiens, gradually develops a new type of faculty: intelligence. I n s t i n c t gives man an innate knowledge of what to do in order to preserve, increase and multiply his generic being at the level of Life, in the Earth's biosphere. I n t e l l i g e n c e makes man become aware of w h a t i s p o s s i b l e under any circumstances, at least provided these circumstances occur within a comprehensible frame of reference and therefore not in a situation of utter chaos or irrationality.

There are always several possibilities for intelligence: a c h o i c e can therefore theoretically be made between these possibilities of action -- and, at a higher level of development, possibilities of reacting to outer pressures, and also of feeling and thinking in new situations involving unfamiliar relationships to other existents. Intelligence becomes aware of the possibilities; but it does not make the decisions as to what is to be done. In the form of "imagination" it may visualize the various possibilities. When it imagines too many possibilities, the mind of the human being may become confused and even the instincts may then fail to operate "correctly."

In primitive man instincts are much more powerful than the more evolved faculty, intelligence. Man then lives within a generally narrow environment and faces relatively simple definable types of experiences in this more or less steady geobiological environment. Nevertheless because man is man, he is able to seek new ways of increasing his chances of survival and his comfort by bringing into his rhythm of existence new forces which his intelligence has shown him are available. These forces, first of all, result from the fact of living in groups, thus from cooperation. By acting together men gain new powers; and they are able to transfer what they have learnt to their progeny. However the problem of how to act together to produce the most effective results must inevitably arise.

There are traditions everywhere which refer to the coming of gods or superior beings who taught groups of primitive men the principles of agriculture, of cattle-raising, and of various arts and religious practices. There may well have been such "visitations" which can be interpreted in various ways. Essentially what takes place is a projection of archetypal Soul-Images upon the receptive and largely passive consciousness of some particularly sensitive tribesmen -- Images which represent the patterns of new evolutionary developments in the species, homo sapiens. The archetypal Image could, through teaching, be impressed upon a "mutant" or a small group of mutants by a Being from a more advanced civilization on Earth or elsewhere; or it could be projected directly upon the nascent minds of such men as inner visions or inspirations. In either case the knowledge received is "revelatory." In it s h r u t i knowledge. It comes

with a powerful impact, a character of unquestionable certainty. It is "right knowledge"; that is, it is knowledge of
precisely how to act in order to get results which answer to
a collective tribal need, even though it may be "channeled
through" a particular human being who thereby becomes
"sacred" -- a term which simply means being an agency for
the focusing of some supernormal power of transformation.
Everything that is related to such a revelation is sacred. It
saves; it heals; it gives control over inimical forces in the
environment.

Because it saves, heals or enhances the capacity to survive, the revelation must be preserved exactly as it was
conveyed. The acts, gestures, words which were revealed
and proved efficacious in a crisis -- or the life-example giv-
en by a leader or seer who had the revelation and radiated
an unusual manna-power -- must be repeated precisely,
invariably. They become rites to be performed -- rites invested with transcendent or specially focused energy. They
constitute "right" action -- rita.

As these methods of acting pass from one generation to
the next they acquire the psychically-innate character of an
instinct. With them are associated, as negative counterparts,
taboos. The primitive tribesman can no more disobey the
taboos of his tribe than he can deliberately stop breathing for
a long time, or make his heart stop beating. (At a later date
men will appear who will do just that -- stop their breathing
process and their heart beats -- as a means of freeing their
consciousness from the tribal-collective state of existence
and become individualized).

Rites are indeed social instincts; and I am not speaking
here only of religious rituals in temples or in some hallowed
locality, but of all traditional ways of behavior which are so
deeply imprinted upon the human mind of a member of a
community, or even of a wider culture, that their value is
unquestioned. The idea of "right" and "wrong" is a generalization of the basic concept involved in the strict perform-

ance of rites. What is still spoken of as a natural instinct for "righteousness," as "moral imperatives" and as the "voice of conscience" are more sophisticated manifestations of the power of tradition to enforce its customary ways of performing certain actions considered essential to the welfare, health and perhaps the survival of a community, a nation, and a particular kind of social-cultural-religious "way of life."

As men develop their intelligence and this intelligence is able to perceive new possibilities of doing things, perhaps in a more satisfactory or more pleasant way -- an ego-pleasing way, as egos take control of "the human condition" -- the instinctual subservience to unchangeable ritual procedures tends to be more and more overcome by this imaginative and creative intelligence which seeks to devise new methods of action. We then see intelligence, imagination and inventiveness struggling against the social instincts which "the Establishment" glorifies under the name of morality. A woman living sexually with a man "without benefit of clergy" is "immoral." An adulteress is even more immoral, and in ancient societies was very often killed in some more or less ghastly manner. Each culture has its own set of moral rules or taboos; yet these crumble when the "revelatory knowledge" which was at the root of the taboos (because it established an opposite type of "right performance of action") is no longer implicitly and unquestionably believed to be valid.

Here a few words concerning the process of "training" would be relevant. Training actually is a process which f r e e z e s a person's capacity to imagine alternatives to the action considered "right" in a clearly defined set of circumstances. Training compels a man, within this sharply defined area of activity, not to be w r o n g. It compels the man not to hesitate should his intelligence and imagination present to his mind other possibilities of action as being perhaps just as valid -- or, at the intellectual level, present him with ways of linking concepts different from the "logical way" he has been trained to follow as the only one that is right, i. e. rational. The thoroughly trained individual actually is made to forget other possible ways of acting, at least within the area of his specialty. Training limits the area of possibilities of which our intelligence might make us aware. It does so in highly specific ways which are not only social but intellectual. It makes entire categories of thoughts -- and as well certain modes of feeling and reacting to specified sets of circumstances -- instantly unacceptable and indeed unthinkable. In this sense our freedom of choice is curtailed, at least in the areas where set procedures are "morally" forced upon us -- i. e. where they refer to social, religious, scientific, or even artistic taboos.

These social taboos are not as rigidly compulsive as tribal taboos because they refer more to the level of mind than to the level of deep-rooted bio-psychic imperatives; yet they certainly powerfully limit the freedom of choice of a socially conditioned and academically trained human being. They constitute a "procedural" type of morality.

Let us consider a physicist in complete charge of complex operations, perhaps related to sending a man into space. He is making the necessary series of checks; he is assuring himself that every apparatus is functioning as it is meant to function. If this scientist should not perform his work "correctly" tragedy would ensue. It is a "performance" in that all his acts follow a formally structured sequence determined by rigidly set formulas. If he has been calculating the orbit of the missile he must be "right" in his calculations. He has no choice, for he can have no doubt as to the truth of the formulas for the calculation of gravitational pull, speed of light, engine-thrust, etc. The possibility that one of these formulas might be inadequate does not, indeed actually cannot, enter his mind at such a time, because he is a man thoroughly trained in the methods and concepts of modern science.

A practically identical situation confronts the old-type

"medicine man" and the celebrant in an archaic magical rite; for these men the efficacy of the ritual depends entirely on the rigorously exact performance of certain gestures, the intoning of precisely determined "words of power," etc. The magician or hierophant has learnt the formulas, rehearsed the exact sequence of gestures. Both he and the physicist-engineer of today are so intent on following the r i g h t p r o-c e d u r e (the "rita") that there is no choice for them and no hesitation between two or more possible acts. They both k n o w without doubt that the acts they perform constitute the correct procedure.

How do they know? The modern scientist acquires his knowledge from books and perhaps through experiments he has made and which his colleagues have check and rechecked; ed; it is knowledge of what he, as a member of our particular society and culture, assumes to be unchanging and reliable "laws of nature." In developing that knowledge all conceivable possibilities of error have been eliminated, or at least minimized to a degree of near-certainty.

Now, it would seem that in this collective and cultural effort which we call "modern science" the faculty of human intelligence operates "freely"; yet can we not see that the whole of modern science has followed a certain line of intellectual-analytical approach and that there may well be other possible lines of endeavor leading to different types of "knowing?" The very objectivity and the "rigorous thinking" (Bertrand Russell) on which are founded our modern scientific methods, their quantitative measurements, and the disassociative procedures interfering with the wholeness of what is being analyzed, all these inevitably constitute a limiting factor. Our science operates within clearly and sharply defined, but therefore limited, areas of possibilities; and in that sense the scientist who is thoroughly endoctrinated is not really "free" to choose between several possible ways of t h i n k i n g. The orientation and character of his thinking processes have been pre-determined by his society in a variety of more or less subtle ways.

The celebrant in archaic rituals or Mysteries no doubt also believes that he has access to a totally reliable kind of "revelatory" knowledge. He was thoroughly trained in that knowledge by tests and initiations. He is no more "free" to choose the basic orientation of his thought-processes and of the way to apply his knowledge, and thus no more free to perform the wrong gestures, than is his modern counterpart, the trained scientist.

Nevertheless a physicist-engineer in charge of some delicate operation might want, for some personal or ideological reason, to perform the "wrong" gesture which would sabotage the operation. Likewise a "medicine man" whose function it is to heal a sick person might also purposefully use wrong formulas because he personally desires to see the man dead. Also a man deeply depressed after an emotional shock could turn the wheel of his car in a wrong direction, contrary to all his training-habits, because the "death wish" in him is overpowering his "life-instinct." What happens in such cases is that a psychological and emotional factor is able to break down the training-pattern. A possibility which this training was at the time unable to block forces its way into the mind charged with the power of an intense desire.

When this occurs we know that the power of the ego has been able to assert itself against the "social instinct." We have reached the level at which the process of individualization operates -- but in such cases in a negative manner. At that level a new factor is operative: the factor of interpersonal relationships.

This factor, when under the control of ambitious, passionate, ideologically fanatic egos, introduces the element of conflict and therefore the possibility of meeting any situation involving some kind of relationship (which indeed means all situations!) in a relatively unpredictable manner. It is relatively unpredictable because of the enormous complexity of factors involved in any relationship. As already stated, it is in relatedness that the element of "freedom" resides; that is, the possibility of choosing from several alternative ways of relating -- and what is more, the possibility of attributing d i f f e r e n t   m e a n i n g s to a particular relationship or type of relationship.

This possibility then forces us to give a new meaning to the concept of "morality." It ceases to refer mainly to correct procedure in the performance of actions. What is now a at stake is actually t h e   c h a r a c t e r   o f   t h e   r e l a t i o n - s h i p entered upon. "Procedural morality" is transformed into "relational morality." The basic issue is not one involving right and wrong action, but right and wrong relationship.

REGIONAL MORALITY
AND THE "GOLDEN RULE"

In the early and unadulterated tribal state of society there are no b a s i c problems of relationship. If interpersonal conflicts occur they may be considered superficial and due to differences in organic and nerve responses to everyday events. Problems of relationship develop as the process of individualization gains momentum within a tribe which, for one of many possible reasons, is losing its homogeneity and whose psychic roots have become ineffectual -- and this probably occurs because of intermarriage with other tribes, or because of some external pressures. The tyrannical powers of the rulers of expanding kingdoms and the conditions of existence almost inevitably associated with large cities to which all kinds of people flock become reflected in the widespread appearance of ego-controlled persons in whom this ego also rules over their fields of consciousness.

Then individuals begin to meet individuals with suspicion, fear, distrust and aggressiveness. The deep psychic rootedness of tribesmen in their land, their folklore and religious practices dries out. Each man for himself, and woe to the weak and the loser! Now the need for what we mainly

understand today, at least in principle, as "morality" becomes imperative. It is met by "lawgivers" who build
a system of laws and rules governing the relationships between individuals; by "prophets" who call men to task and
to repentance for their folly and their many "sins" -- and at
times by "Exemplars" whose pure life and loving radiance
heralds a yet distant future when human beings will have overcome their egocentric fears and passions, their religious
fanaticism and their narrow ideological biases.

A new type of religion, which includes what we now usually call "the Great Religions," develops which supersedes
the tribal cults preeminently stressing the factor of ritual
activity. It is a type of religion fundamentally addressed to
"individuals" -- and to the attempted "spiritualizing" of interpersonal relationships either by presenting a new kind of
thinking-process which counteracts and transcends the
power of the ego (early Buddhism and Zen), or by emphasiz-
ing a new type of feeling-response to interpersonal relationships, a type of feeling-response which is called "Compassion" in Mahayana Buddhism, and "Love" in Christianity.

In these "Great Religions" the ritualistic element is also
present but in a different and more secondary role. The essential need in societies of individualized persons is to neu-
tralize the centrifugal and aggressive tendency of the ego. In
tribal societies whatever there was of centrifugal tendency in
tribesmen could be neutralized by rituals which revivified
the power of the common Root (the tribal god, the Great Ancestor) and made more evident the basic and factual participation of men, women and children in life-processes essential to the strength of the community -- and these included
sexual activities as well as agricultural festivals, dances for
rain, etc.

While some of these ritualistic celebrations and festivals
are still operative in societies of relatively individualized or
individualizing ego-minds, the more essential purpose now
is to present, as vividly as possible, to the feelings and the

minds of individuals and of social groups of individuals the ideal of union -- an ideal even more than a fact; a goal to be striven for with a feeling of more or less individual dedication. Such dedication is considered to be the responsibility -- the free choice -- of individuals, even if the contagious power of group interplay is also seen and used as a potent incentive to the "conversion" of the individual and as a strongly contributing factor in the steady operation of the spirit of dedication.

Such a spirit requires "faith." At the tribal pre-individual level there is, strictly speaking, no need of faith for the determining bio-psychic facts are evident to all. All that is necessary is to emphasize repeatedly this evidence through ceremonials in which the whole tribe participates at two levels, the outer group-level and the more occult field controlled by initiation. But in the societies where ego-differentiation and ego-conflicts are the evident facts of social life, where class fights against class and often ethnic group against ethnic group, what is needed is faith in the possibility of a future condition of unity. It is, in Christianity, faith in the "one God" and His factual incarnation in a divine-human personage whose life is a universal example to be "imitated" by all men, however diverse their racial origins and their egocentric propensities; and, in Buddhism, faith in the possibility of attaining a "state of consciousness" in which all individual differences cease or are absorbed -- a possibility also demonstrated by one great Exemplar, Gautama, the Buddha.

In these societies in which the central preoccupation is how to deal with individual egos bent upon asserting their rights for independent action and minds increasingly eager to have their own opinions, morality has to be enforced by law, and rationality by strict practice and training or education. They must be enforced if the realization of the "collective interest" and of what is required for "collective survival," at the community or the national level, is not suf-

ficient to produce social cohesion and wholesome group-oper-
ation in government, in business, in education and in sports.
The basic and subtler aspect of enforcement is moral indoc-
trination; and at the more material level, propaganda and
overt or hidden persuasion. All forms of persuasion appear
legitimate. The individual has to be made to believe that his
self-interest is to be seemingly unselfish in all interpersonal relationships.

What is called the Golden Rule as usually formulated:
"Do not do to others what you do not want done to you," is a
typical case of the kind of morality which is based on self-
interest and is directed toward human beings who think and
feel egocentrically as "individuals." It is indeed a sad reflection on the nature of a historical phase of the evolution of
mankind and of human consciousness, because it implies that
a man cannot base his action upon any broader and more inclusive concern than his own person, a concern for his own
personal welfare. It implies that the realization that every
human being is part of a "greater whole," humanity, is simply
not any match for the selfcentered drives of ego-controlled
individuals. Relationships are limited to the individual-to-
individual type, actually ignoring the even more fundamental
relationship of the individual to the whole -- the whole of humanity. In the place of the individual-to-whole relationship
religion pictures a purely ideal and transcendent relationship between a man and God -- a mystical I-Thou relationship.

At the tribal stage of evolution (t h e s i s) what happens
to a particular person is entirely secondary to the effect the
action may have on the tribe as a whole. We are now in the
stage of a n t i t h e s i s at which individuals are the main
concern in the ethical sphere -- at least theoretically and
excluding cases of so-called "national interest" or even of
community welfare and health. The characteristic feature
of such an evolutionary stage and of our modern more or
less "democratic" societies is that, in fact, values relevant

to the welfare of the collectivity are constantly in conflict
with values referring to the "rights" of the individual. Such
societies indeed represent transition stages of human
development, and their existence characterizes what I have
elsewhere called "the Age of Conflicts." The type of morality they believe in is a "morality of conflict." It is a morality which seeks constantly to effect a compromise between
a concern for the individual and a concern, not really for the
community, but for a particular condition of existence in the community, that is, for a traditional and
institutionalized collective way of life. It is a morality based
on the danger that would-be individuals still driven by life-
urges cause to an unsteady type of society, always on the
brink of possible chaos.

FREEDOM OF CHOICE

The usual concept of morality in such societies of individuals in more or less constant conflict with each other --
conflicts of personalities, conflicts of interests, conflicts of
religions or ideological beliefs -- rests on the belief that
these individuals are free to choose between alternatives of
conduct. Each individual it is said can make "free decisions," just because he is an individual in whom a God-created Soul or an essentially spiritual principle operates. He
is free to choose between "right" and "wrong," "good" and
"evil" -- between moral and immoral ways of behavior. The
moral issue may not refer to a particular act but rather to a
generalized attitude from which a series of acts inevitably
flows; but in any case man as an individual can choose; he
has moral freedom and thus responsibility.

Thus stated, the issue seems fairly clear. Even an irrel-
igious thinker like the French existentialist, Jean-Paul Sartre
believes that "The human situation is to be defined as one
of free choice without excuse and without assistance" (cf.
L'EXISTENTIALISME EST UN HUMANISME). However when
one looks at the actual facts of the social situation without emotionalism or traditional bias, and with a sense of his-

torical objectivity, one should realize that the concept of freedom of choice and moral responsibility is a very ambiguous one. It is ambiguous because it simply does not question its most basic implication; that is, that every man is an "individual." It does not try to ascertain w h a t i t i s that is supposedly able to make the choice -- what it is that is "free."

We came upon such a situation when we discussed the real meaning of the little word, "I"; also with reference to the problem of reincarnation -- the reincarnation of this mysterious "I." If there is no well-defined or at least relatively stable realization of being "I" there can be no moral c h o i c e, as we usually understand the term; and this fact has been acccpted in our present-day legal system which absolves from moral responsibility and guilt a person judged insane or even temporarily insane, and at the time unable to distinguish between the moral value of his or her actions. The social community may protect itself from the danger of repetition of such a type of behavior and therefore can lock up the person or try to restore him to a "normal" condition of sanity; but this theoretically has nothing to do with moral guilt. The same type of protective behavior would apply to a person who has an incurable but highly contagious disease or who is a carrier of such a disease.

It is obviously very difficult to determine exactly where moral responsibility ceases in a person; and this is reflected in many famous criminal cases, like that of Sirhan Sirhan, who assassinated Robert Kennedy. What our society as a whole does not yet fully recognize is that the very concept of "being an individual" is a very relative and ambiguous one. It does not do so because it is still dominated by the Christian belief that every man has, or is, a God-created soul, and that this soul has the power to make free choices, except in cases of total insanity -- which then implies that the soul has withdrawn from the body.

According to the holistic philosophy of evolution presented in this book, man at the first level of his evolution, what I call the "tribal" level, and also in his early years as a very young child cannot be considered an "individual"; he has only the p o t e n t i a l i t y of becoming an individual.   He functions in the realm of "Life" where there is no individual freedom and instincts are compulsive forces.   Intelligence, as the capacity to see that there are alternative possibilities of action, is not yet developed or only in a most rudiment- ary state completely dominated by the instinct for survival, a survival which usually tends to imply the need for aggres- sive acts.   One can therefore not significantly speak of mor- al choice at that biological and generic level.

It is only when a human being is sufficiently individual- ized to pit his desires for power and for the possession of what he wants a g a i n s t the traditional ways of thinking and acting of his community that the possibility for that man to really "choose" begins.   His moral choice is based on the co-existence of two opposite motives for action, and on the conflict between these motives.   Morality, as the term is usually understood, therefore implies a situation of conflicts: individual against community.

In a sense of course the two principles, "individual" and "collective," always co-exist; again we have here a situation which can be symbolized by the cyclic interplay of the Chi- nese Yang and Yin.   We stated that the principle of individ- uality is l a t e n t in the realm of Life; and that mind exists in a primitive condition in all living beings.   But until the relationship between the two principles has reached a point of near-balance, the principle of individuality cannot assert itself with the character of moral responsibility because the human being is not sufficiently individualized to make really free choices.

In other words there can be no absolute state of moral responsibility any more than there can be absolute states of unity or multiplicity, and no absolute value to individualism or collectivism. It is always a question of m o r e   o r   l e s s.

And this "more or less" depends on the phase of cyclic development which has been reached by the individual and also by his society. There are periods in the cyclic interplay of the two polarities of existence (Yang and Yin) in which one of the two poles gains a definite and outwardly effectual domination over the other. There are periods of crisis in which a basic change occurs. There was one such period in the development of man's consciousness and man's social behavior when the old and long-lasting early tribal state was challenged by the self-assertive power of individuals. We are still living in such a period of evolutionary crisis. And the most acute phase of such a crisis is no doubt represented by the Hebraic-Christian tradition which has emphasized the sense of sin and guilt, and as a result the need for "atonement," divine or human.

For the typical tribesman, what we could compare with the moral issue in our present Western society is whether or not he is open to the dictates of the Great Spirit, or the god of the tribe. The problem is one that involves consciousness rather than action; not how "good" you are, but how "conscious" you are; that is, how able you are to focus in your consciousness as a living human organism the influx of the "god of the Whole."

The ability to focus in a unique human field-of-existence the powers of the Whole, and to be inspired by a vision or by "great dreams" providing some needed answer to the whole community -- this is actually the most basic manifestation of "individual selfhood." But at the tribal level such a focusing or inspiration implies a kind of compulsive, mediumistic process. The human being is "seized by" the god -- the god of the Life-sphere who rules autocratically. It is only when this state of openness to the whole no longer refers to the tribal Whole but to the one-to-one relationship between field-of-existence and Soul-field, that the condition of individual selfhood actually exists. It creates "individual responsibility" which simply means the ability to "respond" to the emanations and the promptings of the Soul-field -- the "Voice of Conscience."

Then, but only then, the human being who has begun to experience a deep feeling of "I am" -- a feeling whose birth is symbolized in our Western tradition by the Mosaic episode -- acquires the moral power to choose, to make relatively free decisions. But Moses' story is characteristic. While he talks to the "I am" God, the people he led "out of captivity" to the Egypt of the flesh, revert to the old pagan worship; and the irascible and violent Moses breaks the Tables of the Law carved by the "I am" out of the rock of Sinai (again the prefix "sin"!). In other words, the first experience of individual self-conscious morality takes a negative turn. The divine experience is reduced to a human experience (the Tables of the Law now carved by human hands); the power of the individual self in the "heart" descends to the level of the solar plexus, at which the social collectivity and the Great Tradition speak in terms of collective Images and symbols on which a society is based.

Then self is superseded by ego; and it is the ego that makes choices. It is the ego that seeks to assert itself, to protest against social regulations or religious ideals which seem to curtail its "freedom," i.e. which run counter to the ego's desires and fears. It is the ego that commits crimes or sins. Then also the ideal of a free society, "democracy," becomes perverted; it cannot work out, nor does it really make sense in a society of egos, by egos, and for the greatest glory of predatory and competitive egos.

In the mean time history has shown us various ways in which the power of the collectivity has sought to control, to minimize and also to guide, with the help of religious and moral exemplars, the growing challenge of individual egos to society. On the one hand society has imposed a system of laws and harsh punishments to try to force egocentric individuals to "choose" the traditional ways of behavior, and of thinking and feeling (family feelings, national feelings, etc.); on the other hand organized r e l i g i o n, as the "spiritual" side of the coin establishing a system of collective values, has sought to compel individuals "to be good" by evoking the imagery of after-death sanctions and speaking to the deepest feeling-needs of the faithful -- the threat of excommunication as well as the dramatization of the great Exemplar, Jesus, stirring collective mass-emotions.

Now these social and religious means to impel and, if possible, to subtly compel individuals to make the correct choices are losing their efficacy. The "rugged individualism" of frontier days has given way to a strange combination of (1) intense eagerness to make "authentic" decisions which challenge the Establishment in all its forms: social, educational and religious; and (2) subservience to patterns of comfortable living imposed from the outside by "hidden persuaders," but also from the inside by the even more subtle pressures of psychological insecurity, neurotic reactions, and fear of losing all the "good things of life."

A tremendously complex industrial society and life in huge, monstrous cities make the choice between alternatives increasingly difficult and therefore the concepts of moral decisions more ambiguous or meaningless. It is for this reason that, on the one hand, society is developing the fantastic paraphernalia of research teams and projections into the future made by trained and supposedly objective specialists aided by computers; while on the other hand masses of distraught and uprooted individuals rush to clairvoyants, astrologers, and mediums, i.e. to anyone who might help make choices on the basis of some presumably transcendent kind of knowledge.

What else can the individual do? Only one thing: that is, to reach beyond egocentric and emotional or strictly intellectual "reasons" on which to base his moral decisions and in a state of ego-less attention and inner quietude a n d f a i t h to "resonate" to the inner images and the promptings which arise in the Ideity-field of which this individual occupies the negative-receptive pole, while the Soul is the positive-active pole. This is what would provide a truly "individual" foundation for "moral" decisions. This is what, in terms of Hindu philosophy, would be to fulfill one's d h a r m a, one's "truth of being." And evidently it is to such a possibility that European existentialists meant to refer when speaking of "authentic" acts; what Dr. Jacob Moreno, founder of Psychodrama and Group-therapy meant when he spoke long ago, with a kind of religious fervor, of "spontaneity and creativity," stressing that he meant by these terms more than they usually convey to our modern individuals so eager to express themselves.

But all these beautiful words -- dharma-fulfillment, authenticity, spontaneity, creativity, self-actualization (Abraham Maslow), etc. -- become not only empty, but masks for egocentricity and in some cases licence, if not chaos, when the actor is the ego instead of the true individual in whose person the power of the individualized "self" (as I defined this term) has been raised to consciousness and to the heart-center. Likewise the very concept of democracy can only be a rather sad and often bitter joke when the citizen, who is theoretically free, independent and "equal," is in fact an egocentric person unable to resist the pressures of "special interests" and indeed to make decisions arrived at in terms of their adequacy to the basic "truth" of the Soul-Image which seeks to find in him, the individual person, an agent for its embodiment.

What then is the next step ahead -- the "synthesis" that would provide valid effective answers to the plight of a society which retains from the early archaic state of "thesis" only a materialized concept of collective power over individuals who, in turn, are led by the appetites of ever more brittle, more sadistic and above all more "alienated" egos, substituting for their true individual selves?

What is needed, fairly obviously, are two simultaneous approaches which in fact represent the two aspects of the same process of human evolution: the individual approach and the social approach. The first refers to the overcoming of the ego and a radical repolarization and transmutation of the energies of the Life-field in man; the second, to the formulation of new ideals, new archetypal Images of society. As society is simply the result of a process of organization of interpersonal and intergroup relationships, this second approach implies the acceptance and demonstration, even against the pressures of our transitional and cathartic era, of a new type of relationship, and especially of a new quality of relatedness.

The term "new" is of course not strictly accurate for, as we have already seen, this quality of relatedness has been extolled by the "Great Religions" of past millennia and demonstrated by a number of individual men and women seeking to attune their consciousness, their feelings and their actions to the great examples of the Buddha, Christ, St. Francis and numerous others. But as a Hindu proverb states: "A few drops of rain do not constitute the monsoon." The beautiful agape-love of a relatively few true Christian saints and their humble followers, and the "compassion" enshrined in the Bodhisattva ideals of Northern Buddhism, at best only herald the future and much longed-for New Age. Something more is needed: a vision of social living in which a totally new concept of society would call for and indeed make possible the world-wide spread of a new type of interpersonal relationships -- relationships based on unpossessive love and the freedom to perform authentic acts in and through which the Soul-Images of the acting individuals would radiate and fulfill their planetary function, i.e. the individuals' dharma.

AN OPEN HOLARCHIC MORALITY

It is impossible here to formulate in detail what is likely to be involved in the future "morality-beyond-morality." I shall only present some points which seem essential -- and which I hope can eventually be discussed in another volume at greater length -- lest their application introduce irrelevant or perverting factors. This is always a serious danger in time of transition from one type of thinking-feeling-behavior to another, and the often strenuous and undiscriminating efforts of today's younger generation to repudiate the standards of our Western culture are not without dangerous elements. The first manifestation of any great ideal always takes the character of a shadow. Yet the shadow is in most cases provided by the people who block the light of the new sunrise by standing rigidly and blindly against the dawn.

If a condition of synthesis is to succeed that of antithesis, the character of the thesis must somehow be integrated with the products of the era of antithesis. This, I believe, is a generally applicable principle of which one should never lose sight. Thus, because the ideal of the man of the tribal "Age of Unconscious Unanimity" was essentially to be open to the voice of the god who represented the "unity aspect" of the tribe and its Root-reality at the level of Life -- so that he might be, whenever needed, a channel or agent for the will of the god -- likewise the man of the "Age of Plenitude" that is yet to come should be "open" in consciousness to a Presence that is both b e y o n d and t h r o u g h his total person -- the Presence of a "greater whole."

The term, greater whole, may be interpreted at several levels; but the basic fact is the readiness of the lesser whole, a particular human person, to enter into a state of total and fully conscious relationship with a greater whole of which it is an operative part. In the present state of existence and consciousness, an individual normally finds himself willingly related to both biological and social greater wholes; that is, as a bio-psychic organism, he recognizes and more or less happily accepts his being part of a particular family and race. He sees himself also as a unit within a social community, group and nation, sharing with many others in the benefits, or negatively the lack of benefits and the frustrations of a culture. Within this social type of greater whole he is a social person, a citizen with many rights and a number of duties (taxes, military service, etc.). But in the type of society in which human beings live today, he is basically considered as a citizen who enters in statistical calculations as a mere unit, i.e. as one child to be educated, one draftee, one voter, one social entity old enough to get social security benefits, etc. He has anonymous, abstract rights of a strictly social character -- and the same type of social duties.

The situation in present day totalitarian regimes is basically the same as in democratic societies. The difference is that in a democracy, the "individual person" has a theoretical "worth and dignity" (whatever this actually may mean!) and the State is said to exist for the sake of the individual; while in totalitarian countries the individual is supposed to exist for the sake of the whole nation and is therefore relentlessly subjected to strict standards of behavior, of thinking and even of feeling, for the supposed good of the whole.

The proportion of individual freedom and of social constraint is different in the two types of societies, but everything still operates at the social level. At that level a human being today feels, acts and thinks basically as an ego, more or less conscious and rational, more or less independent, more or less educated and successful, but as an ego in all cases. The ego develops under social and cultural pressures using a particular language, doing some sort of social work; it is a social unit.

It is that kind of status against which many youths of the present generation are revolting. They do not want to be "social units" and they try by various means, some rather unwholesome, to overcome their ego-condition as well as their social condition. In order to achieve this they are drawn to the use of procedures which imply a "return" to their life-roots, that is, to the experience of the body as such, of natural conditions of life, and of a sexual activity free from social, cultural and religious-traditional restraints. They particularly resent such restraints because their elders officially and hypocritically accept them only to break them on all possible occasions when it is socially safe to do so.

In other words, the youths' protests against a society operating in terms of values of the "antithesis" phase of human evolution tend to take the form of a return to the "thesis" phase. That is why they so often speak of their groups as "tribes." However, these groups are basically different in spirit from the real archaic tribes because the boys and girls who form them are very intent on acting on an individual basis -- on "doing my thing," as they say. The youth of today does not yet realize, exceptions notwithstanding, what it would mean to live in terms of a total, conscious and deliberate dedication to a greater whole which would not be "social" in the modern sense but instead "planetary" in its total dedication to the wholeness of Man. No one has been able to give them a "vision" of such a future condition of human living and of what it implies.

Such a condition has existed at times in the past, but only within specifically limiting religious restrictions, thus in monastic or semi-monastic communities--such as the Therapeutae of Egypt, perhaps the Essenes, then the Druses of Lebanon in the twelfth century, the early Senussi Brotherhoods in nineteenth century North Africa, and probably other "brotherhoods" in Asia and Europe, the Cathari and Albigenses of Southern France who were ruthlessly destroyed by a coalition of King and Pope being by far the most important and influential. Such Brotherhoods, and the few communes of the last century in the United States, could not endure under the pressure of their aggressive environment. They developed prematurely and many had to become "secret" Brotherhoods, or, as we would say today, go underground.

What then of the future? Perhaps a drastic social crisis, or even telluric upheavals, will be needed to make a new type of "commune" possible in a more "open" society. But they will have to embody a very vital and contagious faith in a new kind of interpersonal relationships; and this will mean essentially the development in individuals of a type of consciousness able to experience vividly a superpersonal "greater whole" within which these individuals will act, not merely as spontaneous human organisms and minds illumined by mystic experiences of "unity," but as differentiated parts of the communal whole. Moreover such a greater whole will have to realize, affirm and prove its effectual participation in the still vaster whole of mankind if it is to survive.

Three factors are involved here: the fact that the human beings who enter the new commune enter it as conscious individuals who have more or less definitely freed themselves from family and social status -- then the actual quasi-organic participation of the individual person in the activities of the whole -- and, vivifying, inspiring and maintaining at a high pitch of effectiveness this participation, a constant realization not only of the character and meaning of the communal whole, but of the P r e s e n c e of the Wholeness of the whole as an almost visible and tangible fact of existence.

Mystics of the past have spoken of living "in the Presence of God"; and in an individualistic phase of personal development, the "Presence" has to be personalized and named Christ, Krishna, or the Master, for the small and troubled human individual quite naturally seeks strength, security and emotional comfort in an "I-Thou" relationship with a divine Being. We can envision, however, a condition of communal existence in which the secure human being, sustained by interpersonal group relationships, would have a somewhat different approach and psychological need. As an individual person, he would seek to be as completely attuned as possible to the vibration, the character and the function of the Soul-field with which he is then consciously and wholeheartedly linked, though not yet fully united; but as a member of the commune he would share with all other members in the effectual Presence of the Principle of Wholeness, ONE, per-

haps without the need of personalizing It and thus limiting its
character. This Presence in the commune should be a more
or less constant fact of experience, or at least a deep unquestionable and ineradicable f e e l i n g in all the individual
participants -- i. e. in all the "communicants."

Such an attitude cannot be genuinely and "authentically"
accepted by modern individuals unless they have really experienced a basic change in consciousness and as a result
are willing, able and ready to relate in a new way to other
individuals of like disposition. This new way implies a different concept of ethics -- a new morality. The new morality will be concerned (1) with the character and degree of efficacy of the just mentioned change of consciousness, (2)
with the quality of the interpersonal relationships within the
group and of the relationship of the group to other groups,
and (3) with the ability of the "communicants" to act and work
in a quasi-ritualistic manner, in consecrated service to the
whole -- the commune and mankind-as-a-whole.

The change of consciousness I have in mind here is a
change from a "closed" to an "open" consciousness; and also,
as a result, a change from a sense of personal and cultural
exclusivism and self-righteousness (and there are very subtle
forms of self-righteousness!) to a deeply compelling feeling
of all-human exclusiveness and compassion.

Such a feeling of inclusiveness may be innate and spontaneous regardless of any mental concept and metaphysical
"vision"; but as we are dealing, at this stage in history, with
men and women born into an intellectually-oriented culture
and conditioned by the dogmatic exclusivism of b o t h religion and science, I believe that the mental pictures, subconscious as well as conscious, of the individuals seeking a new
type of communal relationship must also be transformed; and
this is why I have presented a cyclocosmic picture of existence which, if properly understood, does away with the ab-
solutism of values and moral judgments. If every phase of
an evolutionary cycle releases new values and new truths,

no belief or opinion can be absolutely "true" or "right";
therefore no one need be morally or rationally condemned
for his beliefs PROVIDED they are genuinely his own. The
only thing which should be condemned are the conditions in
which dogmatism and fanaticism -- thus exclusivism, self-
righteousness and possessiveness in all their forms -- can
arise and assume an air of legitimacy.

When existence is understood to be a polyphonic, multi-
levelled interplay of different modes of activities, all of
which contribute to the harmony of the Whole, the only "bad"
feature is the fact of being "out of place" and of "hugging the
spotlight" -- i. e. trying to force the attention of the group
by emotional self-dramatization, histrionics or intellectual
fireworks displayed just for show. At its place of
destiny, at the proper time, and in harmonic relationship to other factors, every factor of existence is "right."

This also includes what is called "evil" when considered
from a cosmic and impersonal perspective. This must be
so the moment we realize that every release of potentiality
into actual existence elicits both positive and negative responses -- which means that every cycle of existence produces both success and failure. Evil is simply the way of
failure, a negative response to the release of a new set of
potentiality. Every Avatar or Divine Manifestation whose
life, love and light opens a new Age of human development
also brings the inevitability of evil -- the "Shadow" of the
Light.

A truly "open" consciousness must accept the existence
of the Shadow -- the "dark" Brother -- and learn to deal with
this fact. The illumined person does not emotionally con-
demn the dark facts of existence; he deals with them carefully so as not to be influenced by them physically, psychically and mentally. Because he is securely commited to the
way of Light, he is able to accept without horror or paralyz-
ing fear the fact that by his treading the way of Light it is

inevitable that somewhere in the universe someone is treading the path of Darkness, and that he and his opposite may
actually meet. The supreme Harmony of the existential
Whole always remains dynamically perfect and, because It
includes all forms of existence, It is also "beyond" them all.

Every living organism must feed itself to survive; and
feeding leads inescapably to a process of assimilation and a
process of the elimination of un-assimilatable waste-products. Mankind is, broadly speaking, an organism. There
are waste-products to be eliminated. If the eliminative function does not operate well the system becomes filled with
toxins. Any form of group-relationship will produce toxic
elements that need to be eliminated. BUT these toxic factors
have their source at the level of the mind and the ego. They
use human persons as means of expression, as channels
for release. The evil should not be identified with the human person; it is what forces its way through and
out of the person.

When a new potentiality is released, the negative aspect
of this new potentiality seeks expression through an individual
human being at the level of that person's mind. "Dark" Images of what the new potentiality is bringing are aroused.
Fear, a sense of insecurity, and most often an emotion of
repulsion based on a clinging to old concepts and feelings,
arise in the individual's mind and psyche. A dark whirlpool
is produced which is a negative counterpart of the constructive, evolutionary aspect of the new potentiality. This whirlpool then operates against the development of the new
potentiality; it operates against the creative "flow" of existence -- against the "will of God," the religionist will say. A
heavy mass of fear blocks this flow. As a large stone in the
path of a swift current generates behind it a whirlpool that
hinders the flow of the water, so evil generates anti-evolu-
tionary forces. But these forces are not extraneous; they
are the power of the current, as it were "reversed," or
wasted in concentric (egocentric) motion. Thus occultists

have always asserted that "the Devil is God inverted."

To be open but not afraid is the basic requirement of the future morality of the Age of Plenitude. To be open means, as already stated, to be open as an individual person to a full relationship with the Soul-field, so that the living person may become a projection and embodiment of the Soul-Image; it means also to be open to the fact that one participates in a whole and thus fulfills a function in that whole in relation to other individuals who also fulfill their functions. All these functions are or should be necessary for the health of the whole. Thus they should be performed in terms of the whole rather than as anarchic forms of self-expression -- which actually means ego-expression. They are "anarchic" if performed merely for the sake of the ego. They should become "holarchic," that is, performed with reference to the needs of the whole. But the needs of the whole would not run counter to the individual's self-expression IF it is really the expression of the self and not of the ego, and if the individual acts at the place and in the function which are truly "his," i. e. which are attuned to his Soul-Image. In performing his "work of destiny" (dharma) the individual would serve the purpose of the whole.

This obviously implies that the type of interpersonal group relationship in which the individual participates should be organized in terms of the "organic" adjustment of person to function. A New Age commune should be an "organism." It should be functionally integrated in an attitude of dedicated service to mankind. But it can only operate as such if the Presence of the Principle of integration, ONE, is a vivid, constant realization in the inner life of every participant. And to this end a sense of ritual group-activity would be of extremely great value, for in such a ritualistic activity the individual factor and the group factor could be integrated harmoniously -- if what such rituals should mean today is well understood.

The difference between a future-oriented ritual activity

and the tribal rituals of earlier days resides in the character and quality of the consciousness of the participants. These are today individualized persons; long ago, they were largely unconscious, Life-dominated human organisms at a pre-individual stage of human evolution. The difference is of primary importance. It may not show too much at first in the outer activity, but it is essential at the level of the conscious mind. Life acts in terms of bio-psychic instinctual compulsion; but now man has reached the level of Ideity, of a consciousness focused through an individualized and independently structured mind. The self today can be focused in the heart, whereas of old it was centered in the pelvic or the solar plexus region.

Because of all these human and evolutionary changes, an essentially and spiritually new type of Image of the "Commune Ideal" can be envisioned, then realized. To actualize such an Ideal is evidently a difficult problem, both of individual metamorphosis and of group-organization. But it must be met. It can be met only if the q u a l i t y of the love which illumines the relationships between the participants in the commune is of a conscious and focused character and has not only an unpossessive and non-exclusivistic quality, but is also a truly conscious and focused love. It should pervade the whole community and radiate t h r o u g h the individuals, even more than f r o m the individuals. It should be the very vibration of ONE operating at the level of an all-inclusive Compassion--the "divine" level of operation of the Principle of Wholeness which is as well the foundation of all existence.

In stating this I am not speaking of the usual kind of religious ideal, as expressed in any organized religion, and in its more or less dogmatically formulated m o r a l   i m p e r-a t i v e s. This Love-compassion is not a "Law" somehow replacing or inspiring old "Commandments." It is the very Principle of existence at a level of activity, of wholeness and consciousness which man should now, slowly but surely, strive to reach. But man can only do so if he can clearly imagine such a quality of interrelatedness and communal living without the conditioning factors which races, creeds, nations, sects or classes inevitably introduce. Indeed man can never reach a truly new phase in his evolution as long as he cannot vividly imagine its general character. He must now act consciously, in an individualized manner. He must reach the new evolutionary goal of synthesis and of unity according to the way he selects his approach, or rather the way h e i s, as an individual.

When I speak of "man" I mean the wholeness of an integrated humanity having discovered its place and function within the total field of activity of the Earth. And this implies having realized vividly the complex planetary Archetype that is the Soul-Image of humanity as an integral part of the "divine" potentiality of the Earth. It is this "Form of man" which is "in the likeness" of God -- i.e. of the One Creative Word, the Logos. It is indeed the Soul-Image of the Earth seeking through mankind to actualize itself. Within it is shown the end-result, the omega state, of the age-old process of planetarization of consciousness. A new phase of this evolutionary process is about to begin.

TOWARD A PLENARY SOCIETY

"Communes" within which a new quality of relationship and a new "organic" and therefore ritualistic approach to the problems involved in group-activity can be demonstrated according to the principle of operative wholeness, can be considered small "seeds" which in due time should become the multiformed foundations for a new all-inclusive society. Such a future planetary society need not be a rigidly centralized World State dominated by a class of self-perpetuating managers and technocrats. It should be a multi-level society, for it is fairly evident that only a minority of human beings will be able to reach the level of such communes as I have envisioned in the preceding pages. It should also be a society which, at the level of mass-operation and mass-consciousness, has not lost the feeling of rootedness in specific regions of the globe to the vibrations of which an equally specific type of men are attuned.

As I have shown many years ago (cf. MODERN MAN'S CONFLICTS: The Creative Challenge of a Global Society - New York, 1948) there is a definite relationship between the shape of a continent or sub-continent and the type of culture and society which develops within these geographical regions. Much could be learned from a study of what I called "geomorphy" and "geotechnics." Man has his generic and collective roots in the land; but roots are not the only factor in a plant's life. There are also leaves, flowers -- and seeds that fulfill their destiny as seeds by leaving the parent plant and being blown across space.

What I call the global "plenary" society of the future -- how distant a future, who can tell! -- is a society which must have at least a symbolical organic character. It should operate at several levels. It should be "holarchic" in its overall organization of a c t i v i t i e s, yet individualistically "holistic" in its fundamental recognition of the person as an individualized whole of consciousness and as the potential field of integration of a Soul-Image and a human field-of-existence. As an individualized whole, the person is what I have called an Ideity-field -- a "sacred place" within which the Divine Marriage c a n occur, and eventually will occur if the person has followed the path of Light and Love. (This "sacred place" is symbolized by the Flower, for in the flower the new seed is being formed).

On the other hand, as a p e r f o r m e r o f a c t i v i t i e s which are related to the "greater Whole" constituted by the plenary society of Man on an Earth gradually becoming trans-substantiated by human activity and human minds, an individual person is, ideally, an officiant in the vast ritual being performed by such an all-human global society. As a performer he a c t s; as an individual consciousness seeking an ever more complete attunement with his Soul-field he is

acted upon. The way he is thus acted upon determines
the quality of his acts. It marks him with a definite character and definable -- but not static, always evolving -- capacities for action. These capacities direct him to his "work
of destiny" -- what C. G. Jung called his "vocation."

The reason why young people find it so difficult, in most
cases, to discover anything resembling their true vocation,
is that they live in a chaotic, totally inorganic society from
which their innermost desire is to become separated, because
they feel deeply alienated from all that it stands for. In the
Western world, particularly in the United States, we feel
very proud of living in a democracy in which every man is
theoretically "free" and responsible. We have indeed freedom of the press (relatively), of assembly (within limits), of
voicing our opinions, of choosing our religious and group-
affiliation, etc.; and we have the "four freedoms" extolled
by President Roosevelt, from fear, want, etc. (or have
all Americans such freedoms now?) But no one seems to
tell us what these freedoms are FOR. What should one work
for? What should one perform any social activity for? Our
brand of democracy, as it was conceived by the minds of
earnest men of the eighteenth century, who naively assumed
that they had reached "enlightenment," is a theoretical kind
of democracy in which the unit, the citizen, is abstractly
"equal," "free" only in principle and "fraternal" under limiting social conditions. Men are reduced to abstractions,
even while we speak rather pompously of the worth and dignity of the human person.

Such equalitarianism combined with an ambiguous kind of
majority-rule and a type of parliamentarianism dominated
by powerful "special interests" and wealth -- not to speak of
racial prejudices which are the "karmic" shadow of slavery
in the United States, and in other countries, of colonialism --
lacks the essential characteristics of what I envision as a
plenary society. And I hasten to say that any one of the present forms of totalitarianism is even more deficient and vir-

ulently obnoxious. "Marketplace democracy" sees the free individual as a competitive entity, indeed as an aggressive ego whose purpose in living is to dominate others -- and often to trick them -- in order to accumulate wealth, power, possessions. The purpose of society is to produce more and more goods, even if it means forcing people by all means, fair or foul, to consume often far more than they need or even want, and thus to become ever more enslaved to their appetites and their craving for physical comfort -- and more dependent on psychoanalysis or psychiatry.

This entire social picture should seem crudely and tragically obnoxious to the man of the future living in a plenary society composed of an immense network of regional communes, each with a large degree of independence yet all integrated in a kind of organismic condition of operative wholeness within the global Whole of mankind. In a sense this type of organization retains some of the characteristics of the e a r l y American nation as a federation of small states. The tragedy is that the ideal embodied in the American system became almost completely perverted in the nineteenth century and even more recently by the monstrous growth of the Federation, which made the application of the system impossible. In fact it was only abstractly workable and condemned to become utterly materialized by (1) the maintenance of slavery, (2) the White man's crudely aggressive and predatory attitude toward the American Indians and the land and (3) by the pressures of the other nations of the globe. To become enormously rich and powerful and to out-produce every other country is no mark of "success," as I have used this term. It can mean a tragic moral failure -- tragic indeed because the foundation of "these United States" was originally pervaded with a glorious dream: N o v u m   O r d o   S e - c l o r u m, the New Order of the Centuries, "A new departure in human affairs" (Thomas Paine).

It is not the purpose of this book to criticize conditions present today. Yet it is at times necessary to compare reality with the ideal, and to show how this ideal failed to include the very fundamental principles of the future society of which a few basic characteristics are here outlined. Democracy, parliamentarianism, majority rule, free enterprise, these really mean nothing definite and concrete unless one specifies (1) the character of the human units in such a quantitative system of social organization, (2) the quality of the relationship between these units, and (3) the human, spiritual and metaphysical purpose, and the expected results, of the social system.

Our democratic Western world is essentially a society of egos, even if increasingly unconvincing religious organizations talk pompously of God-created souls and of saving souls; and in that world of egos, by egos and for the greater glory of egos, interpersonal relationships are based on competition and acquisitiveness, on possessiveness and a false, because abstract, notion of equality -- quantitative equality, the equality of units in statistical computations. The most basic facts of such a social and egocentered type of organization preclude the realization of Love, because true Love and Compassion demand a constant realization of the Presence of That which is the very principle of Wholeness and high-level integration. The official purpose of our Western democracies is either to build strong nations or to insure the pursuit of liberty, happiness and comfort to their citizens through constantly increased productivity and expansion, with the unspecified but apparently inevitable results of wasteful exploitation of the very substance of the Earth, and in a great many cases of its inhabitants as well.

It will be said that, justified as such criticisms may be, they simply indicate that the vast majority of human beings are operating at an egocentric, aggressive and possessive level of consciousness, and that the best devised system of organization will fail to live up to its ideals under such conditions. This is perfectly true. However, my purpose is not, I repeat, to show how wrong the present situation is --

this is being done by a great many writers today -- but to try to point our clearly the actual differences between the ideal of the past, even of our American democratic past, and the one I envision for the future. What I wish to stress is the obvious fact that today no one that I know of -- with one exception -- is able to present to our rebellious young generation the vision of a future worth working for, and if needed, dying for. And without such a "vision," based upon an all-encompassing picture of the universe and of the interplay of metaphysical Principles beyond any limiting personification, there can be no really integrated and sustained efforts, because there will be no powerful vivid sense of the possibility, nay, the evolutionary inevitability, of the actualization of the vision.

The one exception just mentioned is the movement begun in India by Sri Aurobindo and his surviving co-worker, Mother Mira who for many years has skillfully and powerfully managed the Aurobindo ashram in Pondicherry. The writings of Aurobindo provide the vision-- particularly his monumental work THE LIFE DIVINE and the Commentaries on old Hindu "sacred books" to which he gave a revolutionary new meaning. And now the activities of "the Mother," past the age of 90, are directed toward the realization of the vision; they have given the needed "Creative Word" for the building of an ideal city-community near Pondicherry, named Auroville.* It could become, if successful, a seed-pattern for a number of similar endeavors.

The essential factor, I repeat, in all such community-building is the Presence of ONE, the Principle of Wholeness,

---

*Anyone wanting information concerning the Auroville project which was formally started in an impressive ceremony in February 1968 in which youths of many countries participated, bringing some soil from their native lands, can write to Sri Aurobindo Ashram, Pondicherry 2, India.

the Integrator at the heart of all existential forms of integration. Today, because we are still in an Age when individuals find it so difficult to find enough vividness and drama in an impersonal Principle and cosmogenic Power, this Presence may require the intermediary of a living (or dead) personage who has become the effectual symbol of this Presence. If he, or she, is content to be a symbol of integration, all is well. But alas, personification leads to worship, to singling out the one that is worshipped as "the only one" -- the "only begotten Son of God"! -- and this inevitably leads to the feeling of exclusive ownership of a capitalized Truth and to a host of subsequent evils and perversions of the original Creative Impulse which has become differentiated along many paths.

There is not only one Truth, not one Way only toward the actualization of a plenary society encompassing all men and regional cultures and communities in their diversity of approaches and responses to the new evolutionary step which is ahead of mankind. The Auroville project just mentioned could be a most significant response to the call of Man -- or God -- for a new human "mutation" in consciousness and in the quality of interhuman relatedness. But there will certainly be others, in which a somewhat different metaphysical approach will be accepted as a basis for group-action. And the holistic and essentially impersonal approach formulated in this book accentuates the basic realities of existence in a way which definitely differs from and perhaps in a way complements the metaphysical realizations of Sri Aurobindo. He follows the traditional line represented by the Bhagavad Gita, while my approach has probably greater kinship to that of Mahayana Buddhism. The basic realities are the same, but different formulations emphasize one or the other of these realities, seeing them in a somewhat different light.

This is "good"; for the ways of the search and the forms taken by the great realizations of evolutionary Archetypes as they reach the human mind are many. Integration does not lead ultimately to a dictatorial type of "unity," but to a polyphonic state of "multi-unity." The unanimous condition of consciousness of the many perfected Beings constituting the Seed-Pleroma at the end of a great cycle does not exclude the active remembrance of the different paths these Beings took to reach union with their Soul-Images and to become consecrated Agents of the one power of evolution to which devotionally inclined individuals refer as the Will of God. Unity in consciousness does not preclude functional distinctions.

At the level of the new communities which should become seeds for the New Age there should also be a unanimity of purpose and of dedication, an utter readiness to reach beyond individualism and to vibrate to the nascent reality of the transformed whole; but there will still be individuals at work, acting in different capacities and each fulfilling his or her own dharma -- not as an ego dictates or as Life-energies crave compulsive fulfillment, but in the clear light of a unanimous consciousness and dedication to the whole.

EPILOGUE

EPILOGUE - Planetarization and Plenitude

The social situation in the Western world - Non-conforming youth vs. middle-class inertia and fear - Similarity with the confrontation between the early Christians and the Roman empire - A new world-religion? (327-328); The global character of the present crisis and the planetarization of consciousness (329); The change of state from solid to liquid (330); The new world of physics (331); Human interdependence and world-citizenship (332); Organization vs. aggressive-expansion - a reversal of all values (333); Plenitude and the Age of Synthesis - Definition of "plenitude" (334); The Man of Plenitude (335-36); The need for "Seed men" and the emergence of global man (337); The new symbols: the Globe and Heat (337-338); The new type of man: what it demands (339); Mankind's "mentalizing" function for the Earth (340); The power of symbols (341); The symbol of the Incarnation - God becoming concrete as global Man (342); Facing the future in creative faith (343).

PLANETARIZATION AND PLENITUDE

As we watch present developments in the Western world with a mind detached from ancestral traditions, we face a complex and ambivalent situation. On the one hand we are aware of a powerful ferment of fascinating new ideas and of the dynamic and world-wide discontent and often passionate revolt of a youth refusing to accept the role which the generations in control of the political, industrial and military machinery of society have prepared for it. On the other hand we are confronted with the dull but bitter and frightened middle-class, middle-and-old-age masses of "the people" clinging to their comfort, their Sunday Church religion, their inept but familiar leaders, and somehow believing with a blind fanaticism that Science and Technology, their twin-Gods, will solve all problems and usher in some sort of mechanized Golden Age.

All "sensible persons" may well bank on the victory of normality, "good sense," and technicians who perform seeming miracles. However, historians should remember that a handful of irrational, starry-eyed and utopian fanatics from an insignificant corner of the Roman Empire successfully challenged the might of the Rome of the Caesars and grew in power and influence within a society which, in spite of splendid administrators and a strong army, was inwardly disintegrating in rootless boredom and moral vacuity under outer and inner pressures which it took lightly and, in fact, before which it was helpless. It was helpless because it was built on a basic fallacy -- the fallacy that efficient administrators and a powerful army can take the place of a spiritual tradition which is slowly dying of meaninglessness, and that pride in social-political and economic achievement can be a solid basis for the building of a new society.

The situation today is of course very different. America has tremendous power it dares not and cannot use if nearly total destruction is to be avoided. It has many, many thousands of churches, but they are mere facades to hide deep, gnawing insecurity; and though frightened people cling to their pews and the printed words still declaimed by confused and wavering priests or ministers, the spirit is either dead or fast asleep, drugged by suburban comfort and the tamed mediocrity of officeholders. Yet the middle class people and the drugged masses of retired T.V. watchers and golf addicts still have enormous inertial strength made comfortable by self-righteousness. Goliath may scorn the little fool, David; but David won through mobility and faith. Is our non-conforming, dreamy-eyed, love-entranced youth, fascinated by drugs that help dissipate the ego-lure, often at heavy cost to their bodies and minds, the new David?

One may wonder if a radically transformed Christianity could again stir the imagination of the new generation, after it tires perhaps of Oriental symbols and occult tales -- possibly after a nuclear holocaust. Or does the future of humanity belong to a new world religion, perhaps the Bahai Movement whose followers so often glow with a faith that evokes the stories one has heard of early Christians, and who more than any other world-wide group have a definitely planned, indeed a God-revealed "World-order" to reintegrate on a global scale a humanity disorganized by an expected radical catharsis? Perhaps also -- who knows! -- a contact with Intelligences coming from another planet will upset, arouse and recast into a new mould man's collective response to a broadened awareness of the universe around him.

No one can convincingly answer these questions and many others just as crucial. One thing seems certain: the world-crisis through which we are passing and which very likely will soon become sharper and more focalized is not just one of those crises which, we are told, occur periodically and to which society becomes adjusted, after which the good old days come back again.

The crises of the past were relatively l o c a l and the consciousness of even the broadest Roman mind never actually encompassed the whole of mankind; great kingdoms and empires existed when Rome collapsed. Now, the crisis is g l o b a l. It might seem to manifest as a struggle between two different approaches to social and economic organization; but the now very ambiguous and shifting cold-hot war in which many shades of human temperament and doctrines face one another in a confused array of big propaganda words and menacing gestures is not the basic factor in the global crisis. The struggle between the idealistic and protesting section of the youth of a l l countries and the various types of "Establishments" is far more significant, at a time when the whole future of Man is at stake. Not only is the whole of humanity indirectly if not directly affected by the critical world-situation, but all the kingdoms of life on this Earth are more or less menaced -- and as well the water, the air, the soil of the planet. Should a large-scale nuclear holocaust take place, the electro-magnetic state of the entire solar system might even be altered with totally unknowable consequences.

Such an enormous potentiality for change of a catastrophic nature also indicates the possibility of an evolutionary transformation on a truly planetary scale. The title of this book, THE PLANETARIZATION OF CONSCIOUSNESS, should indicate what I consider this possibility to be. What is at stake is not some minor modification in the structures of society. It is a fundamental transformation which transcends local or national conditions and the normal behavior of greedy egocentric men hankering for power to fill their inner soul-emptiness. It is a change as radical as the change from one state of matter to the next in the scale of temperature -- let us say, from the solid to the liquid state. It occurs at a time when atomic scientists speak of a new state of matter, the plasma state -- and perhaps there is some kind of parallelism between such a discovery of the plasma state and the dissolution of all objects, concepts and traditions to which one can apply the concept of "solidity" into a condition of increasing "liquidity." Is not our whole philosophical and psychological approach to reality leading us to a completely dynamic, unsolid, fluidic reality?

FROM SOLIDITY TO LIQUIDITY

Solid matter is the matter which we experience as "objects," an object having a more or less precisely defined and constant form. It is in this realm of objects and as well in the "solid" world of traditions and standards of value -- gold, for instance, as a concrete basis for interpersonal and international transactions --that humanity has functioned for millennia. The growth of "cultures" has taken place in terms of objects, of solid land, of sacred idols; and as the ego-sense developed it led to a kind of idolatry, of dependence upon "solid" character and static beliefs. Interestingly enough ancient cultures took form mainly along the banks of great rivers, whose inundations were life-giving, so that there also developed a sort of mystical response to and identification with the flowing water. The old Mediterranean cultures grew around a nearly closed sea -- somewhat as a primitive living organism born of the sea is a pocket of water surrounded by a layer of more differentiated cells. Yet this Mediterranean sea also became a potent symbol of the inner mystery of life, and Crete -- an island -- may have been the cradle of the vitalistic Mysteries which spread to the later rationalistic Greece, Aristotelian in her outer mentality but with an inner life deeply influenced by oracles and mystic rites.

With the Renaissance and the Great Voyages around the

globe, the entire world-picture began to change. The ocean became the controlling factor in an ever-expanding commerce. England dominated the world-scene as a sea-power, extending in all directions her tentacular greed and pride as "ruler of the waves." While until then it was the coastal region which appropriated the seas on the shores of which they solidly stood, giving them local names, men now began to realize that there is but one global ocean, and that all the land was born of it and may one day return to its majestic tidal breathing, its unfathomable rhythm.

The mystery of the fluid and tidal ocean has now been violated by man's avidity and armed power; and paralleling this violation is the conquest of the "sub-lunar realm" of ancient lore -- the "aura" of the Earth; and perhaps soon will follow man's penetration into the space of the solar system, another even vaster, even more open oceanic expanse which we at last realize to be a plenum of vibrations and of vast tides of solar energies, rhythmed not unlikely by a slow 11-year cycle of in and out breathings.

Where is anything "solid" left upon which man can rest his yearning for static peace, unquestioned security and safe ego-boundaries? The world of modern physics is a world of fantastic motions, a world in which change is the only fact that does not change -- as the old Greek seer-philosopher, Heraclitus, intuitively felt. Yet, as has been shown throughout this book, this constant and inconceivably rapid rhythm of change is ordered. It is rhythm. But the rhythm of the motions of atomic particles and of galaxies seemingly rushing away from us in all directions is a tremendous challenge to minds whose consciousness is still attached to some tiny homeland for the possession of which horrible wars seem worth fighting. The consciousness of most men is still bound to the land of their birth and of their ancestors. How senseless this must seem to our "space travelers!" And yet they too are most likely caught in the web of local regional or national feelings and the moral or religious paraphernalia of local creeds. A President of the United States could push a button which might destroy most of the world's population; yet he has to cater to local business interests and dutifully attend church services every Sunday and football games.

What is the way that would lead us to the planetarization of consciousness? Can a sufficient number of individuals reach this planetary stage of mind and truly become "world citizens"? Is nationalism an incurable sickness today, even though in the past it fulfilled a necessary function in the development of a frame of reference larger than the narrow provincialism of the Middle Ages or the even narrower worship of the "tribal land" to which a small group of men fanatically believed they had been given eternal possession by their tribal god?

It should be clear today -- though it obviously is not, insofar as most people's minds are concerned -- that mankind has reached a stage in its historical development where the basic fact is the nearly total interdependence of all human groups, the larger nations included. We are all living now inside of a field of ever more closely related activities. Every move on any continent immediately affects the behavior and the welfare of people on other continents. Nothing therefore is any longer an external factor, because all nations and communities are linked by an actually unbreakable web of relationships. Hatred, too, is a form of relationship; but it has become such a senseless type of relationship in a world already so unified by ever more pervasive interchanges at all levels, that this hatred and all nationalistic feelings have to be fed and sustained by the lies of governments and large business groups capitalizing on the inertia of old historic antagonisms.

Presumably for the first time in the evolution of mankind, a people need not expand aggressively in order to survive; or at least it would not need to do so if the political, social, religious and cultural leaders were not blind to the potentialities of our modern world. Abundance for all is possible only if minds controlled by greedy egos and cultural traditions would let go of their fears and their ambitions. But this, of course, means a reversal of the type of thinking which has controlled human minds through long millennia of scarcity and of conflicts for survival. Whereas in the past man's energies had to be directed o u t w a r d toward conquest, now these energies should be directed i n w a r d, which means toward the accomplishment of an inner harmony in the planet-wide organism of an integrated humanity. The key to survival and all-human peace is no longer aggressive expansion in the outer world peopled with competitors and probable enemies, but the internal organization of resources and their distribution among the various human collectivities, each collectivity willingly and effectively fulfilling its function in the economy of the whole, i. e. in the global organism of Man.

What this means practically is a r e v e r s a l o f a l l b a-s i c h u m a n v a l u e s, and first of all an irrefutable awareness that we have come to a turning point in human evolution, that we have left behind the "Age of Conflicts" and entered the "Age of Plenitude."

THE MAN OF PLENITUDE

I have already spoken of "plenitude" several times in this book; and nearly thirty years ago I wrote a long but still unpublished work called THE AGE OF PLENITUDE. It is a sad reflection on the average American mentality that almost everywhere I have spoken or written of plenitude, the audience or the linotype men have understood it as "plentitude" -- an inexistent word monstrously derived from "plenty" as, say, autobus is derived from omnibus, a Latin term meaning broadly "for everybody." Plenty, and its synonym, abundance, indeed express the ideal for the realization of which the people in our "consumers society" yearn. The craving for bigness is, alas, typical of our people. We have not learnt from the fate of the dinosaurs and other immoderately and cumbersomely large animals.

The word, plenitude, well known in all European countries, has nearly the same meaning as "fullness," but it is used almost exclusively with reference to an inner state of human or divine being and consciousness. The Greek term, pleroma, is related to it, and I have used this term, pleroma, to indicate a condition of existence in which the most complete plenitude of being and consciousness is experienced -- a truly "divine" state, the omega state.

Each of the great periods of human evolution brings to the fore a type of man who not only is associated characteristically with such an historical era but whose appearance on the stage of human evolution heralds and contributes greatly to the building of the kind of society which flourishes during such an era. During what I call the Age of Conflicts, which is witnessing the gradual process of the individualization of man, we have seen appearing, then ruling the human stage, such basic types of men as the Warrior, the Priest, the Merchant. Today the Executive and the Manager or Technocrat type are dominant in the United States and other Western nations, polarized, as it were, by the general type of the Workingman, organized and full of its importance since the glorification by Karl Marx of the Proletariat, the "virgin masses" from which a revolutionary renewal of society and human relationships was supposed to come. One should also of course speak of the Scientist as a type which should be very different from the Technocrat, though today the difference has lost much of its significance in a great many cases.

When I wrote about the Man of Plenitude in 1941 just before and after Pearl Harbor I had a very broad evolutionary concept of a type of human being who would herald the coming Age of Plenitude, the Age of Synthesis which marks the third phase of the dialectic process of the development of man's consciousness and capacity for relationship. All preceding types converge, as it were, toward the coming to birth of the Man of Plenitude: the man who, freed from his egocentric

clinging to security and to "local" conditions, in time as well
as in space, can resonate totally to the vast rhythm of the
cyclic process of transformation acting through the whole
planet--his home and indeed the very substance of his being;
the "man-globe" who can thus become an utterly consecrated
agent for this process, who can focus in his global, because
fully developed and polyphonic being, the energy of world-
evolution. Having focused this power in full awareness, he
can then release it and also formulate the multi-level meaning of the great crisis the whole Earth is facing. It is a crisis in consciousness, because it is conscious and individualized men who have brought it about.

"Who is the man of plenitude? It is he who lives the
fullest, the deepest, the most creative life possible
under any condition: a life most individually formed,
yet utterly consecrated to the greatest whole of which
he can realize himself an organic part. It is he who
lives a life rooted in the common humanity of all men,
but unfolding through functional differentiation of activities toward an ever higher level of fulfillment -- a
life glorious with a vibrant and integral understanding
of the meaning of all activities within himself as within the social and universal wholes. It is he who realizes in the fullest possible way that at the core of
any whole flows the cyclic stream of formative power
of the Divine Mind, and who becomes that stream.

"What is the goal of plenitude? -- It is to live a life
of organic totality; of multi-levelled rhythmic integration; of eager intensity in love as in thought; of serene understanding, yet creative fervor; of unflinch-
ing honesty to oneself, as well as to the whole; of el-
egance and ease; of service and consecration; -- a
life structured by self yet rooted in the greater Whole
and filled with its total life; contained in form, yet
radiant in freedom; a life beautiful and noble, in which
earth mates with heaven in the generous bestowal of

creative meaning, and man unites with his companions for the work of the Seed.

"Thus indeed it is to live the life of plenitude -- the life of the Spirit, by the Spirit, as the Spirit.

"... To be plenitude -- to be consecrated -- to accept responsibility -- to assume the burden of those who deny Man and worship stultified gods -- to go on and on, never looking back save to understand and to accept, to bless and transfigure the roots which have become flowers and seed -- to smile and laugh at the little joys which trickle as dew from sun-drenched trees at dawn -- to be silent and open as the desert under the stars -- to enfold and to bless the depths as well as the heights -- to be beautiful and clear, with the purity of water which is only its chemical self and contains no sediment -- to be honest with oneself and with the world, because Personality creates within forms that are unblurred and steady -- to be a song of Destiny and a chord of power in harmony with the universal Whole -- to be Incarnation and Transfiguration, Christos become a man and man divine. These are words; they may be goals; they may be realities. It is for everyone to decide, for everyone to accept the meaning and the fullness of what he c a n live, of what he wills to live."

(from "The Age of Plenitude")

In this century which has seen a fantastic growth of specialization and technology, this century which once Henry Wallace, one-time Vice-President, called "the century of the common man," the ideal of the man of plenitude may well seem far-fetched and utterly utopian or out of place; yet, as Count Keyserling, the great German thinker, unfortunately rather forgotten these days, wrote repeatedly: "It is the few minds whose thoughts run in counterpoint to the popular trend of the time who are most significant and who really matter." They are the "seed men," the true Fathers of tomorrow. What the technology and specialization dominating the lives of our contemporaries represent is simply the means to the end; and most people are blind to that end. Modern science and technology were necessary in order that men might circumfly the earth and thus, through them, that Man might become objectively aware of the globe from whose gravitational pull they had become free. Because these astronauts experienced the planet as a whole from the outside, they could actually realize its global character, and they opened the door, as it were, to the emergence of "global man" made in the image of the planet.

SYMBOLS FOR THE NEW AGE

One can only become consciously the likeness of that to which one has become exterior and from which one has been liberated. The seed must leave the dying plant in order to fulfill its dharma. A human being must emerge from the womb of local and ancestral traditions in order to be individually human; or as an old occult statement proclaimed: "When the son leaves the mother he becomes the father." Man circling the globe in conscious wakefulness and in control of the forces he is using can be remade in the symbolic image of a globe. Indeed the greatest symbol of the future is the Globe, and no longer the Cross; not the Man of Sorrow but the Man of Plenitude who, having learnt how to suffer, has overcome the schizophrenia of futile conflicts in pain and reached the peace that is found at the core of the sphere, where all radii converge and gravitation is annihilated -- at the core of the sphere, rather than in external "space" where men can only exist by means of technical subterfuges. Crises are inevitable; suffering is the great Liberator. What matters is the end, not the means -- provided these means really lead to the omega state, the plenitude of man. The Cross has been for us the way to the Globe. Our Christian culture has conditioned a global crisis which can be the foundation for individual victory; and it should now be seen and justified as an inevitable prelude to Man's fulfilling tomorrows.

Heat, the tremendous heat released by atomic fusion, and the Globe -- these are the two great symbols of this New Age to which so many people today aspire. Alas these aspirations and the intellectualized extrapolations and previsions of science-fiction writers and scientific planners seem most of the time to offer us but quite unpleasant prospects for the future. The gadgets are exciting, the men unimpressively similar to modern college-graduates who have run the gauntlet of the many tests worshipped in our "factories of knowledge." These factories of knowledge are no longer universities; they do not bring to our youth a sense of the unity of the existential and human process; rather they take pride in being multiversities -- the very opposite of the global ideal, and indeed the manifestation of a new type of intellectual materialism. This is the most basic reason for the recent revolt of youth all over the world.

Yet for anyone who is not blinded by the superficialities of this period of crisis and transition and by the inevitable readjustments of society and human psychology during such a period, the final outcome should not be in doubt; but it does indeed require the emergence of a new type of human being. The great Indian yogi-philosopher, Sri Aurobindo, gave to this type the name of "Gnostic being." Starting from a very different base of thought the French priest-archaeologist, Teilhard de Chardin, has spoken in Christian terms of a magnificent apotheosis for man at the end of the universal cycle, the omega point. The American philosopher, Charles Morris, in his splendid book, PATHS OF LIFE, also written at the beginning of World War II, presented us with the vision of "Maitreyan Man" -- the man of a future of all-inclusive synthesis. Other thinkers also have more recently outlined what this new type of man might be, giving it a variety of names. These are not dreams; or if so, then let us admit that the future is always, at its highest point, the dream of a few seer-philosophers of the past who were totally aware of the momentum of evolution and could already see, even if only dimly, the butterfly in the chrysalis. Could there be a new planetary cycle without its seed-men?

We need such men today, men of creative imagination, or as was said during the last World War, "imagineers" combining engineering skill with imagination. We need new symbols to fecundate the minds of the youth of tomorrow, perhaps after a momentous crisis. Whatever form this crisis may take matters little, perhaps, provided it brings humanity to "the dead-end to end all dead-ends" (quoted from a text of Zen). Man usually tries all conceivable means to escape from total self-transformation until they all fail; then left alone and hopeless, and for all practical purposes "dead," he realizes that, though all strength is gone from him, yet he lives. What makes him live after the collapse of all he believes in as a means of strength? -- the self.

The self is the center of the globe. It is the depth beyond all depths, which negates the very concept of depth or height. From the self -- this basic vibration which sustains changelessly all the ever-changing organic activities of the total person -- man can go with creative power in every direction. From the self, man can act as "man of plenitude" attuned to the Great Harmony of the universe, the Brahman beyond all gods, the infinite Potentiality of any and all universes, each presenting a different solution to the problem of existence, every universe a cyclocosmic whole structured by its particular logos, its "time-formula" of change, beginning in unity (alpha state) and ending in multi-unity (omega state).

Always increasingly awake to the needs of all lives and progressively more vitally aware of all activities within the several spheres enveloping the solid globe of Earth, man in the condition of plenitude will be able to fulfill, individually and collectively, the function of humanity on this planet. Let me repeat, as this book closes, that this function is to make the planet conscious; it is to "mentalize" all the activities occurring within the vast Field of the earth; to increase the level of consciousness of all existents and indeed to transubstantiate or "etherialize" the very matter of the globe.

To perform this alchemical "Great Work" of human destiny, men of all races and cultures must act together. The greatness of modern science resides primarily in having brought together in a common endeavor and in a remarkable fraternity men of all countries and most varied backgrounds. In a concrete and highly effective manner science has demonstrated the possibility of a global brotherhood of men polarized by a common quest and an effectually structured effort. That this effort leading to the release of new potentialities can have destructive as well as constructive results is inevitable. What is needed among scientists is the realization that their methods, fertile of results as they may be, cannot lead to a total understanding of universal reality because they are conditioned by limiting types of cognition based on a past rebellion against religious dogmatism. They need as well the courage to stand up for mankind-as-a-whole and against local and national interests and passions.

I spoke in a preceding chapter of the one vast creative effort of Man which has left remarkable artistic achievements in every century and on all continents. In Art too therefore we witness a unity of human endeavor though manifesting through a multiplicity and great variety of forms. Likewise in Religion, underneath the different dogmas loudly proclaimed by priests and moralists, there is one vast millennial effort, circuitous though it may be, toward the planetarization of consciousness and the ultimate achievement of the plenitude of Man.

Science, Art, Religion operate essentially through the

use of symbols; and indeed nothing is more important than the emergence of new symbols. Each field uses its own special type of symbolism, but a society or a culture considered as an organized Field of human activity is always dominated by some especially powerful symbol, and by some archetypal "heroic" act which inspires the multitude. Today the symbol of the Globe is emerging as the dominant factor of the civilization slowly forming out of our confused and tragic Western society which ruthlessly and blindly managed to spread over the surface of the earth; and I repeat its twin-symbol is that of the generation of fantastic heat through an organized effort in which scientists of all nations collaborate -- heat that destroys, but also heat that gives us the possibility of adventuring beyond the pull of Earth's gravitation, and to reach the moon and eventually other planets as well. In this adventure, which is now fascinating men's imagination, as the Crusades and the great voyages of the early Renaissance fascinated the imagination of men five centuries ago, man will find himself reaching the paradoxical goal of discovering himself as a citizen of the Earth just because he is now able to free himself from its gravitational pull. The next step may be the discovery that intelligent beings exist on other planets, perhaps in other solar systems. Then humanity will ineluctably have to stress above all else its unity -- the wholeness of planetary Man; and human beings will be able to call themselves "Terrans" and have no home but the whole Earth.

Today fear and pride are straining the hearts of multitudes of men; and perhaps a third of mankind is nearly starving. Human bodies are proliferating at a fantastic pace, possibly to offset some impending cataclysm; but if there is to be no death-dealing event, then such a proliferation will in itself be the cataclysm, in spite of the eventual possibility of having vast new sources of food made available for human use, for any adequate production and distribution of such food would come too late. Yet we must have faith in Man;

not this or that man or this or that country, but global Man
as the emergent consciousness of Earth -- as the Mind of the
planet. The planet will act if men are too inert or blind to
do so. Some will sneer at these statements, saying that such
a faith is of the order of the naive faith in God held by long
generations of Christian men and women. What if it is?
What if the most profound and vital clue to the crisis of our
epoch were that G o d   i s   b e c o m i n g   c o n c r e t e? As
Oliver Reiser once wrote: "When God is known he becomes
Man."

This is the great symbol of the Incarnation. But while
twenty centuries ago it was one particular human being who
was believed to have assumed the awesome responsibility of
God becoming known in and through him alone, today at this
time when many expect and await a "Second Coming," we
should realize that the Incarnation of God is occurring in
humanity as a whole, in global Man. It is indeed taking place
at the center of the Earth -- a "planetary" Incarnation in
which we may all participate if we have sufficient faith and
the courage to vanquish the ghosts of our yet unredeemed
collective past.

To understand with one's mind and even more to feel with
one's heart the reality of this Incarnation, we must enshrine
in our consciousness a new Image of God, and as well a new
Image of Man and of the planet Earth. The transcendent
"mystic Body of Christ" in which all men live, move and have
their being has become a concrete, vitally effective Presence. It is surrounding us; Humanity is surrounding us, taking multifarious forms on our television screens; the planet
is enfolding us as closely as did the walls of our ancestral
home enfold our childhood; do we not romp around in it in
often meaningless excitement just as we did as children?
And beyond all forms, all globes, all finite universes we
should be able to feel -- within and through, as well as beyond, our limited beings and minds -- the immanent power of
ONE, the very Principle of existence, the Wholeness in ev-

ery whole.

We cannot escape the facts of our tumultuous and perhaps cataclysmic era. We can only refuse to see them, panicking when aware of their implications. We are afraid, just as the Jewish rabbis were afraid in Jesus' presence; because men are always afraid of a new Image of God and Reality unless they are courageous enough, or perhaps desperate enough, to remain open and spiritually naked before the vision; unless they are forced to see that there is nothing to lose and plenitude of being to gain.

Plenitude of being! I want to end this book, which is an act of faith in the creative power of Man, by these words, annunciating what is latent in all human beings simply because they are human. Plenitude of being, which means that the infinite and boundless Potentiality of existence and the Presence of ONE is also latent in every man, and that every individual person can become an agent for the "divine" Power which silently, perpetually, ineradicably vibrates at the core of the Earth and in the heart of every human being. All we need do is to focus our attention, to hold steady our thoughts, to feel deeply the Presence that is now incarnating in the Earth toward the transfiguration of Man -- and above all to be totally, vividly, dynamically awake, and in our wakefulness to have faith, faith in Man, faith in the Earth and in the Power that structures the immense Field of activity which is our global home, faith in the plenitude of being that is Man's incorruptible destiny.

Idyllwild, California
Summer, 1969

DANE RUDHYAR was born in Paris and at the age of 18 already had a small book on Debussy and piano compositions published. He came to New York late in 1916 for a performance of some of his orchestral works in a festival of modern and abstract dances at the Metropolitan Opera. He remained in America and became active in various progressive artistic and spiritual movements both in Hollywood and in the East, lecturing extensively on modern music, Oriental philosophy and psychological topics. A number of his books were published, including three books of poems, and his non-objective transcendental paintings were exhibited in several Western states. After 1933 he devoted the major part of his time to reformulating in modern philosophical terms the old "art-science" of astrology, as it became popularized by national magazines, integrating its most significant features with Jungian depth-psychology and developing their symbolical contents on the background of a "humanistic" yet deeply spiritual approach to existence.

COLOPHON BOOKS ON PHILOSOPHY AND RELIGION

*In Preparation